MICHAEL'S MISSION

Revealing the Essential Secrets of Human Nature

MICHAEL'S MISSION

Revealing the Essential Secrets of Human Nature

Twelve lectures given at Dornach, Switzerland, between 21 November and 15 December 1919

TRANSLATED BY JOHANNA COLLIS

INTRODUCTION BY DAVID JONES

RUDOLF STEINER

RUDOLF STEINER PRESS

CW 194

The publishers gratefully acknowledge the generous funding of this publication by the estate of Dr Eva Frommer MD (1927–2004) and the Anthroposophical Society in Great Britain

Rudolf Steiner Press
Hillside House, The Square
Forest Row, RH18 5ES

www.rudolfsteinerpress.com

Published by Rudolf Steiner Press 2015

Originally published in German under the title *Die Sendung Michaels* (volume 194 in the *Rudolf Steiner Gesamtausgabe* or Collected Works) by Rudolf Steiner Verlag, Dornach. Based on shorthand transcripts and notes, not reviewed by the speaker. This authorized translation is based on the latest available (fourth) edition of 1994 edited by Hella Wiesberger

Drawings within the text are by Leonore Uhlig and Assja Turgenieff, based on Rudolf Steiner's blackboard sketches reproduced in the Plate Section

Published by permission of the Rudolf Steiner Nachlassverwaltung, Dornach

A catalogue record for this book is available from the British Library

ISBN 978 1 85584 517 6

Cover by Mary Giddens
Typeset by DP Photosetting, Neath, West Glamorgan
Printed and bound by Gutenberg Press Ltd., Malta

CONTENTS

INTRODUCTION

The lectures included in this volume were given in November and December 1919. During the First World War and immediately after, Rudolf Steiner's activities were focused in Dornach around the building of the first Goetheanum. The centrepiece of the interior of the building was to be a sculpture carved by Rudolf Steiner and his co-worker Edith Maryon, known as 'the Representative of Man', with Christ at its centre. This work of art visualized the dynamic of forces through which the earthly development of humanity takes place. In this course of lectures—one of several given by Rudolf Steiner during this period in which he presents a spiritual account of human evolution—he explains the unique and essential effect made possible by the 'Mystery of Golgotha' in the development of humanity.

As part of this overview, Steiner refers to the philosophical work of Aristotle in relation to Socrates and Plato (see lecture 4). The 'ethics' of Aristotle presents a theory of the human being in which 'nature' develops a person only up to a certain point.* This, however, includes a number of 'potential abilities' that have become known as the Aristotelian 'Virtues' (for example, *courage* and *temperance*). These Virtues refer to human qualities that can only come to expression through free will and the 'right judgement' of the individual; for example, the ability to perceive the appropriate mean, in the case of *courage*, between *rashness* and *cowardice*. These are *moral skills* that, like other skills, have to be developed and practiced.

According to the above view, there is no natural necessity for human beings to fulfil their complete developmental potential. Good

* See Aristotle, *The Nicomachean Ethics*, Oxford 2009.

judgement of the given circumstances, and a correctly practiced initiative, is required to exercise each type of virtuous action, without the lapse into the 'too little' or the 'too much'. 'Nature' provides us with the materials through which we can complete our development, but the actual fulfilment of human completion, or *eudaimonia*, is dependent upon our own freely chosen action.

Rudolf Steiner presents a broader context of human evolution and development which might be seen as analogous to that presented by Aristotle more than two thousand years previously. Human development has passed the point that is provided by outer nature. The remainder of Earth evolution depends upon the individual, inner spiritual activity of human beings.

Steiner describes two quite different impulses in human evolution, whose effects appear on the outer stage of human history, for which he uses the historical names 'Lucifer' and 'Ahriman'. Both of these can be viewed from the aspects of cosmic-spiritual events, cultural history, and the personal experience of the soul in the current stage of human development. Steiner presents them as essential for the progress of human evolution, provided that they can be held in balance. This is similar to the way that each person makes use of both their left and right sides, in order to progress in a chosen direction. This coordination and balance is only possible with the use of another force that provides a higher perspective, over and above that of the other two, and thereby is able to make use of them without falling to either side.

These lectures do not have the introductory character of Rudolf Steiner's public presentations. Rather, they presume prior knowledge of anthroposophy—of a good and detailed acquaintance with the spiritual world conception set out in the author's basic books. However, they are integral to the development of a clear picture of the being and activities of the Archangel Michael within the context of the cosmic and human evolution that is set out in Rudolf Steiner's book *Occult Science, An Outline*, particularly chapters 4 and 6. Out of this cosmically broad context, the nature and activities of different spiritual beings are characterized through a description of the roles they play in the development of human nature during our present epoch.

The simplistic moral dualism of 'good' versus 'evil', that often shapes the judgement of modern consciousness, is contrasted with an altogether more subtle and nuanced account of human development. For instance, if each individual person did not possess the possibility of being selfish, then no deeds would be free and all actions would be determined. If knowledge was never restricted and narrow, but rather always true and complete, then no new individual perspectives could be added to the existing cosmos. It is only through the discovery of a third 'imperative'—that Rudolf Steiner identifies with what he calls the Christ Impulse—that human beings can hold in balance the two kinds of one-sidedness. Otherwise, such one-sidedness would propel us away from further human development. Each of the two potentially negative tendencies are necessary for the advancement of free actions and rich, multiple and individualized perspectives of experience and knowledge. This virtuous power of the Christ Impulse to keep balance is not by a cancellation of the two opposing forces, but by a *dynamic interaction*. That virtue, like those of Aristotle, is also one which nature does not automatically provide to human beings. Each person can only discover and participate in such a virtue freely, towards the further completion of human development.

David Jones, October 2015

LECTURE 1

DORNACH, 21 NOVEMBER 1919

OVER the coming days I shall be speaking about how we human beings of the present time have the opportunity to form a relationship with that spiritual power about which it can be said that as the power of Michael it is able to intervene in spiritual and thus also in all other events on the earth. Today it will be necessary to prepare for what we shall be saying. We shall have to approach the subject from various points of view which will make it possible for us to give a proper account, on the basis of the symptoms we see all around us, of the different interventions emanating from the power just mentioned. In order to speak in all seriousness about the spiritual world we must remember always to pay attention to what is visible in the physical world in the shape of revelations from the spiritual powers. One must endeavour to penetrate, as it were, the veil of the physical world in order to reach what is at work in the spiritual world. What is present in the physical world can be observed by any one of us; what is at work in the spiritual world then helps us solve the riddles posed by the physical world. The important thing is to develop a real sense for the riddles posed by the physical world. In these important matters entirely serious attention must be paid to what I have been saying during the period of time that has preceded these current lectures.[1] One cannot apply one's personal views about the world when endeavouring to reach a true understanding of something that involves not only humanity as a whole but indeed the whole world as such. One must divest oneself of merely personal interests. The best way for us to gain an understanding of our task in the world and of how we can be of value there is to free ourselves from what is personal in the narrower sense.

As you know, our evolution, the evolution we understand to be that of the earth, was preceded by another evolution, so that in fact we find ourselves planted firmly within an entire cosmic evolution. You know, firstly, that this evolution is progressing and that it has reached a point beyond which it will continue to develop further, towards more advanced stages. And, secondly, you also know that when we consider the world as such we are involved not only with the beings we encounter here on earth, those of the mineral, animal, plant and human kingdoms, but also with entities who stand above those kingdoms, whom we have described as beings of the higher hierarchies. Whenever we speak about evolution as a whole we have to pay attention also to those higher hierarchies.

These beings in their turn also evolve. The analogy of our own human evolution and of the other kingdoms of the earth can help us understand this. Please consider how we human beings have made our way through a Saturn, a Sun and a Moon evolution and have now arrived on our Earth. Looking at our cosmic evolution in this way, we can say that in our present, earthly surroundings we now find ourselves in the fourth stage of our evolution.

When we consider the beings who are at the stage immediately above our own human stage, the Angeloi, we can say of them, simply as an analogy: Although their forms are entirely different from those of human existence and although we cannot perceive them with our physical human senses, they have reached the evolutionary stage of Jupiter.

And as for the Archangeloi we see that they are at the evolutionary stage which humanity will have reached on Venus. And the Archai, the Spirits of Time, those beings who have a very special significance for us in our earthly evolution, have meanwhile progressed to the Vulcan stage of evolution.

This now brings us to the meaningful question concerning the next higher class of beings, those belonging to the hierarchy of the Spirits of Form. If we ask what stage these Spirits of Form have reached, we have to say that they have moved beyond what we as human beings can discern as the Vulcan evolution, beyond what we can as yet conceive of as our future evolution. These Spirits of Form have reached a stage beyond the seven stages of which we can have any understanding and they are now at the eighth stage of evolution. We can say that while we human beings are now at the fourth stage of evolution, the Spirits of Form are at the eighth stage.

But we cannot imagine this sequence of evolutionary stages as happening one after the other, for we must realize that everything is jumbled together. Just like the atmosphere surrounding and penetrating the earth, the eighth sphere of evolution to which the Spirits of Form belong penetrates the sphere in which, as human beings, we find ourselves at present. So let us now look closely at these two stages of evolution.

As human beings we are now in a sphere which has reached the fourth stage of evolution. But, while initially ignoring everything else, we also find ourselves in the kingdom which the Spirits of Form consider to be theirs, yet which is all around us and within us too. We can now consider the human being in his development. We have frequently made distinctions between the various components of this human being. We have differentiated the head development from the other aspects of the human being's development. We also divide the rest of the development into that of the breast and that of the limbs but we shall ignore this further division for the present. For now let us take the standpoint that the human being consists of everything belonging to the head and everything present in the other parts of his makeup.

If you see this [drawing (Plate 1)] as a picture, you can think of the surface of an ocean in which the human being is wading and moving forwards, with only his head above the surface. This is of course only a picture, but it shows the present situation of the human being. Everything in which the head is rooted would have to be counted as belonging to the fourth stage of evolution, while that in which he is wading or swimming forward would have to be described as the eighth stage of evolution. The remarkable fact is that with his head the human being has, in a way, grown beyond the element in which the Spirits of Form unfold their own specific being. With regard to the formation of his head, the human being has become, you might say, emancipated from what is fully impregnated by the characteristics of the Spirits of Form.

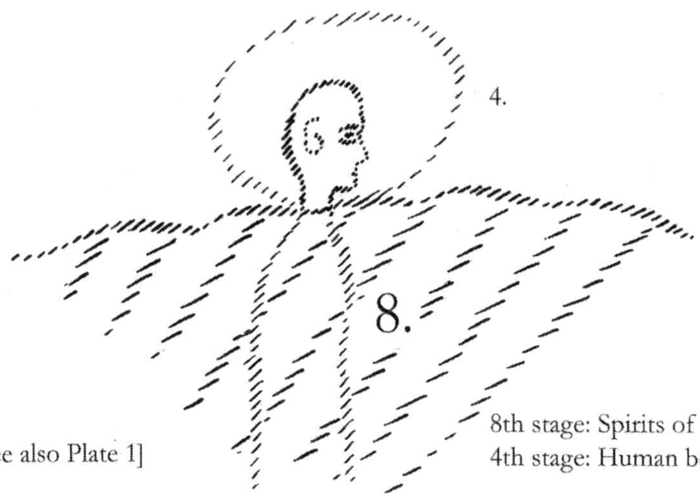

[See also Plate 1]

8th stage: Spirits of Form
4th stage: Human being

Only by fully understanding this can one truly acquire an understanding of the human being. Only through this can one fully grasp the special status the human being has in the world. Only on this basis can we rightly grasp the fact that although the human being senses a certain creative influence within himself that emanates from the Spirits of Form this influence reaches him not through the capacities of his head but through the effect the other parts of his organism have on his head. As you know, we breathe and, speaking in ordinary physiological terms, our breathing is connected with the circulation of our blood. Our blood is also driven up into our head. In this way our head lives in an organic connection with the other parts of our organism. It is nourished and enlivened by the rest of our organism.

You must distinguish clearly between these two facts. The one is that the head is in direct contact with the outside world. When you see something, you are seeing it with your eyes. This is a direct connection between the outside world and your head. But on the other hand, when you consider how your head lives through the breathing process and the circulation of the blood, you see how the blood shoots up into your head. Here there is no direct link between your head and the environment, but only an indirect one.

Of course you shouldn't be pedantic about this and say that we inhale the air we breathe through our mouth, so breathing also belongs to the head. That is why I said that this is only a picture. Organically, what we inhale through our mouth is not really connected with our head; it belongs to the other parts of our organism.

The basic concept here is that we are living in two spheres: firstly in the sphere into which we have been placed by having undergone the Saturn, Sun and Moon evolutions, so that we have now arrived at the Earth evolution and are thus at the fourth stage of our evolution; and secondly we are also living in a sphere which belongs to the Spirits of Form in the same way that the Earth evolution belongs to us—while our head is excluded from it, the other parts of our organism with all our sense impressions exist in this eighth sphere. Once you have taken all this into account you will have some basis upon which to consider what is to follow.

But first I want to mention yet other concepts to contribute to this basis. Further necessary influences to be considered are the beings who also participate in world events, as I have often mentioned: the luciferic and the ahrimanic beings. Let us look first at what one might call the most external elements belonging to the luciferic and ahrimanic beings. Together with us they inhabit the spheres which we also inhabit. In considering the most external characteristics of the luciferic beings we have to regard them as possessing those forces which we human beings feel when we want to give way to fantasy in a one-sided way, when we enter into visionary reverie, when—speaking in pictures—we want to fly up beyond the confines of our head. When as human beings we want to rise up beyond our head, the forces in our human organism that play a part in this are the universal forces of luciferic beings. Imagine beings entirely formed out of something in us which strives to rise beyond our head. These are those luciferic beings who have a certain relationship with our human world. And now think the reverse; think of everything that presses us down into the earth, wanting to make of us sober philistines and causing us to develop materialistic attitudes which fill us with dry intellectual ideas and so on. These are the ahrimanic powers.

All these things, which I have mentioned more from the angle of the soul, can also be expressed in a more bodily way. One can say: The human being is always in a kind of central position between what his blood wants to do with him and what his bones want to do with him. The bones perpetually want to rigidify us; in other words they constantly want to harden us and make us ahrimanic in our body too. Blood, though, wants to drive us out of ourselves. Pathologically speaking: Blood can become feverish, so that the human being is also driven organically into the realm of fantasy. And the bones can envelop the whole organism in their nature, making the human being bony and sclerotic, as happens to almost all of us in old age to some extent. That is when the human being carries the death-bringing element within himself: the ahrimanic element. One could say that everything in the blood tends towards the luciferic, and everything in the bones tends towards the ahrimanic, while the human being holds the balance between them; from the point of view of the soul he must hold the balance between too much sentiment and too much sober philistinism.

In a certain way we could also characterize these two beings more profoundly. When we consider what is interesting for the luciferic beings in matters of the cosmos, we find that their main interest is to make the human world disloyal to those spiritual beings whom we should consider to be the creators of humanity and the human world. The luciferic beings want nothing other than to make the world stray from the divine beings although not, in the first instance, in order to take over the world for themselves. From various comments I have already made about the luciferic beings you will understand that this is not their main aim. For them the main aim is to disengage the world from that which the human being feels to be his own divine beings, to keep the world free of these.

The purpose of the ahrimanic beings is different. It is their firm intention to bring the human realm, and thus the rest of the earth, into their own sphere of influence, to make it, and especially first of all the human beings, dependent on them. Whereas the luciferic beings have always been and still are intent on making human beings defect from what they sense to be their own sphere of divinity, the ahrimanic beings tend more towards capturing humanity together with all that is related to it and integrating it into their sphere of influence.

Thus there is in our cosmos, the cosmos with which we as human beings are interwoven, a battle between the luciferic beings who are perpetually striving for freedom, for universal freedom, and the ahrimanic beings who strive unceasingly for power and strength. This battle, which is all around us, permeates everything. So now I ask you to retain the second idea that is important for our considerations. The world in which we live is permeated by luciferic and ahrimanic beings, so that there exists the tremendous contradiction between the liberating tendency of the luciferic beings and the urge of the ahrimanic beings to exercise power.

Once you pay attention to this, you will say to yourself: I can properly comprehend the world only when I look at it in relation to the number three. On the one hand there is everything that is luciferic, and on the other everything that is ahrimanic. And between the two is the human being as the third element, who cannot help but create a balance between the two in sensing his own divinity. We can only reach an understanding of the world if we take this trinity as the basis and realize clearly that our human life is like the balancing beam of the scales {drawing}. Here is the balancing beam, and on this side is one pan of the scales, the luciferic one, pulling upwards. And here, on the other side, is the ahrimanic one, dragging downwards. What maintains the balancing beam in the horizontal position is the being of man.

Initiates who understood such mysteries in the past always maintained, with regard to human evolution, that the world existence into which humanity has been placed can only be comprehended on the basis of the number three. In its basic structure it cannot be comprehended on the basis of any other number. Speaking in our language, we may therefore say that in world existence Lucifer represents one pan of the scales and Ahriman the other, while between them the balance is maintained by the Christ Impulse. {Plate 2}

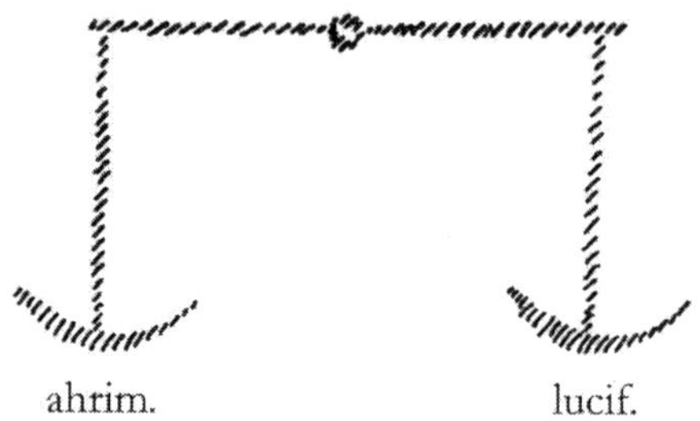

One might well imagine that the luciferic and ahrimanic powers would be rather interested in hiding this mystery of the number three. After all, a proper understanding of this mystery of the number three would enable human beings to bring about a balance between the ahrimanic and the luciferic powers. In other words on the one hand they would be free to use what is luciferic for the good of cosmic aims, and on the other hand the same would be the case with regard to what is ahrimanic. The most normal spiritual state of mind for the human being consists in entering in the right way into this threefoldness, this trinity of the world, this world structure in so far as it is based on the number three.

As we shall consider in more depth tomorrow and the next day regarding influences which are brought to bear on human spiritual and cultural life, there was and is a strong tendency to confuse human beings with regard to the significance of the number three. There is a strong tendency to bamboozle them with regard to what we may truly call this sacred number three. In more recent human culture we can observe very clearly how this structuring in accordance with the number three has come to be almost entirely obliterated by the number two.

Just consider, as I have frequently discussed here, that even to understand Goethe's *Faust* rightly one has to know how confusion regarding the number three plays into this great drama about the world. If in his day Goethe had fully understood the true situation, he would have confronted Faust not only with Mephistopheles who, as we know, represents the ahrimanic power, but also with the luciferic power. Then Lucifer and Mephistopheles would both have appeared in *Faust*. I have frequently explained this here. If you study Goethe's Mephistopheles character you will see clearly how Goethe everywhere mixes together the luciferic and ahrimanic elements in the character of Mephistopheles. In Goethe's work the figure of Mephistopheles is a compound of two elements. He is not a uniform character. Luciferic and ahrimanic elements are thoroughly mixed together. I have gone into this more deeply in my booklet about Goethe's *Faust*.[2]

This confusion, which also played its part in *Faust*, is the result of a delusion which has taken hold in more recent times—things were different earlier on—that the number two is applicable in place of the number three: good on the one side and evil on the other, God and the devil.

Please remember, therefore, that to gain any insight into the structure of the world we must take account of the number three, where the luciferic and the ahrimanic elements are in opposition to one another and where the divine element of God consists in holding the balance between the two. In opposition to this we have the mistaken illusion of the number two which has entered into humanity's cultural development: God and the devil, with the divine powers above and the diabolical ones down below. The human being has been as though squeezed out of the balance by having had concealed from him the fact that the true salvation of world understanding lies in a proper comprehension of the number three and by having been shown instead that the structure of the world is governed by the number two. Despite everything, even the best human endeavours have fallen prey to this error.

If we want to enter into this matter, we must do so very much without any prejudice; we must absolutely place ourselves out there in the sphere where there is no prejudice. And then we must also make a clear distinction between things and names. We must not be tempted to assume that by having given a being a specific name we have already gained a full sense of what that being is.

When we look at those beings whom we should feel to be divine beings for humanity, we must realize that we can only have a true sense of who they are when we think of them as holding the balance between the luciferic and the ahrimanic principle. In seeking the divine, we shall never fully find it if we do not enter properly into this matter of threefolding. Look at Milton's poem *Paradise Lost* or Klopstock's *Der Messias* which was influenced by *Paradise Lost*.[3] These show no true comprehension of a threefold universal structure; they tell of an assumed battle between heaven and hell and in this way contribute to bringing the delusion of a duality into our cultural development. Here we have the illusion of a combat between heaven and hell being brought into our popular culture by two universally known more modern poems.

There is no point in the way Milton or Klopstock speak of the beings of heaven as divine beings. They can only be what human beings should know as divine beings if the foundation on which they stand is the threefold structure of the world. Only then would one be able to say: Here is a battle between the good principle and the evil principle. But as things stand, goodness is attributed to a duality, with names taken from what is actually divine and given to beings who are devilish, who are an anti-divine element. What is the consequence of this in reality? This actually amounts to nothing less than pushing the divine out of our consciousness; the luciferic element is given the name of the divine, so that the battle is between Lucifer and Ahriman, with Ahriman being accorded luciferic characteristics while the divine characteristics are attributed to the realm of Lucifer.

This shows us how momentous such a view can become. A confrontation such as that shown in Milton's *Paradise Lost* or Klopstock's *Messias* is said to be a conflict between divine and diabolical elements, whereas in truth it is about the luciferic and the ahrimanic element. There is no awareness of a truly divine element but instead the divine names are attributed to the luciferic element.

Milton's *Paradise Lost* and Klopstock's *Messias* are spiritual creations arising out of more recent human consciousness. What takes place in these works belongs to the general consciousness of humanity. The illusion of the number two has taken up residence in more recent human consciousness while the truth of the number three has been pushed into the background. Profound creations emanating from humanity in recent times, which with some justification are regarded as being among the greatest productions of these times, are a cultural *maya*, a great delusion which has arisen out of recent humanity's great delusion. What is at work in this illusion is basically a creation emanating from ahrimanic influences, those influences which will one day come to full concentration in the incarnation of Ahriman about which I have already spoken to you.[4] This illusion in the midst of which we find ourselves is nothing other than the result of that false view of the world, which has been making its appearance everywhere in recent civilization, and which places heaven into opposition with hell. Heaven is looked upon as being divine while hell is seen as being diabolical, whereas on the one hand it is the luciferic elements that are termed divine while on the other the ahrimanic elements are termed diabolical.

We need only consider what interests have come into play during more recent cultural history. Even the threefold ordering of the human organism, or indeed of the human being as a whole, was abolished in a certain sense by the Ecumenical Council of Constantinople in the year 869.[5] The dogma was established that Christians must believe not in the threefold but in a twofold being of man. Belief in body, soul and spirit was frowned upon, and medieval theologians and philosophers, who still knew a great deal about the truth, had great difficulties in getting around this because belief in body, soul and spirit was declared a heresy. They were obliged to teach the dichotomy: the human being consists of body and soul, not body, soul and spirit. And this is why replacing the trichotomy with the dichotomy makes such an immense difference for human spiritual life, as certain individuals know only too well.

One must face up to such depths if one wants to understand what the Jesuit, Father Zimmermann, is referring to in the November issue of *Stimmen der Zeit*.[6] It states that a recent decree promulgated by the Council of Rome prevents Catholics from receiving absolution after confession if they read or possess theosophical writings or participate in any way in theosophical matters. This Jesuit father interprets that article in *Stimmen der Zeit*, which used to be known as *Stimmen aus Maria-Laach*, as a specific reference to my anthroposophy, so that everything ought to be done to prevent Catholics who want to be regarded as genuine Roman Catholics from occupying their minds with anthroposophical literature. One of the main reasons given is that the human being is seen to consist of body, soul and spirit, in other words that we teach something heretical, since the proper belief consists in regarding the human being as having a body and a soul.

I mentioned just now that the distinction between body and soul has come upon modern philosophers without their being aware of this. They think they are conducting unprejudiced scientific thought, they genuinely believe that observation has shown them that the human being consists of body and soul. Yet in actual fact all they, too, are doing is following that dogma which has entered into more recent scientific development. What is nowadays regarded as science is actually entirely dependent upon ways of thinking which have been imposed during the course of more recent human evolution. Do not imagine that the few kind words you feel you ought to address to these people will convert their conviction that anthroposophy is a heresy or that you can persuade them to regard anthroposophy sympathetically. Anthroposophy must find its own way into the world without protection from any other powers however strongly Christian they may consider themselves to be. Anthroposophy can only achieve through inner strength what it is intended to achieve in the world.

You must remember that the Christ Impulse can only be comprehended if it is regarded as the impulse of balance between what is ahrimanic and what is luciferic, if it is properly installed within the trinity. What is it that can be done, one might ask, in order to mislead people regarding the true Christ Impulse? One would have to distract them from the true structure of the world based on the number three and lead them instead to the illusion of the number two which is solely justifiable in matters that are outwardly manifest but not in matters that lie hidden behind what is outwardly manifest but are present in the sphere of truth.

We must begin to realize that in such matters one has to progress beyond mere names. Merely by using the name of Christ does not mean that we have properly characterized the Christ. And one can prevent the Christ from being properly characterized solely by being named if one puts the number two in the place of the number three. If someone wanted to steer people away from a proper conception of Christ that person would merely need to put the number two in the place of the number three. So if the Christ Impulse is to be spoken of in the true sense, then it is necessary to replace the number two by the number three.

There is, though, no need as of today to condemn people on account of their heresy. You do not have to describe Milton's *Paradise Lost* or Klopstock's *Messias* as infernal writings of the devil, for you can of course still enjoy the beauty and greatness of these writings. But you must be clear about the fact that such works, in so far as they represent the flower of popular human civilization, have absolutely nothing to say about Christ. Such writings are based on the erroneous assumption that whatever does not comply with human evolution has to be counted among what comes from the devil, while on the other hand one also has what is divine. No! All that one has is something luciferic. And if one then writes about a 'lost paradise' one is in reality describing the expulsion of mankind from the realm of Lucifer into the realm of Ahriman. So what is being described is not the yearning of mankind for the divine but the yearning of mankind for the realm of Lucifer. What you are seeing in Milton's *Paradise Lost* and in Klopstock's *Messias* are descriptions of humanity's longing for the realm of Lucifer. And this is all you should see in them.

Certain ideas that have been taken up by modern humanity are therefore very much in need of reassessment. In preparing seriously to think and feel anthroposophically, we are today not faced by small decisions but by momentous ones. We are faced with having to take very seriously something frequently said by Nietzsche.[7] His words about the reassessment of certain values must be taken very, very seriously. What humanity has achieved in recent times will have to be very much reassessed.

There is no need, however, to condemn heretics out of hand. We continue to perform scenes from Goethe's *Faust*,[8] and I have devoted decades to the study of Goethe.[9] You will read in my small book *Goethes Geistesart* that this has not blinded me to Goethe's wrong characterization of Mephistopheles. But merely to say that Goethe's Mephistopheles is wrong, so let's get rid of him, would be rather a narrow-minded reaction. That is how those who pronounce judgement on heretics behave, and as modern individuals we ought not to place ourselves in this position. On the other hand, though, we should not take the easy way out by allowing the newer pronouncements of general cultural life to become ingrained in us. It will be necessary for humanity to learn a very great deal. We shall have to revalue many things.

All these things are bound up with the mission of Michael in regard to those beings of the higher hierarchies with whom he, in his turn, is connected. Tomorrow and the day after tomorrow we shall have more to say about how we may comprehend those impulses which radiate from him into our human existence on earth.

LECTURE 2

DORNACH, 22 NOVEMBER 1919

I spoke yesterday about the error which has entered into our present cultural life while having as yet been correctly comprehended by only a few individuals. From what I said you will have sensed that in drawing attention to this error we have arrived at a very important point regarding the views expressed by spiritual science. For a fruitful development of humanity's spiritual and cultural life it will be essential for us to gain clarity in this matter. I drew your attention to cultural phenomena such as Milton's *Paradise Lost* and Klopstock's *Messias* which have arisen out of general popular thinking in recent centuries. I also pointed out the dangers with which human soul life is confronted through the artistic and cultural excellence that imbues such works if people do not see beyond this in order to reach a proper concept of God and thus also of Christ rather than being led astray by a conception of spiritual life based only on the number two.

By perceiving only a duality of good on the one hand and evil on the other, people have fallen into the error of attributing all evil to what we have come to call the luciferic and the ahrimanic. They have failed to notice that two universal elements have become conflated. As a result it has come about that the luciferic element was pushed to the other side, to the side of the good, so that in worshipping the divine and in recognizing the divine we spoke of God while mingling that name with the luciferic element. That is why it has become so difficult in our time to reach a clear concept of the Christ Impulse within human and world evolution.

Through the culture of centuries, the recognition of this duality has led us to speak on the one hand of the soul and on the other of the body, the bodily nature. And we have lost the connection between the images which tell us what is soul-spiritual and those which tell us what is bodily. Nowadays when we, and especially our academic psychology, speak of our thinking and will, of our soul-nature and feeling, we are merely playing with the sounds made by words. We do not attain any real inner, content-filled idea of the element of soul. And on the other hand we speak about what is matter devoid of any spirit, about something soullessly materialistic; we as it were knock upon this externally hard, calcified, soulless matter and are unable to build any bridges across to the element of soul.

What is spiritual has everywhere fallen apart and become two elements; and what is bodily is at the same time something spiritual. We cannot reach a bridge between what is bodily and what is spiritual by merely theorizing. And because we are unable to achieve this, our whole way of thinking scientifically has acquired this characteristic of a dichotomy between what is of the body and what is of the spirit or soul. Or we could put it like this: On the one hand the various belief systems have ended up pointing to a spiritual element without being capable of working out how this spiritual element enters into what is bodily and physical, how it works creatively upon what is bodily and physical; and on the other hand a soulless knowledge, a soulless view of nature views the body in a way which renders it incapable of seeing through the bodily processes and finding beyond these a spiritual and soul element at work.

Observing from this point of view how present-day science has evolved during the nineteenth and on into the twentieth century, one has to say: Everything we see here reveals itself as a consequence of what we have just been describing. By adding up everything that can be derived from the various aspects we have been discussing here, we shall be able to reach a full comprehension of the misapprehension which today hides what is right.

We speak today about a human being as though he were a homogeneous entity, without taking any account of whether we mean the soul element or the bodily element. We speak today of the soul element as of a unitary entity, and we speak of the bodily element as of a unitary entity. And yet, everything we have been discussing will have shown you that there is above all in the human being a great contrast between what goes into making up his head and—without just now going into all the details—what he has within him apart from his head. [The right-hand part of the drawing on p. 18 is drawn (Plate 3).] When asking about how the human being has evolved our questions must be quite different with reference to his head from the questions to be asked with reference to the rest of his bodily development.

When we observe the formation of the human head—now entirely in its bodily nature—with regard to what it contains for perception by means of the senses and also for thinking and imagining, we have to look far back into the cosmic evolution of the human being. We here have to say: What is now expressed in the formation of the human head has taken a long time to be developed and transformed. It has been developing during the time of Old Saturn, during the time of Old Sun, during the time of Old Moon and now even during the time of Earth evolution. But this is not the case with regard to the other parts of the body. It would be an utter mistake to look for a uniform history of the development of the human being as a whole. So we say [drawing continues (Plate 3)]: The formation of the head points backwards to previous planetary stages of Earth's evolution, the Moon stage, the Sun stage, the Saturn stage. The final result now arrived at by the development of the human head reaches far back into the past. But in order to add the other parts of the human being we cannot return to the Saturn stage, for here we have to say: What the human being has within him apart from his head can be traced back at most, in so far as the formation of the chest is concerned, to the planetary Moon stage [the vertical dividing line is drawn]. And as far as the limbs are concerned, they only arrive during the formation of Earth.

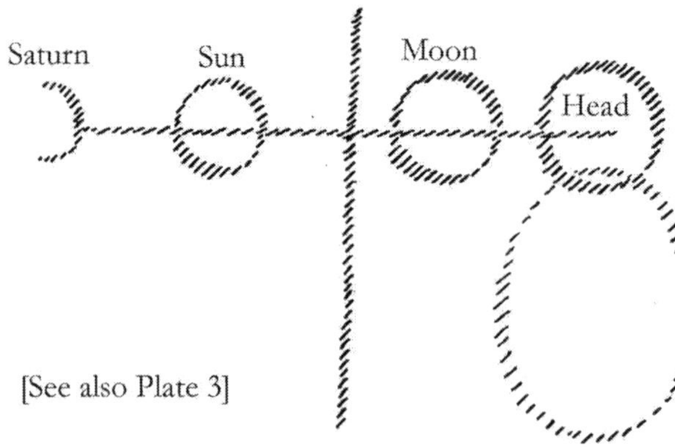

[See also Plate 3]

We only observe the human being correctly if we make a comparison as follows. Please note that a comparison is meant. Hypothetically it would be very easy to imagine, on account of some organic situation or other in the cosmos, on account of some adaptation or other connected with the conditions for growth, how the human being then adds new members. But you would not be tracing the human being as a whole right back to the earlier evolution. You would be saying that one must go back to a certain point where this member or that member was added. We are tempted to think like this because purely in the matter of external size the other parts of the human being together are larger than the head. But the truth is that the formation of the head reaches further back, while the other parts represent later developments. Indeed, when speaking of a connection between the human being and the world of animals in the matter of evolution one can only say that what exists in the human head points back to a former animal evolution. The human head is a transformed animal development, a very much transformed animal shape.

Externally, of course under entirely different physical conditions, the human being had an animal shape before any animals even existed. The animals came into existence later, in addition to human beings. And what was then added to the head as the other parts of the organism only became added to the head at the same time as the development of the animals took place. So this has nothing to do with being descended from animals, and we really do have to say the following. What at first seems to be the noblest element in the human being, his head, points back to an animal nature; it was in this respect that the human being earlier had a kind of animal form. And whatever else we bear in us came into being in parallel with the evolution of the animals as an organic addition and cosmic development of the head.

Now in a certain sense our head has become our organ of thinking. In other words, our organ of thinking is that in us which has been inherited from the animals. But of course it is a rather special kind of inheritance. Looking at a human head today it is, seen anatomically, not exactly something which points back towards an animal shape. But when you look more closely you will see, when you rightly interpret the form of the organs in the head, that they are indeed transformed organs of animal nature, very thoroughly metamorphosed animal forms.

In examining this one must also mention that this transformation of the human head from an animal nature came about because a backward evolution has already commenced in the head. That which was full of life in earlier stages of evolution is, in the human head, already in decline; in the human head it is a backward evolution. I once said that if as a human being we were to consist solely of a head we would never be capable of living. We would be constantly in a process of dying because organically the forces of the head, rather than being life forces, are a process of dying. That which is in our head is constantly being re-enlivened by the rest of our organism. It is owing to the life in the rest of our organism that our head participates in the overall life of our organism. If the head were able to surrender itself entirely to those forces for which it is organized, the forces of sensory perception and thinking and imagining, then it would be in a permanent process of dying. The head tends constantly towards death; it is constantly in need of being enlivened. When we think and when we perceive with our senses, what goes on in our head and in our nervous system in its links with our sensory organs is not a life process connected with growth, for if it were we would be capable only of sleep, we would sink into deep sleep and be entirely incapable of clear thinking. Thinking and sensory perception can only take place in our head because death constantly passes through it, because there is a permanent backward evolution, because the organic processes are constantly being withdrawn.

Those who want to explain thinking and sensory perception in a materialistic manner on the basis of brain processes have no idea what takes place in the head; they believe that the processes going on there can be compared with organic processes of growth and the like. But this is not the case. What takes place in sensory perception and in thinking involves processes of dying, processes of wear and tear, processes of destruction. What is organic and material in its character first has to be worn away and destroyed, and then, above the organic process of destruction the process of thinking rises up.

People today presume that such things can be comprehended in an external way. They think they are perceiving with their senses, but they remain entirely oblivious of what is going on in parallel with this within their organism. Through the processes I have described in my book *Knowledge of the Higher Worlds* they can gradually gain an understanding of what really goes on in the soul processes of sensory perception and thinking. When the soul has developed sufficiently it can occupy itself with thinking and sensory perception while at the same time perceiving what is going on in the brain. The perception there is not of growth processes but of reduction processes which constantly require renewal from the rest of the organism.

Here we have the disappointing concomitant of a true understanding of what goes on in the activity of our head. When thinking and perceiving with his senses, a clairvoyant person has no enjoyment of a burgeoning in the head's organic processes; instead he has to come to terms with a process which is destructive. He has to become acquainted with the fact that a materialist assumes that processes take place in the head which are in fact impossible during thinking or sensory perception. Materialism presumes the very opposite of what actually occurs.

In the case of the human head we are thus concerned with a

development which, while going beyond the animal nature, is actually a backward development, a process of degradation. It is the rest of our organism which is progressing. But we must not assume that this other part of the human organism plays no part in the soul-spiritual processes and our experience of them. Not only does the rest of the organism constantly send blood up into the head. What also rises up in the blood are those soul-spiritual thought forms from which the world is woven and from which our own organism is woven.

These soul-spiritual thought forms are not yet perceived by human beings in their normal state of awareness. But we have now entered an age when it will be necessary for us to begin to become aware of what rises up out of our own being into the forms of thought. As you know, we are asleep not only between falling asleep and waking up; with a part of our being we remain asleep all day long. We are only properly awake in our thinking, in our imagining and in the way we perceive with our senses. We dream in so far as our life of feeling is concerned; and we are fast asleep in the life of our will. As far as our will is concerned we are aware only of the ideas we have but not at all of how the will functions. As far as our consciousness is concerned, what our will actually does is as unconscious as our life of sleep between falling asleep and waking up again.

If we ask after the paths through which knowledge about what is truly divine can reach the human being, then it is not right to point to the path through the head, the path through sensory perception or thinking; the only path to which we can point is that which goes through the other parts of our organism. The great mystery is the fact that our head developed through a long developmental sequence, that what is the rest of our organism developed after that, and that what we can feel to be divine in us must speak to us through the rest of our organism and not through our head. It is important to be clear about the fact that it was only the luciferic beings who initially spoke to us through our head. What we can say is that in addition to our head the rest of our organism was created so that through it the gods are able to speak to us. The Bible does not begin with the sentence 'And God sent a beam of light to the human being so that he might become a living soul'. What it says is that God breathed the living breath into him and he became a living soul. Here we have the correct realization that the human being received the divine impulse through a deed not connected with the head.

This enables you to understand that initially the divine impulse could only reach the human being through a kind of unconscious clairvoyance, or at least through an understanding of what was given through an unconscious clairvoyance. As we know from other considerations, when you look at the Old Testament of our Bible you will discover it to be an outcome of an unconscious clairvoyance. Those who gave their assistance in the creation of the Old Testament also knew this. I cannot just now describe to you how the Old Testament came into being. But I do want to point out how we have considered such things many times. You will find everywhere among the teachers of the ancient Hebrew people the awareness that their God spoke to them not through direct sensory perceptions, not through ordinary thinking, not through all those things for which the head is the mediator. Their God spoke to them through dreams which they understood were not ordinary dreams but dreams steeped in reality; God spoke to them in clairvoyant moments such as that in which he spoke to Moses out of the burning bush, and similar instances.

If one asked the initiates of those ancient times how they imagined that those divine messages came to them, their reply was: The Lord whose name is unutterable speaks from out of his countenance. And the name they gave to the countenance of their God was Michael, that spiritual power whom we count among the hierarchy of the Archangeloi. They felt their God to be the one who remained unknown beyond the visions even of those who are clairvoyant. And when the clairvoyant raised himself up to his God through the state of his soul, the one who spoke to him was Michael. But this Michael spoke only to those who were able to bring themselves into a state of consciousness which differed from that of ordinary consciousness, a certain kind of clairvoyance through which that consciousness arose which otherwise only lives and moves in the human being between falling asleep and waking up, or through the will which remains in the unconscious and is asleep even when we are wide awake.

So in ancient Hebrew the secret teaching of the Yahweh revelation was termed the revelation of the night; one felt revelation through Michael to be revelation of the night. On the one hand people looked into the world through sensory perceptions and through human thinking and said: The knowledge and understanding which reaches the human being along this path does not yet contain the divine. But when, from this form of consciousness, they developed a different form of consciousness, they then found themselves addressed by the countenance of God, Michael, who revealed the true secrets which are connected with the human being. That which was then revealed to them built a bridge between the human being and those powers who cannot be perceived in the external world of the senses and cannot be comprehended with an understanding that is bound to the brain.

We are therefore obliged to say: In pre-Christian times human beings lived in such a way that they were able to perceive sensory perceptions which gave them guidelines for their deeds on earth; but on the other hand they would only have—but did not have—what was appropriate for ordinary consciousness if they were to retain consciousness between falling asleep and waking up again. While one is awake one is in the company of spiritual beings—and the people knew this. But these spiritual beings are not—as people supposed during the time of the Old Testament—those beings who created them, for those are in fact the luciferic beings. The beings who were sensed to be creative for humanity worked on the human being between falling asleep and waking up, or on those parts of the human being which also slept during the day. During Old Testament times, the God Yahweh was spoken of as the ruler of the night, and the servant of the ruler of the night, Yahweh's countenance, was Michael. And it was Michael who came to mind when one referred to all those prophetic inspirations through which more could be comprehended than through knowledge of the sense-perceptible world.

And what consciousness is it that lies behind all this? Behind all this lies the consciousness that has grown out of the sphere of existence in which those beings who surround Yahweh are at work while the creation of the human head is surrounded by luciferic beings. A secret which was maintained through all the temples, and which was indeed very close to the truth, was that in protruding above the human organism the human head was that part of the human being which was directed towards the luciferic beings. In that the head protruded above the human organism, people knew Lucifer was protruding above the human organism. The power which has led the human head beyond its animal-ness and into its present form is a luciferic power. And the power which the human being should sense to be divine will have to stream up into the head out of the night-time situation of the rest of the organism. This is what human beings were able to know during pre-Christian times.

And then the Mystery of Golgotha burst into earthly evolution. As we know, the Mystery of Golgotha signifies a coming together of a supersensible being with earthly evolution through the body of Jesus of Nazareth, a coming together which, through the death on Golgotha, brought about the uniting of the Christ Being with the earthly human being. What did this bring about in earthly evolution? This is actually what brought meaningfulness into earthly evolution. The earth would have lacked meaningfulness if the human being had developed here with his intellect tied to his head, an intellect which was luciferic in origin and would thus have had to remain in a state of sleep in order to perceive the divine while looking at the external earthly world with the light of sun and stars shining upon it. The earth would never have become meaningful because it is when he is awake that the human being belongs to it. A sleeping human being is not aware of his connection with the earth's existence.

The Christ Being lived in a human body which had to pass through death. This gave the earth a jolt in its development and through it everything in earthly evolution received new meaning. First of all it became possible for the human being gradually to recognize his creative divine powers also during the daytime, in ordinary wakefulness, in his ordinary state of consciousness. The only reason why this is still misunderstood today is because insufficient time has as yet passed since the Mystery of Golgotha for the human being to be able also in daytime consciousness to look into that world into which the prophets of the Old Testament were able to look in the days which they sensed to be permeated with the revelations of their ruler of the night, Yahweh, and his countenance Michael. A time of transition has been necessary. During the course of the nineteenth century—the whole of oriental wisdom, although from an entirely different point of view, points to the importance of this process of the nineteenth century[10]—the time began to arrive in which human beings must recognize that something has been fulfilled, something which has hitherto not been fulfilled, namely that latent in them there now exists the ability to see through daytime revelation what was formerly only revealed during the night, through Michael.

This had to be preceded by a great error, a night-time of knowledge. I have often said that I do not agree with those who maintain that our age is a period of transition. Of course I know that every age is a period of transition. But I don't wish to come to a halt in such an abstract formulation, for what is important is to explain what the transition is which is undergone during a certain period. The transition of our time is the following. Human beings must recognize that what was formerly only night-time awareness must now come through daytime awareness. In other words, Michael was the one who revealed through the night and must now become the one who reveals during the day. Michael must be transformed from being a night spirit to being a day spirit. For him the Mystery of Golgotha signifies the transformation from being a night spirit to being a day spirit.

But this understanding, which ought to be entering more rapidly than we can imagine into general human knowledge, is preceded by a still greater error, the greatest imaginable error which has been possible in human evolution despite the fact that today in many circles it is still regarded as an especially important and essential truth. The origin of the human head has remained fully hidden from more recent humanity; the luciferic spirituality linked with the human head has remained fully hidden. As I have said, the human being was seen as a unit. When questions were raised as to his origins, the answer given was that he is descended from the animals, whereas in reality only that part of the human being which is luciferic stems from the animals. That, however, through which formerly his divine creators spoke to him from out of his state of sleep only arose—after the animals had come into being—as an addition to the human head. Everything connected with the human being has been lumped together, so that one speaks of humans as being descended from the animals. This is something like a punishment of knowledge which has come upon humanity, although in my use of the word 'punishment' here I am giving the word a somewhat different interpretation.

What might be the origin of the tendency to invent the idea that the human being is descended from the animals whereas the true facts are as already described in our depiction of the origins of the head and of the other parts of the organism? What has misled humanity to believe that the human being as a whole is descended from the animal realm?

Well, in the stretch of time between the Mystery of Golgotha and our era, a stretch of time which was in a sense also intended as a preparation for an understanding of the Mystery of Golgotha while the ancient heathen wisdom was gradually withdrawing owing to that endeavour to comprehend Christianity, the new comprehension of the spirit had not yet fully developed. And thus the ahrimanic element gradually insinuated itself into human evolution. And because one had failed to recognize the luciferic element in the human head, so had one also failed to recognize in the other parts of the human organism the ahrimanic element, with which the divine element does battle. Thus the purely ahrimanic invention arose of the human being stemming from the animal succession.

That the human being stems from the animal succession is an

ahrimanic inspiration. Such knowledge is purely ahrimanic in character. The wisdom showing the human head as a luciferic formation became obscured; this led to the error which stated that the human being stemmed from the animal succession. Because people no longer rightly comprehended the origins of the human head they could also no longer comprehend the other side of the matter. This is how the error crept in of believing that the human being as a whole was descended from the animal kingdom. And this is also how in more recent civilization a whole world-view has arisen in which the human head is regarded as the noblest element, with the other parts of the human being beside it, just as good and evil, or heaven and hell, are juxtaposed in the world, a duality instead of a trinity. What should in truth have been known is that the human being initially owes his head to the wisdom of the world, to the luciferic wisdom of the world, and that this luciferic wisdom must gradually become imbued by other elements as well.

Once human evolution has passed through the Saturn, Sun and Moon evolutions and reached the beginning of Earth evolution, the spiritual power which brings the luciferic element into the human head is the Michael Power. 'And he threw his opposing spirits down on to the earth.' This means: Because of this throwing down of the luciferic spirits,[11] the spirits who were in opposition to Michael, the human being became imbued with reason, with that which comes into being out of the head.

Thus it was Michael who sent his opponents to the human being so that by taking in this opposing, this luciferic element, the human being might receive his reason. And then the Mystery of Golgotha entered into human evolution. The Christ Being passed through the death of Jesus of Nazareth. The Christ Being united Himself with human evolution.

The era of preparation has now passed. In the supersensible world, Michael himself participated in the events of the Mystery of Golgotha. Since the final third of the nineteenth century Michael has occupied a very special place within human evolution.[12] The first thing that should come about through a proper understanding of the human being's relationship with Michael is that we begin to comprehend those secrets which are revealed, for example, in the situation of the human head and its relationship with the other parts of the human organism.

It is essential for us to realize that because of our lack of comprehension regarding the true origin of the human head we have fallen into error with regard to the origin of the human being as a totality. Through not wishing to understand that a luciferic formation had come about in the human head, human beings succumbed to the illusion that what belonged to the human head could be attributed to the same origin as that of the other parts of the human being. Humanity must now come to grips with these mysteries. Human beings must become able boldly and bravely to face up to the knowledge that they have to improve their comprehension of divine mysteries which are new to them concerning their understanding of the head and their purely earthly wisdom or intelligence. And the first thing must be a correction of the great error inherent in the materialistic interpretation of evolutionary doctrine which states that the human being as a whole stems from the animal succession.

This will be the only path we can follow in order to see in the human being as he stands before us not, on the one hand, something purely of the spirit and soul living in a body with, on the other hand, something that is purely bodily without any soul. No, we must look at something concretely spiritual which is, however, working in a luciferic manner in the human head, while there is also at work in the human being apart from the head an opponent who is ahrimanic in nature.

Speaking in imaginations, we may point backwards to how the luciferic was incorporated into the human being through the Michaelic Impulse. But now, through that which Michael has become, the human being must be deprived of the ahrimanic aspect. We are presented today by our external science with a human being who, in view of anatomy and physiology or what our external senses observe, is presumed to be a reality. We must, though, now become capable of perceiving the human being in such a way that with every fibre we see in him what is spiritual, what is concretely spiritual as well as belonging to the body. We must come to realize that the blood running in the living human being is not the blood which might drip away; for this blood is filled with spirit in a special way. We must come to know this spirit which pulses through our blood. We must come to know the spirit which pulses through our nervous system when that nervous system is in a dying phase, and so on. We must come to see the spiritual element in every single expression of what is living.

Michael is the spirit of strength. In entering into human evolution, he must empower our capacity to see not on the one hand an abstract spirituality and on the other what consists of matter which we can thump and cut up and of which we do not realize that it is, in fact, only an external manifestation of what is spiritual. Michael must permeate us as that strong power which is able to see through matter by seeing within it both what is material and what is spiritual, so that the spiritual is everywhere seen in what is material.

During an ancient phase of human consciousness it was said: In that ancient phase the Word was spirit, but now it became flesh and lived among us—as expressed by the Evangelist. The Word united with the flesh, and this was preceded by the Michael revelation. All these things are processes within human consciousness. It is now time for the reverse process to begin which consists in adding other words to those of the Evangelist. A force must begin within our consciousness which will enable us to see how the human being absorbs that which comes from spiritual worlds through the Christ Impulse, that which must unite itself with humanity, so that humanity need not perish when the earth perishes. We must be able to see how the human being absorbs the spirit not only in his head but in his whole being, so that he becomes entirely permeated by the spirit. The Christ Impulse alone can assist us in this. And for this to happen the interpretation of the Christ Impulse by the Michael Impulse must help. Then we shall be able to add to the words of the Evangelist: And the time must come when the flesh once more becomes the Word and learns to dwell in the realm of the Word.

When we read at the end of the Gospels that 'there are also many other things',[13] this is not an invention by some later author. It refers, rather, to what can only be revealed to humanity piece by piece. Those who regard the Gospels as a finished work never to be altered do not understand them correctly. They must be interpreted according to the words of Christ Jesus: I am with you always, even unto the end of the world.[14]

What this means is: I have revealed myself to you not only in the days when the Gospels were being written; through my Day Spirit Michael I shall always speak to you when you seek to find me. You will be permitted to add to the Gospels through the continuing revelations of Christ, not only those of the first millennium, but also those of the second millennium; and in subsequent millennia there will always be more to add. However truthfully the Gospels may speak, 'In the beginning was the Word, and the Word became flesh and lived among us,' however true this may be, it is also equally true that we must add the revelation: And the flesh of man must become permeated by spirit so that it may be capable of living in the kingdom of the Word and of beholding the divine mysteries. That the Word becomes flesh is the first Michael revelation. That the flesh becomes spirit must be the second Michael revelation.

Lecture 3

DORNACH, 23 NOVEMBER 1919

I mentioned here the day before yesterday that as members of the human race we are at present living in the fourth sphere of our evolution. We know that what is now earthly evolution has evolved gradually from the Saturn evolution out of which firstly the Sun evolution and then the Moon evolution emerged. When we look at this sequence of four configurations of the earthly planet, to which of course humanity as such belongs, we may consider the human being only in so far as he is a being of the head. And we must realize that in speaking in this way we include everything which belongs to the head in that it symbolizes whatever belongs to our perception through the senses and whatever belongs to our human intelligence together with whatever flows into our social life through these. We must include all the experiences we have which arise on account of our being creatures with sense perceptions and creatures of intelligence. All of this is encompassed in my expression 'the human being as a being of the head'.

We speak light-heartedly about being surrounded by the air as physical human beings. We must understand that this orb of the air belongs to us. After all, the air which is at this moment inside us was, only a moment ago, outside us. As human beings we are inconceivable outside this orb of the air. As modern individuals we have become accustomed to imagining that this situation also persisted in earlier times, that we can speak about the air and suchlike in this modern manner also when referring to earlier times. But this is not the case. Today we find it peculiar to speak in the same way as we do about being surrounded by air, when we want to express that we live in a sphere which provides the conditions necessary for beings of the senses and beings of intelligence—for beings of the head when expressed symbolically as I explained just now.

Well, as I said, this is only one of the spheres in which we find ourselves. Actually we exist in various spheres, so now let us proceed to another sphere for humanity and investigate what surrounds us now that we are living on our earth which, having passed through three former stages, is now in its fourth stage of development. The area of this circle denotes everything in which we live now that we are in our fourth sphere of development [the inner circular area below is drawn: orange (Plate 4)].

In addition we live in a further sphere of development, a sphere of development to which the spiritual beings belong who are our creators. Let us initially disregard ourselves, the human beings, and turn our attention to those beings among the higher hierarchies whom we have named the Spirits of Form, those spirits who create all that is inherent in form. In doing so we realize that the sphere which belongs to these divine spirits can only be reached by us as human beings when we have passed through

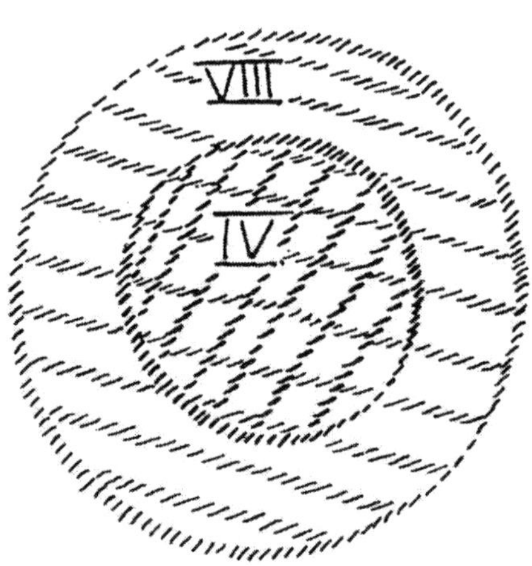

[See also Plate 4]

three further stages of evolution (described in my book *Knowledge of the Higher Worlds* as the Jupiter stage, the Venus stage and the Vulcan stage) and then arrive at the eighth stage. These creative spirits are now at the stage which we as human beings shall reach after the Vulcan stage. This is their sphere, which belongs to them just as the fourth sphere belongs to us. However, we must picture these two spheres as being one within the other, as permeating one another [a larger circular area is drawn over the first one: yellow (Plate 4).] So if I call this other sphere the eighth, we do actually live not only in the fourth but also in the eighth sphere[15] owing to the way in which our divine creators live together with us in this sphere.

If you now examine this eighth sphere, you will see living there not only our divine creator spirits but also the ahrimanic beings. So in the environment of the eighth sphere we live together with those spirits whom we sense to be divine powers, but also with the ahrimanic beings. This is what the distribution of these spiritual beings looks like. And we can now go into more detail regarding these spiritual beings by examining which aspects of ourselves are connected with these spheres.

First of all we observe through the clairvoyance of initiation science that because we are living in the fourth sphere of our development we are, as I have said, perceptive and intelligent beings. But we must never forget that in this very intelligence—which always denotes a combination of sense perceptions and intelligence—the power of what is luciferic is involved. This luciferic power is always closely bound up with the specific type of intelligence which human beings today still regard as their own and with which they most prefer to be involved. Yet this intelligence has only been apportioned to the human being because that higher being of whom I have spoken as the Michael Being has driven the luciferic spirit down into the human sphere, the fourth sphere of humanity, and that is how the intelligent impulse actually entered into the human being.

You can sense what this intelligent impulse signifies in humanity when you examine the impersonal element of what still remains as human intelligence. We human beings do possess many personal interests. We meet one another with our personal interests, and we are individualized through those personal interests. But this individualization is brought up short by the intelligence. As far as our intelligence is concerned, as far as our logic is concerned, we human beings, all of us, possess the same intelligence, and we count on this. We would not all possess this same intelligence if the luciferic influence, imparted by Michael, had not come upon humanity.

It is easy for us to understand one another only because we share our intelligence, only because our shared intelligence is derived from luciferic spirituality. This luciferic spirituality came into being through the way in which Michael imbued, influenced, human beings with the being of Lucifer. And these luciferic influences have developed further during the course of human history. Alongside these, much else has also developed in the human being. Yet still today this luciferic intelligence, which we describe as our own intelligence, is regarded in the widest circles as that which sets the human being apart.

To make this even clearer, you should cast the eye of your soul also over something else which is capable of uniting us throughout the whole earth once it has extended right across the earth. And that is the Christ Impulse. The Christ Impulse is something other than the intelligence impulse. There is something compelling about the intelligence impulse. You cannot make the intelligence of humanity your personal affair. You cannot suddenly personally determine something which has to be decided through intelligence without becoming excluded from social life as being mad.

But on the other hand the only relationship you can gain with the Christ Impulse is a personal one. No one can interfere in the relationship someone else wishes to establish with Christ. This is absolutely a personal matter. But because Christ underwent the Mystery of Golgotha, thus uniting himself with earthly evolution, however many individuals establish their own personal relationship with Christ it will nevertheless be the same. This means that individuals are brought together by something which each one carries out individually, not through compulsion, as would be the case through intelligence, but because the Christ Impulse brings it about that every individual builds his own relationship with Christ in such a way that with every individual it is the same. That is the difference between the intelligence impulse and the Christ Impulse. Throughout all of humanity the Christ Impulse can be the same while also being a personal matter for each individual. Intelligence, on the other hand, is not a personal matter.

Now, what was it into which the Christ Impulse descended? I have already hinted where the answer lies in regard to this. We know that the development of the head is now in regression. With regard to his head, the human being is now constantly dying away. We can point to the cosmic fact that Michael pushed the luciferic beings down into the realm of humanity. In this way the luciferic beings came to reside in the human head, but a human head that is dying away.

And here these luciferic beings began to combat the dying of the human head. So now we come to a secret of human nature which has always been known, in various forms, but which is now almost entirely hidden. In respect of his divine evolution, the human being carries a perpetually moribund development in his head. But this dying away is running parallel with a constant rekindling of life by Lucifer. Lucifer is constantly endeavouring to make our head as alive as the rest of our organism. But from the point of view of the organic realm, Lucifer would deflect the evolution of humanity from its divine tendency if he were to succeed in enlivening the head in the same degree as the rest of the organism is alive.

The divine tendency of human evolution has to work against this. The human being must remain connected with the evolution of the Earth in order to be able to move forward with subsequent Earth evolutions through the Jupiter, Venus and Vulcan evolutions. If Lucifer were to reach his goal, the human being would be unable to follow this predetermined path but would instead become embedded in a cosmos which would be intelligent through and through.

What one could say is that physiologically Lucifer is constantly at work in us by sending up into our head from the rest of our organism the life forces which want to permeate the human head. As seen from the aspect of the soul, Lucifer constantly wants to fill our intelligence, which consists merely of thoughts, of images, with a content of substance. Lucifer always persists—having just now spoken of the physical aspect, I now refer to the soul aspect—he always persists in forming images in the soul in such a way that something which should be of an artistic nature becomes filled instead with something substantial, in other words so that our thought content, our imaginative content becomes permeated instead with ordinary earthly reality. The consequence of this would be that we human beings would move away from that other reality and flee across to a reality of thoughts which would be actual reality and not merely thoughts. There is in our being constantly a tendency for our fantasies to become realities; indeed, the greatest imaginable efforts are made to transform human fantasies into realities.

All things in humanity which cause internal illness are linked with this luciferic tendency. If we can fully comprehend the work of Lucifer in this respect—as he strives to press forces of vitality into the dying forces of the human head—then we shall be able to diagnose every internal illness. And the scientific development of medicine must work towards being able to build on an understanding of this luciferic element. To give matters a push in this direction is one of the tasks of the Michael influence which is now beginning to enter into human development.

Now, on the other hand, the ahrimanic influence is also here. This influence asserts itself from out of the eighth sphere from which the rest of our organism—with the exception of the head—obtains its full vitality; in its own organization it is fully open to vitality. And into this the ahrimanic powers work. They endeavour to send forces of death into the forces of vitality belonging to the other parts of our organism, those forces of death which, according to divine development, otherwise belong to the head. In this way, via the detour of

Ahriman, we receive from the eighth sphere the forces of death—physically speaking.

With reference to the soul element I would have to say the following: Everything that exerts its influence from this eighth sphere is here working on human will, not on human intelligence. The wish for it is based on the human will; the will always contains an aspect of wishing. This wishing aspect is founded on the will into which Ahriman constantly endeavours to bring a personal element of the human being. And it is because the aspect of wishing always lies hidden in the personal element of the human being that our progress towards death is always an image of our soul activity of will. Instead of allowing ourselves to be permeated by the divine ideals, instead of permitting them to enter into our wishing and therefore our will, something personal is always brought into our wishing and our willing.

So we really do find ourselves in a situation of balance between the luciferic and the ahrimanic elements. In the physical realm the luciferic-ahrimanic element transmits to us what is sickness and death. In the soul realm illusion develops caused by the way we regard one thing or another as reality when it actually stems from the world of thought or imagination or fantasy. And regarding the spiritual element, furthermore, the cupidity of egoism enters into the human being by this means. [See also Plate 5]

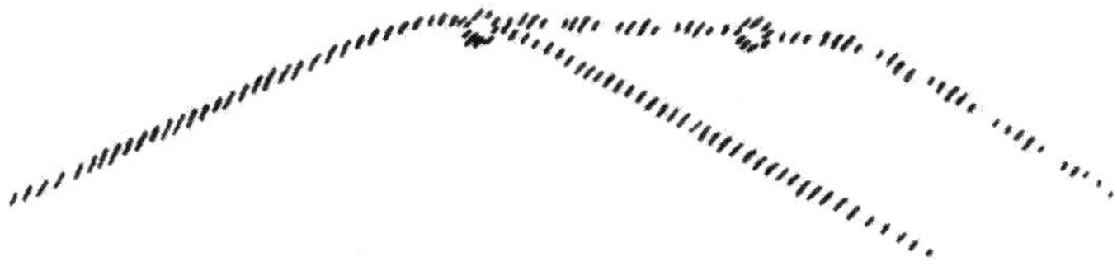

Well, so now we see how the Lucifer-Ahriman duality is bound up with the nature of the human being. And based on Milton's *Paradise Lost*, on Klopstock's *Messias*, and on Goethe's *Faust* I have explained to you how modern, civilized humanity can become mistaken with regard to this duality. And now, as humanity, we have passed the halfway point of our evolution. This is how the situation looks now [drawing]: Initially, earthly evolution ascended until it reached its highest point, after which it began to descend. For reasons we need not explain today, it remained at the same level for some time, from the Graeco-Roman era until the fifteenth century. But since that time earthly human evolution has been properly on the descent.

Physical earthly evolution has been on the descent for much longer. Physically, the descent of earthly development began during the period which preceded our last Ice Age, that is before the catastrophe of Atlantis. This is something we anthroposophists do not need to tell people, for it is already known to geologists,[16] as I have often mentioned. As we walk upon the face of the earth there are many places where we find ourselves stepping on the deteriorating crust of the earth. You need only consult the more superior geological descriptions of the earth's development in order to find verification in natural science that the earth is indeed now on a downward path of its development. And what lives and works in human beings is also on a downward path of development. As human beings we can no longer hope for any improvement in the development of our body. We must look for an upward path by learning to see what there is in the human being that leads onward to further formations of earth development. We must learn to observe the human being of the future. To do this we must think in the way of Michael. Let me now describe more closely what is meant by Michaelic thinking.

When you encounter a fellow human being today you do so with your entirely materialistic consciousness. You say, but not out loud, or indeed not even in your thoughts, but you do say it in the more intimate foundations of your awareness: This is a human being made of flesh and blood, this person consists of earthly substances. You say this of animals, too, and of plants as well. But when you say this with reference to man, to animal and to plant, it is correct only with regard to the mineral realm; it refers solely to the mineral nature.

Let us consider the most extreme case: the human being. In his outer appearance he looks like this [drawing (Plate 5)]. But you do not see this external figure, you do not encounter it with your

physical capacity of perception since more than 90 per cent of it is filled with fluid, with water. What you do see with your physical eyes is its mineral content. What you see is the external mineral content which the human being unites with himself. What you do not see is the human being who brings it all together. You speak correctly when you say: That which is standing before me here are the physical particles with which the human form is filled; these are what make this invisible form visible for me. The human being himself is completely and utterly invisible. All of you sitting here are imperceptible to the physical senses. A certain number of figures are sitting here, and through some inner capacity of attraction they have gathered up particles of matter [drawing (Plate 5)]. These physical particles are what we see. We see the mineral element. The real human beings who sit here are invisible, they are supersensible.

When we say such a thing in full consciousness during every moment of our waking life, this is what we describe as Michaelic thinking: we cease to see the human being in this agglomeration of particles which he has merely organized in a certain way. The animals do likewise, and also the plants; the minerals alone do not. When we become aware of the fact that we are living and moving among invisible human beings, then we are thinking in a Michaelic way.

We speak of ahrimanic beings and of luciferic beings; we speak of the Angeloi, Archangeloi, Archai and so on, the beings of the hierarchies. These are invisible beings. We come to know them through their deeds. We have spoken, in recent days as well, about many of those deeds. We learn to recognize these beings through what they do. Yet is this different as far as human beings are concerned? Here in the physical world we get to know the human being, who is invisible, through the way in which he arranges the mineral particles in a form that resembles a human being. But this is merely an activity, a working of the human being. The fact that we have to be clear about the workings of Ahriman and Lucifer, of the Angeloi, Archangeloi and Archai and so on in a different way merely means getting to know these beings in a different way. But the fact that these beings are supersensible does not distinguish them in any way from us so long as we are aware of what a human being actually is.

We are employing Michaelic thinking when we understand that in our being we do not differ in any way from the supersensible beings. So long as the minerals had something to give them, human beings were able to cope without having this awareness. But now that the mineral world has entered into a downward development, the human being is obliged to grow into a spiritual understanding both of himself and of the world. We can find the inner strength to realize that we need no longer go through the world thinking that this collection of material particles is a human being. The human being is a supersensible being while those particles are merely gestures from the external mineral world pointing to what a human being is.

It has been possible for us to have greater strength to realize these things since the seventies of the nineteenth century. It is solely on account of the ahrimanic influences I described here a week ago that people are rejecting this through not being willing to approach this inner awareness.[17] This is linked to something else in human life. As long as we carry on believing in the error that the human being is a sense-perceptible being and not a supersensible being, so long shall we also be prone to other errors as well. We speak of development and imagine that it will just continue on and on as a matter of course. As you know, it was not possible to depict such a development artistically in our building.[18] When designing the capitals of the columns I had to show the first three in an ascending development, the fourth one in the centre, the fifth in a descending development, the sixth somewhat simpler and the seventh the simplest of all. There, added to the ascending development I had to depict the descending development.

We do actually have the latter in our head. Whereas the rest of our organism is still in an ascending development, our head is already in a descending development. To believe that development can only ascend is to distance oneself from the truth by speaking in the same vein as Haeckel who wrote under the influence of certain errors, maintaining that what was simplest came first, to be followed by further developments which grow ever more complicated and ever more perfect, on and on into infinity.[19] This is nonsense. Every progressive development in turn enters into a regression. Every ascending development is followed by a descending development, every ascent already bears the potential for descent within it. It is one of the most awkward errors of more recent humanity that they have lost touch with the connection between evolution and devolution, between ascending development and descending development. Every ascending development bears within it the potential for descent. At the moment when an ascending development begins to descend, the physical begins to enter into the spiritual. Wherever the physical begins to decline, space arises in which the spiritual can develop. There is room in our head for spiritual development because a physical decline has set in.

We shall not be capable of understanding our human nature or with it the rest of the world until we become able to see things as they really are by bringing our intelligence into connection with luciferic development in the manner I have described. When we have succeeded in this we shall be able to evaluate matters correctly by knowing that our intelligence needs a boost like this if it is to bring us properly to our goal. Lucifer must be prevented by the Christ Principle from turning the human being away from his predestined divine direction.

As I have said, one thing is bound up with another. So, under the influence of that error which has added luciferic characteristics to the divine powers, the human being has a tendency nowadays to be idealistic about how to represent something beautiful. It is of course possible to represent beauty as such. But one must be aware that if one were to devote oneself solely to beauty one would be cultivating within oneself those forces which get caught up in the wake of what is luciferic. For just as in the real world devolution belongs to evolution, so is beauty by itself not one-sidedly present here. Beauty alone, of which Lucifer makes use in his endeavours to delude human beings, would free us from earthly evolution rather than binding us to it. In reality, as with the interplay of evolution and devolution, we are involved with an interplay, or indeed with a fierce battle between beauty and ugliness.

If we wish to understand art in a proper way,[20] we must never forget that the ultimate task of art in the world is to show how beauty and ugliness are bound to be at loggerheads with one another. Simply by taking account of the balance between what is beautiful and what is ugly we find our place in reality, rather than being one-sidedly in a reality which is not ours, but rather that of Lucifer or that of Ahriman.

It is most important for ideas such as these to find their way into human cultural development. In ancient Greece—and you know how enthusiastically I have often spoken in this very place about Greek culture—it was still possible to devote oneself one-sidedly to beauty because at that time human beings, or at least the Greek people, had not yet become bound up in the descending earthly evolution. But since that time we ought no longer to grant ourselves the luxury of cultivating only what is beautiful. This would amount to an escape from reality. We must bravely and courageously face up to the battle between what is beautiful and what is ugly. In this interplay we must become capable of sympathizing and empathizing with both the dissonances and the consonances in the world.

This will bring strength into human evolution, and from this strength will come the possibility of building an inner attitude which will really succeed in taking us beyond the illusion that the human being is no more than a conglomeration of mineral particles which he has heaped up inside himself. We could today already say regarding the physical that the human being does not show the signs of external mineral nature. External minerality is heavy. But that in us which enables us to develop soul qualities—and I don't mean intelligence—is linked not to heaviness but to the opposite of heaviness, namely to that which we might call the upwelling of fluidity. I have described on other occasions how our brain floats in the cerebral fluid. If it did not float in this way, the tiny blood vessels in it would be crushed. When Archimedes[21] was in his bath he discovered that he was less weighty and was so delighted that he uttered his famous 'Eureka'. Of course you learnt about all this in physics. We do not, then, live from being dragged down in our soul but from being lifted up. As far as the soul is concerned we live not by our brain being heavy but by it being lighter on account of the cerebral fluid. We live through that which draws us away from the earth. This can even be a claim made physically today.

What I have been wanting to draw your attention to during these three days has been that we need, with regard to modern life, an attitude of soul which is aware in every waking moment of what is supersensible in our immediate surroundings and which does not succumb to the error of thinking that human beings are real because we see them and spiritual beings are not real because we do not see them. We do not see human beings. This is the error: that we believe we are indeed seeing them. We are in fact no different from the beings of the higher hierarchies. The task facing modern humanity is learning to comprehend the similarity between the beings of the higher hierarchies and ourselves, and even the animals and plants.

We speak of the fact that through the Mystery of Golgotha the Christ Impulse entered into earthly evolution, initially into the evolution of humanity with which it is now intertwined. People say they cannot see Him. Well, they cannot see Him so long as they are in error about the human being, so long as what they are looking at is something entirely other than what the human being really is. As soon as this is no longer a theory but a livingly felt reality of soul enabling us to see something supersensible in the human being, as soon as this is so we will develop in us the ability to perceive the Christ Impulse everywhere among us and say with conviction: Do not seek Him in external gestures, for He is everywhere among you. But it will be necessary to develop modesty and humility in order to believe that it is really important to generate an awareness of the human being primarily and everywhere as a supersensible being.

Merely making a theoretical claim is not sufficient. Only when we really believe it to be—and indeed feel it to be—an absurdity that what confronts us is the actual human being, only then shall we be in the state of soul about which I am speaking.

If you were to go out there to the building site[22] and gather up some of the bits and pieces lying around and clutch them all in front of you so that anyone meeting you would see only broken bricks and scraps of boards, you wouldn't say all this debris arranged in a certain way was a human being. Yet you are doing just the same with the mineral substances arranged inside you when you encounter a fellow human being. You say that because you can see these mineral substances with your eyes they are a human being. The truth is, however, that all this is merely a gesture pointing towards the true human being.

Looking back to pre-Christian times we will find that God's messengers came to the earth in visible form; they revealed themselves to the human being who was then able to comprehend them. The greatest messenger from God to come to the earth was at the same time the One who was able to reveal Himself in the greatest event that took place on the earth without any collaboration by human beings.

We are now living in the age of the Michael revelation. This is another revelation, just like that other one. But it now no longer obtrudes upon human beings because they have entered into the evolution of their freedom. We must go out to meet the revelation of Michael; we must prepare ourselves in order that he may fill us with the greatest strength with which to become aware of what is supersensible in the immediate vicinity of the earth. Do not fail to recognize what this Michael revelation, if approached in freedom, will entail for human beings now and in the near future. Do not fail to recognize how nowadays people are endeavouring to solve the social question on the basis of the remnants of former states of consciousness. Yet everything it was possible to solve through the old states of consciousness has indeed been solved. The earth is on the downward path of its evolution. The challenges facing us today will not be resolved by the ways of thinking arising from olden times. They will only be resolved by a humanity which possesses a new constitution of soul. Our task is to work towards enabling this new constitution of soul to arise among human beings. What we see today weighs on our soul like a terrible incubus: that human beings are unable to extricate themselves from ideas which have been cultivated for thousands of years. We see today how the consequences of these age-old ideas run their course almost automatically; we see how these ideas, practically void of any content, continue to exist as mere husks of words.

All around us people talk of human ideals. Yet what those ideals actually contain is nothing; they are the hollow sounds of words, for humanity now is in need of a new constitution of soul. Once upon a time a call was heard by humanity which in our language we may translate as follows: Change your mind, for the time is fulfilled![23] In those times people were still able to change their mind based on the old soul constitutions. But that is no longer possible. If that demand of old is to be fulfilled now, it must be done out of a new constitution of soul. Michael brought the Yahweh tradition, the Yahweh influence to human beings. Since the end of the 1870s he has been proceeding to bring us an understanding of the Christ Impulse in the true sense of the word if only we are able to go out towards Him. It is up to us to do this. We go out towards Him by fulfilling two things.

As regards our own soul constitution we can say to ourselves: We must turn away from a certain error. I do not want to burden you too much with narrow abstractions or philosophical world-views, but there is one thing to which I must draw your attention because it is a symptom of more recent human evolution. For example, the philosopher Descartes lived at the dawn of the new age.[24] He still knew a certain amount about the spiritual element which, for example, plays in through the dying human nervous system. Yet at the same time he also said: I think, therefore I am.

This is the opposite of what is true. We do not exist because we think, for in thinking we have only an image of what is real. We would gain nothing from thinking if we really did exist within our thinking, if thinking were not actually a mere mirror image, a reflection. We must become aware of the reflective character of our world of thinking, of the mirroring character of our thought world. The moment we become conscious of this reflective character we shall begin to turn to a different source of reality within us.

It is of this that Michael wishes to speak to us. So we must endeavour to recognize our world of thinking in its character as a reflector; and we shall then be working to counter the luciferic development. It is this development which is most interested in pouring substance into our thinking, in projecting the deceptive image of there being substance in our thinking. It is image, not substance, which is in our thinking. We shall bring up the substance from elsewhere, from deeper layers of our consciousness.

That is the one thing. If we are aware that our thoughts make us weak we appeal to the strength of Michael. He is the spirit who draws our attention to that within us which is more strongly in us than our thoughts, whereas through more recent civilization we have learned to pay attention primarily to the thought. The reason for our having become weak human beings is that we have regarded thought as being something real. However much we endeavour to turn away from mere abstract intelligence, we are only seemingly doing so. As modern human beings we are completely under the frightful lash of intelligence. We do not send into our thoughts what comes from the deeper layers of our being and what ought to dwell in them.

The second thing is that we must bring into our wishes, and thus our will, the reality which arises solely from what we recognize as supersensible reality. I have frequently mentioned here that our failure to take seriously the character of the Mystery of Golgotha has wreaked bitter revenge upon us. I have drawn your attention to views such as, for example, those of the liberal theologian Adolf Harnack.[25] There are many such liberal theologians who are quite relaxed about stating that there is no proof in historical documents as to the reality of the Mystery of Golgotha. While one can prove historically that Caesar existed, or Napoleon, it is not possible to prove in the same way that Christ Jesus existed. Why is this? It is because in the Mystery of Golgotha human beings were to have been presented with an event to which they could only have supersensible access. It was not intended to be a sense-perceptible event. It was not supposed to have any sense-perceptible, any external historical proof for the very reason that humanity was to learn how to rise up to the supersensible world through the Mystery of Golgotha.

All this points to two aspects which we should approach. On the one hand we must recognize what is supersensible in the immediately sense-perceptible world, in the world of the human being, of the animals and of the plants. This is the Michaelic path. And to take this further: in the world which we recognize is a supersensible one, we must find the Christ Impulse.

In describing this I am at the same time also describing the most profound impulses of the social question. That abstract League of Nations[26] will not solve the international problem. Such abstractions will not create unity among all people on earth. It is the spirits who lead human beings into the supersensible world, about whom we have been speaking in the last few days, who will bring humanity together.

Externally humanity is now approaching tough battles. And from these tough battles, of which we are now only at the beginning as I have often said, and which make a nonsense of the old impulses of earth evolution, there will arise no political, economic or cultural cures which might be taken from the apothecary of ancient historical development. From what comes to us from ancient times the ferments will arise which have initially placed Europe at the beginning of its abyss, and which will see Asia and America at loggerheads with one another; and this in turn will generate a struggle covering the face of the whole earth. The one and only remedy for this nonsense being made of human evolution will be that which can lead humanity to the spirit: to the path of Michael, which finds its continuation in the path of Christ.

LECTURE 4

DORNACH, 28 NOVEMBER 1919[27]

CARRYING on from various points I made during last week's talks, what I have to say today will be a preparation for the lectures tomorrow and the day after. This will be a matter of reminding you in a different way about certain aspects which we shall need in order then to continue with our theme.

In order to gain clarity about the course of earthly evolution it will be best to proceed by always relating events to a specific focal point as regards their significance for earthly evolution. Relating them in this way will enable us to perceive a degree of structure in which the individual human being's own development is involved through the development of humanity as a whole. This focal point is, of course, as you know, the Mystery of Golgotha through which the whole of earthly evolution has gained its meaning, its true inner content.

When we refer back to the development of western humanity, which received the impulse of the Mystery of Golgotha like an impact from the Orient, we can describe how, around the fifth century before this Mystery of Golgotha, a kind of preparation for it began to emerge from the culture of ancient Greece. We can say that there was a certain consistent trend in Greek thinking, feeling and will throughout the four centuries and a half which led up to the advent of the Mystery of Golgotha. This consistent trend received its introduction through the figure of Socrates, before continuing on in all of Greek culture. The same trend is noticeable even in art, and in the prodigious, towering personality of Plato, before gaining an increasingly learned character in Aristotle.[28]

As you know from various descriptions of mine, the Middle Ages, and especially the period after Augustine,[29] was a time when efforts were especially made to gain guidance from the thinking of Aristotle in order to comprehend everything connected with the Mystery of Golgotha, its preparation and its ongoing resonance. That is why Greek thinking in particular became so important, also for the development of Christianity in the Occident up to the end of the Middle Ages; it was Greek thinking which was used to penetrate the content of the Mystery of Golgotha. So it will be useful to gain an understanding of what was happening in Greece during the centuries leading up to the impact of the Mystery of Golgotha.

What was taking place in the thinking, feeling and will of Greek human beings was the finale of an early culture of humanity which is no longer appreciated today. Current historical considerations are truly not capable of seeing such things as they really were because our current historical considerations do not reach back to a mystery culture which ranged across the whole of the civilized world and imbued all human will and feeling. It is important for us, in going back to the millennia no longer reached by historical research, to apply the methods which are at least hinted at in my book *Occult Science*, in order to understand the nature of that ancient human culture.

That culture originated in the mysteries, those ancient mysteries to which the great leading initiates admitted individuals who were objectively deemed fit also to receive direct initiation. Through those leading initiates the knowledge they had received from the mysteries streamed forth into other human beings. It is not really possible to comprehend ancient culture as a whole without paying attention to the matrix of mystery culture. If only we want to listen, Aeschylus[30] tells us quite clearly about that matrix of the mysteries. We can also sense it in Plato's philosophy. But the revelations about the divine which humanity actually received through the mysteries have become lost historically. Only in a most primitive sense is there anything left of them in the culture now discernible to history. Well, what actually happened in those times can best be assessed by investigating what of the ancient mystery culture actually remained behind in the post-Socratean age of Greek culture. It is a certain kind of thinking, a certain kind of imagining which has been retained.

As you know, in external history one is told how Socrates founded dialectics, how he was actually the great teacher of thinking, of that kind of thinking which Aristotle subsequently developed more scientifically. However, what was actually incorporated in Greek thinking and imagining was only the last remnant of mystery culture, a mystery culture which had actually been brimful of content. In the overall view of human history certain spiritual facts are known about what are the fundamental causes of our world order. But the real content, the great and mighty content, has gradually faded away.

What has remained is the type of thinking developed by the mystery pupils, the way of imagining, the configuration of thinking, and this has become historical. First it was historical in Greek thinking, and then in medieval thinking, the thinking of the Christian theologians who for the most part adapted Greek thinking for their theology, using the thought forms, the ideas and concepts emanating from Greek thinking in order to comprehend what flowed into the world through the Mystery of Golgotha. Medieval philosophy, so-called Scholasticism, is certainly a coming-together of the spiritual truths of the Mystery of Golgotha with Greek thought. The elaboration, the working-out in thought of the Golgotha Mysteries was certainly accomplished using—not to put too fine a point on it—the tools of Greek thinking, of Greek dialectics. Prior to the Mystery of Golgotha there had been four-and-a-half centuries during which the fading of ancient mystery content had been going on while its merely formal thought content had come to the fore.

Yes, approximately four-and-a-half centuries. So we have to imagine a period of pre-history spreading the mystery culture across what was the civilized Earth. This is then further developed in such a way that only a distillation remains: Greek dialectics, Greek thinking. And then the Mystery of Golgotha comes to pass. In the West it is initially comprehended on the basis of Greek dialectics. Those who want to enter fully into the science upon which the theology was still based, let's say in the tenth, eleventh, twelfth, thirteenth and fourteenth centuries, cannot use our present way of thinking because our thinking is based on the manner of the natural sciences. Those who nowadays want to form a judgement about Scholasticism can usually not do it justice because their schooling is the schooling of the natural sciences, while Scholasticism presupposes a different way of schooling one's thinking.

Today we are living at a point in time when a further four-and-a-half centuries have passed since that other way of thinking, the scientific way, took hold of humanity. This began in the middle of the fourteenth century. That was when in the West people began thinking in the manner well developed to some extent by Galileo[31] or by Giordano Bruno.[32] This way of thinking has lasted into our own time. It has the appearance of being the same logic as Greek logic, and yet it is utterly and completely different. It is a logic which has been derived from natural processes in the same way as Greek logic was derived from what the mystery pupils beheld in the mysteries.

So now let us endeavour to be clear about the difference that exists between the four-and-a-half centuries which preceded the Mystery of Golgotha in the virtually only civilized world of that time, the Greek world, and our own four-and-a-half centuries during which humanity has been trained by natural science. The best way for me to demonstrate this is by drawing {drawing begins (Plate 6)}.

Imagine the mystery culture as a kind of Chimborazo[33] of human culture in very ancient times {white}. This mystery culture then becomes logic in Greece until the Mystery of Golgotha {red line up to the first red vertical line}. This is then continued in the Middle Ages as Scholasticism {white line up to the second red vertical line}. *Here* {upper red bracket} we have the final tailing-off of the old mystery culture through four-and-a-half centuries {*4½ cent.* is written above the red bracket}. And now, from the fifteenth century

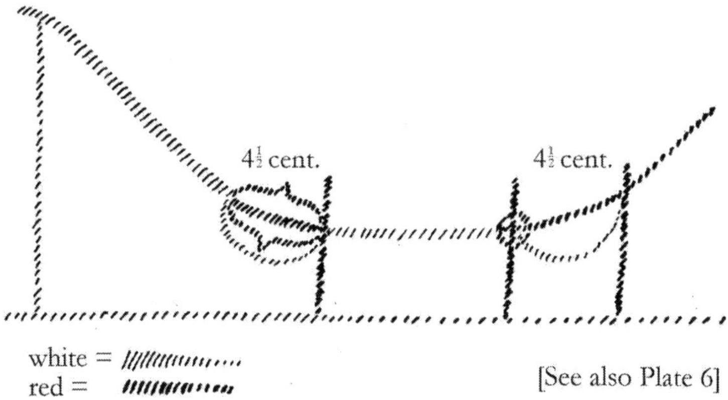

[See also Plate 6]

onwards, a new kind of perceiving begins; we could call it the Galileo perception. We are just about as far in time from the starting point {small red circle and third red vertical line} as is the Mystery of Golgotha from the beginning of the Greek way of thinking {lower red bracket before the first red vertical line}. But while that is an ending {white curve under the lower red bracket}, a red evening sky, *we* are here involved in a beginning {white curve between the second and third red vertical line; *4½ cent.* is written}, in something which must develop upwards, something we must take up to a considerable height. The culture of Greece was at an ending. We are at a beginning.

We shall only be able fully to understand this juxtaposition of an ending and a beginning if, with the help of spiritual science, we study the evolution of humanity from a specific point of view.

As I have frequently told you—and often repeated—it is not without reason that attempts are being made now to bring about an understanding of the human being on the basis of the spiritual science of anthroposophy. The reason is that by far the greater part of humanity is now confronted by a significant possibility for the future. You see, it is important to take seriously the fact that humanity, which has been evolving throughout history, is an organism continuing in its development. Just as the individual organism reaches sexual maturity, with subsequent epochal transitions, so have similar epochal transitions taken place throughout history. Today people still frequently counter teachings about repeated earth lives with the argument that one doesn't remember any former lives on earth.

Those who interpret the historical evolution of humanity as being that of an organism in development, as I explained just now, ought not to be surprised—if they are entirely realistic about that evolutionary history—by the fact that individuals today do not recognize their former earthly lives in the ordinary sense. Let us ask ourselves what it is that we remember in ordinary life. We remember something we thought about. We do not remember what we did not think about. Think of all the daily happenings that go by unnoticed. You do not remember them because you did not think them, even if they perhaps took place in your immediate vicinity. You can only remember something which you have thought.

Well, the evolution of humanity in former centuries and millennia was not such that individuals thought in a reasoning way about their own being. Of course 'Know thyself', like a kind of yearning, has been familiar since the age of Greek thinking, but this 'Know thyself' can only be fully realized through the medium of true spiritual knowledge. Only after spending a whole lifetime thinking properly about our self—something for which humanity has only now become sufficiently mature—shall we be prepared, in our next life, to remember the previous one. One must have thought about something before becoming capable of remembering it. In our present time, only those—and there are more than a few—who formerly learned through initiation, though not necessarily in the mysteries, to look properly at themselves are capable of looking back to former earth lives.

It is also the case that human beings undergo a transformation with regard to their bodily development. These things can be observed through spiritual science but not physiologically. Humanity is not now as it was two thousand years ago with regard to its bodily constitution. And in another two thousand years it will again not be the same as it is today. I have often spoken about this. Human beings are now living towards a future time in which—to put it simply—their brains will be externally different in their construction by comparison with today. The brain will be capable of remembering back to former earth lives.

But those who have not prepared for this by contemplating their own self will only experience this capability as—to use a modern expression—a kind of inner nervousness, an inner deficiency. They will not discover what they are lacking in a humanity which has become capable through its bodily maturity of looking back to former lives on earth. If they have not made preparation for looking back, then they will not be able to look back. They will experience this capability only as a deficiency. That is why, by recognizing the capacity for transformation possessed at present by humanity, the spiritual science of anthroposophy can guide human beings to self-knowledge. What I am hinting at is that even today we can already indicate what that special experience will be like when it becomes possible to take earlier lives on earth into account.

In our present time these nuances of feeling will be possible for only a few individuals, although there will be more and more as time goes on. These nuances of feeling are not much taken into account as yet. But let me describe what they will be like when they begin to occur.

Individuals will be born into the world and will say: As I live among others, I am indeed being educated for a specific type of thinking, either consciously or unconsciously. Thoughts rise up in me. I am being born and educated into a certain type of imagining. But at the same time, as I observe my external environment my thinking and imagining do not really fit in with that external environment. This nuance of feeling is already present in some individuals. They are obliged to think in a way which makes it appear as if external nature were telling them something entirely different, as if external nature were asking something quite different of them. Formerly when such individuals appeared who sensed this discrepancy between what they should think and what external nature was telling them, they were laughed at. Hegel,[34] for instance, is a classic example of this. He expressed certain ideas—of course not all Hegel's thoughts are foolish—about nature and compiled them systematically. Then the philistines came and said: These may well be your ideas about nature; but look at this process or that process and you'll see that's not how it is. To which Hegel replied: All the worse for nature.

Of course this is quite paradoxical, and yet there is subjectively something perfectly reasonable in this attitude. It is quite possible to adopt innate thoughts on the one hand while at the same time saying that nature would have to manifest quite differently if it were to match these. But then, after a while, one begins to grow accustomed to what one has learned from nature. Most people do not notice, once they have come to terms with what they have seen in nature, that they have within them something akin to a double soul, really something resembling two truths. Those who do notice it may suffer considerably because it brings a mismatch into their soul. What I am talking about is so far present only in a few individuals, and even when it is present they often do not notice it, but it will gain the upper hand more and more. People will more and more say: In the way I am through having been born my head is compelling me to form a certain image of nature, but it does not really conform to nature; as I live on in my life I begin to adopt what nature is telling me, but then I have to create a way out.

These ambivalent feelings will be present even more strongly in our soul when we once again return to the earth. We shall have a kind of inner fount of thoughts and feelings which will oblige us to say: Yes, I do sense how the world ought to be, but it is not like this, it is different. And then we shall once again live our way into this world, learning a second kind of conformity and having to search once again for compensation. What will be the cause of this?

Let us assume [drawing begins (Plate 7)] that the human being is coming through birth into physical existence. He brings with him whatever in his thinking and feeling is the result of his previous life

[See also Plate 7]

on earth. During his absence from the earth, external earthly life has changed in some way. He senses a discrepancy between the thinking he brings with him from his former life on earth and what has come about while he has been absent from the earth. And now he gradually grows accustomed to his new life but does not become fully aware of what might be learned by him about his environment. He becomes aware of it, you could say, as though through a veil. He only processes it after death, and then again brings it with him into his next life. Again and again he will live in the duality of his soul life. Again and again he will realize: I am bringing something with me, but in comparison with it the world is new into which I am entering through birth and in which I am growing up as a physical human being; through my physical being in this world I am absorbing something which does not entirely enter into my soul and which I will again have to work on after death.

Present-day human beings ought to find their way intensively into this way of feeling about life. Only by entering in a living way into such things does one become aware of the forces pulsing through one's existence but of which one otherwise remains entirely unaware. Yet we are interwoven with them. If we do not endeavour to enter into these forces with our consciousness they remain in our subconscious and to some extent make us ill in our soul. We will become increasingly aware of this discrepancy between what we retain from our former life and what we prepare during our present life for the next one. And because we will feel this discrepancy ever more strongly, we will need an inner mediation, a genuine inner mediation. And the question will become ever more urgent as to how we can find such an inner mediation. We can only find an answer to this question if we consider the following.

I have often explained that as human beings in ordinary life between waking up and falling asleep we are only fully awake in our life of thoughts and concepts. [As the speaking continues, the left-hand and middle parts of the scheme on p. 57 are written (Plate 7).] The life of thoughts and concepts signifies full wakefulness. But even when we are awake, full wakefulness is not present in our life of feeling. Even when we are fully awake in respect of our concepts and thoughts, our feelings are at the level of dreams. Those who are able to investigate this sphere know through direct insight that in our consciousness our feelings are no more alive than this; it is only the concepts by which we describe our feelings that make this seem otherwise. Our feeling life as such surges up from the depths of consciousness in such a way that what thus surges up resembles a dream. And in the way our will lives it is for us something which is asleep, even when we are awake. We are asleep as regards our will. So we bear within us three states of consciousness even when we are awake. We go about during the day in a state of wakefulness as regards our life of thoughts and concepts, but we deceive ourselves that we are also awake in our will because we make concepts about what our will accomplishes. What rises up into our consciousness is only a concept of what our will accomplishes, not what it actually experiences. We dream in our feelings, and we sleep while our will is at work.

However, when we apply Imaginative insight to what is dreaming in our feelings we see that wisdom (although in many it is 'un-wisdom') is present not only in our thoughts and concepts but also in our feeling life. There is wisdom in our thoughts and also in our feelings and in our will. [The word 'Wisdom' is added to the scheme on the blackboard (Plate 7).] As regards human existence as it is today, we can really only speak clearly about what lives in our thoughts and concepts. And as to what lives in our world of feeling, our ideas are really no different from dreams; nevertheless, wisdom is there also.

Someone seriously applying to his own soul the exercises described in my book *Knowledge of the Higher Worlds* is most likely to discern a certain inner surging of his soul, rather dreamlike, and no more

Life of thoughts:	fully awake:	Wisdom
Feelings:	dreaming:	"
Will:	sleeping:	"

[Plate 7]

regular, for most people, than ordinary dreaming. But it is possible fairly soon to create enough order in this inner experience for someone to notice that the logic in this inner experience—sometimes a very grotesque logic, and the most varied shreds of thoughts come together, running as though in a dream, certainly sometimes a most peculiar logic—we notice that the logic in this inner experience, while not the same, is nevertheless something which is, as I said, a first inner experience, still very primitive, of a kind which can be recognized by someone who even not very often applies to his own soul what is described in *Knowledge of the Higher Worlds*.

When one immerses oneself in this surge of waking dreams a new reality emerges with regard to the ordinary reality of external life. One notices quite soon that a new reality is emerging. One also notices quite soon that there is wisdom in all this, too, but a wisdom which one cannot quite grasp, for which one feels insufficiently mature with regard to bringing it into full consciousness. It eludes one again and again, and one doesn't know what to do. So then one notices, or may notice, that not only does wisdom surge through the upper layer of one's consciousness in ordinary daytime wakefulness but that below this there is also another layer of consciousness which only seems illogical because that is how one describes it through being unable to grasp its wisdom. We can say that once we have fully attained Imaginative insight these waking dreams cease to be as grotesque as they appear to be in ordinary life, for they are now permeated with a wisdom which indicates another kind of reality, namely a world which differs from the sense-perceptible world we can comprehend with our ordinary wisdom.

In ordinary life, it is only the world of feeling which surges up into our consciousness from that lower layer of consciousness. And from an even lower layer the world of will surges up, which in its turn is also permeated by wisdom. We, too, are linked with this wisdom, although we are most certainly incapable of bringing it up into our ordinary consciousness. We can say, then, that as human beings we are ruled by three layers of consciousness. The first is the consciousness of thoughts and concepts in which we live during the daytime. The second is an Imagination consciousness. And the third is an Inspiration consciousness which remains very deeply buried; it certainly works, really works within us, but in ordinary life we are unable to perceive it [writing (Plate 7)].

I. Consciousness of thoughts and concepts

II. Imagination consciousness

III. Inspiration consciousness

If our present-day philosophy were somewhat less obtuse it could not fail to notice—I'm not talking to those who know nothing of this philosophy, but actual philosophers really ought to grasp this, though they don't—our present-day philosophy really ought to notice very clearly, indeed much more intensely, what a great difference there is between the truths we observe on the basis of external nature and what we find in the sciences, for example mathematics and geometry, which we also use in our endeavour to comprehend external nature.

With some justification we can say that regarding the truths we gather by means of external observation—in the history of philosophy this has been said so often that the philosophers themselves ought to find it superfluous—we can never actually claim total certainty. Kant or Hume have demonstrated this very clearly by their grotesque statement: Although we observe that the sun rises, our observation will never give us the right to claim that it will rise again tomorrow; we are merely concluding from the fact of the sun having always risen hitherto that it will rise again tomorrow. So this is what happens with truths we have gained externally through observation. But this is not the case with mathematical truths. Once we have understood them we know that they will hold good for ever. [Plate 6] Those who know and can prove for inner reasons that the square on the hypotenuse equals the sum of the squares on the other two sides will also know that no one will ever be able to draw a right-angled triangle to which this does not apply.

There is a difference between these mathematical truths and those we know from external observation. We know this as a fact but we are not in a position to understand the reason for it by using the means provided by present-day research. The reason for it is that mathematical truths arise out of the lowest layer of our consciousness and, without us realizing it, come shooting up into our uppermost consciousness where we then see them inwardly. We possess the mathematical truths because we ourselves act mathematically in the world. We walk, we stand and so on, we follow straight lines. We receive our inner view of mathematics through our will-based relationship with the external world. Mathematics arises down below in the third layer of consciousness [see scheme on p. 61 (Plate 7)] whence it shoots up.

So strictly speaking, even though in this case the origin is not present in our ordinary consciousness, we have a very clear idea of at least a part of this lower-down consciousness. It is from there that mathematical and geometrical ideas rise up to us. It is only the middle layer which is dreamlike, confusing. The middle layer has a quality of dreamy confusion. Up here, in our little upper storey, where our ordinary daytime consciousness resides, we are quite clear. That is why there is clarity in us with regard to what rises up to us from the third layer of consciousness. But what lies in between is for most of us a confused waking dream. It is very important that we should be clear about this fact. In those four-and-a-half centuries the Greeks were very familiar with this consciousness. They took into themselves this consciousness (I), this consciousness which they held as a remnant of mystery culture. And this is a purely luciferic element, it is purely luciferic. I described it to you the other day. It is the intellectualistic culture. It is very clear in our head. It is permeated with wisdom, with a generally accepted wisdom. It is a luciferic element in us ['luciferic' is written on the board (Plate 7)]. And down there is what present-day scientists are so fond of, what Kant[35] was already so fond of that he said: There is only as much science with regard to nature as there is mathematics in it. This is the ahrimanic element rising up through our human being. This is the ahrimanic element ['ahrimanic' is written on the board; the scheme is now complete (Plate 7)].

life of thoughts:	fully awake:	wisdom
feelings:	dreaming:	"
will:	sleeping:	"

I.	consciousness of thoughts	luciferic
II.	Imagination consciousness	
III.	Inspiration consciousness	ahrimanic

It is not enough to know that something is correct. We know that the things we understand intellectually in our head are correct, but this is a gift from the luciferic element. And we know that mathematics is correct, but we owe this mighty correctness of mathematics to Ahriman who sits within us. And the most doubtful element resides in the middle: those dreams which seem to surge illogically.

And let me now introduce a further feature to help you comprehend fully the whole importance of this matter. The fact is that all this mathematical comprehension of the world put forward by Galileo or Giordano Bruno stems from that deeper layer of consciousness. Four-and-a-half centuries have elapsed since we began to take this in, four-and-a-half centuries since we have been endeavouring to introduce this ahrimanic element into our human thinking and feeling. While the last echoes of the mystery culture in Greek thinking shone into the brightest clarity of consciousness, that which will not attain its Chimborazo until the future begins to rise up in the deepest, darkest layers of our consciousness.

The soul life which we human beings possess is really like the beam of a pair of scales holding the balance between the luciferic element on the one side and the ahrimanic element on the other [Plate 6]. The only difference is that the luciferic element is located in the awakeness of our head while the ahrimanic element lies down

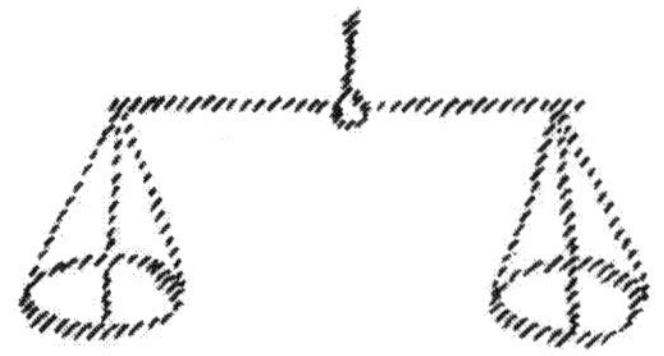

below in the realm of wisdom which permeates our will. In between we have to search for balance in something which initially does not appear to be permeated by anything.

How does wisdom enter into this middle part of the human being? As he exists in the world at present, his head is held by Lucifer while his metabolic wisdom, his limb wisdom is held by Ahriman. But as far as the heart is concerned, this is the sphere which must receive order just as much as is already present in the wisdom of the head through head logic and in what contains the ahrimanic influence through mathematics, through geometry and whatever arises through rational observation of nature. Through what does inner logic, inner wisdom and orientation enter into the middle part of the human being? Through the Christ Impulse, through that which entered into earthly culture by means of the Mystery of Golgotha.

The view of anatomy in spiritual science shows us what is meant by the culture of the head. It also shows us the culture of the metabolism. And in addition it shows us the sphere of organization which lies between these two, and also what it needs. To be permeated by the Christ Impulse is what belongs to our nature as human beings.

We may ask, hypothetically, what would be the situation if the Mystery of Golgotha had not entered into earthly evolution. Well, the human being would still possess the wisdom of the head. And he would also still have what has come into being within him since the fifteenth century. But as regards the middle part of his being he would be empty and void. He would increasingly feel the dichotomy between those other two inner spheres. And he would be incapable of creating a situation of balance. We can only bring about a situation of balance by imbuing ourselves ever more and more with the Christ Impulse which creates the balance between the luciferic and the ahrimanic element.

So we can say that the four-and-a-half pre-Christian centuries bestowed upon us the last remnants of the ancient mystery culture as a preparation for the Mystery of Golgotha which has established itself in us like a head-memory of that ancient mystery culture. And in more recent times another four-and-a-half centuries have been preparing our being for a new spiritual direction, a new kind of mystery culture. For these two to become linked together it was necessary for the Mystery of Golgotha to be placed objectively into human evolution. Seen from outside, human evolution follows its course in such a way that the Mystery of Golgotha is placed into it as an objective fact. Inwardly, however, human evolution proceeded towards the fifteenth century after which it received a new impetus which I have described to you as an Ahriman impetus. Through this you will truly sense that humanity needs the possibility of building a bridge between the one and the other.

It is in this way that we can inwardly comprehend the threefold human being. And we shall comprehend him even more exactly when we link what I have said today with something I have also mentioned repeatedly. For the ancient Greek with those last remnants of the old mystery culture it would have been impossible—except in a few decadent individuals, and even then not to the extent that is possible now—it would have been impossible for him to be an atheist. Atheism is basically a new phenomenon, at least in its more radical configurations. But an ancient Greek properly imbued with dialectics still had feeling in his thinking.

When we know this and then have a look at atheism, at that utter denial of the divine, we can see what is really at the bottom of atheism. Of course one must apply the methods of spiritual science to recognize this: atheists are solely those people who have—usually in very delicate structural conditions—some organic disorder. Atheism is in reality a disease.

This is the first thing we have to take into account: that atheism is a disease. When our organism is entirely healthy its various components cannot work together in any other way than in the feeling that our origins lie with the divine—*ex deo nascimur*.

There is, though, also a second aspect. An individual can have a sense for the divine and yet be incapable of having a sense for the Christ. We do not differentiate very clearly in such matters nowadays. We too easily make do with words, in other matters too. When one investigates the real spiritual content of many western individuals without taking account of their words—they say they believe in the freedom of the will and so on—it becomes obvious that the whole configuration of their thinking is at odds with what they are saying. It is only in this cultural setting that they are accustomed to speaking of Christ, of freedom and so on. In reality a great many of those who live among us are nothing other than Turks. What they believe is just as fatalistic—even though this fatalism is often described as a natural necessity—as the beliefs of the Mohammedans. Mohammedanism is much more prevalent than we imagine. When one pays attention not to the words but to the spiritual and soul content, many a Christian is actually a Turk; many Christians are Turks. Thus people call themselves Christian even when they are unable to find how the God whose existence they sense is connected with the Christ.

I need only point out the classic example of a modern theologian, Adolf Harnack,[36] who wrote the book *What is Christianity?* Please carry out this experiment: When reading *What is Christianity?*, cross out the name of Christ wherever it occurs and substitute the name of God. You will find that this in no way alters the content of the book. There is no need for the author to refer to Christ in what he says; all his utterances are generalizations referring to the Father God who is the foundation of the world. There is no necessity for him to relate what he says to the Christ. Both outwardly and inwardly what he professes is untrue when he derives his statements from the Gospels; there is no reason for the way he relates them to the Christ. One must find ways of understanding the Christ without equating Him with the Father God. Many, especially among the newer Protestant theologians, are unable to make a distinction between the generalized concept of God and the concept of the Christ.

Not finding Christ in one's life is different from not finding the Father God. You know of course that I have no intention here of doubting the divinity of the Christ. It is just that it is necessary, with regard to the sphere of the divine, to distinguish clearly between the Father God and the Christ God. This is also expressed in the soul life of the human being. Not finding the Father God is an illness; not finding the Christ is a misfortune. The human being is bound up with the Christ in such a way that he is inwardly dependent on Him. He is dependent on something which took place as a historical event. The human being must find a connection to the Christ here on earth. If he does not, this is a misfortune. To be an atheist, not to find the Father God, is an illness. But it is a misfortune not to find the Son of God, the Christ.

What does it mean not to find the spirit? Not to have the possibility of comprehending one's own spirituality and thus not to discover the interconnection between one's own spirituality and the spirituality of the world is a mental deficiency, a weakness of spirit; it is a weakness of soul not to recognize the spirit.

Please remember these three states of the human soul so that we may tomorrow continue in the right way with these considerations. Please remember what, from a different perspective, I have told you today about those three consciousnesses: that to be an atheist, not to find the God from whom we are born—and whom we must find when we are in full good health—not to find Him is an illness, not to find the Christ is a misfortune, not to find the spirit is a weakness of soul.

It is in this way that the paths of the human being differ from one another. It will become ever more important to enter into these concrete matters of soul life and not to remain always in generalized, indistinct, hazy views. Yet nowadays people are very much inclined towards the hazy view. It is an essential task of our time to replace the inclination towards the hazy view with a view which enters into the concrete aspects of soul life.

LECTURE 5

DORNACH, 29 NOVEMBER 1919

THE human being can only attain a true, soul-supporting consciousness by assimilating at least the most important and essential laws of human evolution. We must recognize and include in our life of soul what has taken place throughout the evolution of humanity. This is the task of human beings at the present time. As I have hinted in the last few days, this involves taking seriously the fact that as such the evolution of humanity is a kind of living development of the human being. Just as growth takes place in the individual human being in accordance with certain laws, so it is with the evolution of the human race as a whole. In our present age a point in time has been reached when certain things must rise up into consciousness, and during repeated lives on earth the individual human being has participated in the various configurations of human evolutionary history. It is thus also necessary for us to develop an understanding of the various moods of soul which have prevailed in the different epochs. As I have often said, what nowadays goes by the name of history is actually no more than a *fable convenue* because in all the abstract accounts about events and in all the searching for causes and effects in the most external sense regarding historical happenings, no account at all is taken of the transformations, the metamorphoses of human soul life as such.

If one were to embark on a historical investigation, one would certainly realize the degree of prejudice involved in assuming that the constitution of today's souls is more or less the same as it was back in the days covered by the earliest historical documents. For this was certainly not the case. Even the most simple and primitive human beings of the ninth or tenth post-Christian centuries had a mood of soul utterly different from the mood of those living after the middle of the fifteenth century. This can be investigated with regard both to the lowest and the highest echelons of humanity. You could, for example, look into Dante's extraordinary treatise *De Monarchia*.[37] If you read something like this not as a matter of curiosity but with some degree of cultural sensitivity, you will notice how a book by a representative of that time contains things which could not possibly be expressed by the soul of a present-day person. There is just one point I want to make.

In this book,[38] which is intended as a serious treatise, from his point of view, about the political basis of the monarchy, Dante endeavours to demonstrate that the Romans were the most excellent people on earth. He endeavours to show that it was the primeval right of the Romans, in so far as would have been possible in their day, to conquer the whole globe. He endeavours to show that victory over the whole globe by the Romans was a greater right than, for instance, the right of independence of individual small nations for, as he says, it was God's wish that the Romans should rule over individual, small nations for the good of those individual small nations. Dante quotes many proofs out of the spirit of his time for this justification for the Romans to rule the globe. One of those proofs reads as follows. The Romans stemmed from Aeneas. Aeneas married three times. His first wife was Creusa. Through his marriage to her he had won the right to rule over Asia. Secondly he married Dido. Through this marriage, as progenitor of the Romans, he had won the right to rule over Africa. And then he had married Lavinia, thus gaining the right—that is, for the Romans—to rule over Europe. When speaking about this, Herman Grimm[39] once remarked—in my opinion not without some justification: How lucky that America and Australia had not yet been discovered!

Well, for an enlightened intellect of Dante's day, indeed for the most enlightened intellect of Dante's day, the conclusion drawn was perfectly obvious. At the time, such a discourse amounted to a legalistic declaration. So now try to imagine any lawyer of the present time presenting a conclusion like this. You cannot imagine it. And similarly you would be unable to imagine with regard to other matters that a train of thought such as Dante's could arise from the soul make-up of a present-day individual.

From this very obvious fact we learn how to view the metamorphosis of human soul configurations. Such things are now incomprehensible, but until quite recently they were in some respects still acceptable. Now they are no longer acceptable and they will in future not be acceptable, although up till our time or at least until the end of the eighteenth century—things began to change after the French Revolution—humanity did still possess certain instincts, certain remnants of those soul configurations. From those instincts it was still possible to develop a consciousness which upheld the soul. But the ever-developing organism of humanity has become such that these instincts are no longer present, so that human beings must now work in a more conscious way towards understanding the coherency of humanity as a whole. This surely constitutes the whole significance of today's social question. What people now say often amounts to no more than partisan formulations. But what surges in the depths of the human soul cannot be expressed in such formulations. What surges there is what humanity feels, namely that one must consciously seek what binds the individual to the whole of humanity—which means that one must adopt a social impulse.

But one cannot do this without seriously taking a comprehensive view of the law of evolution. So let us do this once more, having already done it repeatedly in respect of other questions. For example let us look at the period from the fourth post-Christian century up to about the sixteenth post-Christian century. Here we see Christianity spreading across what was then a civilized Europe. We find that this spreading out can be characterized as we did yesterday and on other occasions. We find that during this period great care is taken to comprehend the Mysteries of Golgotha on the basis of all human ideas and concepts stemming from Greek culture. But then a changed form of development begins. We know that in fact it commenced somewhat earlier, around the middle of the fifteenth century before becoming fully visible in the sixteenth century. That is when thinking based on science begins to take hold of the upper echelons of humanity, before becoming ever more widespread.

So now let us look at this thinking based on science with regard to one specific characteristic. There are many such characteristics which can be applied to scientific thinking, but today we shall focus on one of these, namely that if one is one of the stalwart, newer thinkers in today's sense one cannot cope with the distinction between natural necessity and freedom. Today's thinking based on nature has increasingly seen the human being as a part of the rest of nature, which is conceived of as a stream of firmly interlocking causes and effects. Of course there are also many individuals today who understand clearly that freedom, the experience of freedom, is a fact of human consciousness. Nevertheless, this does not necessarily prevent one from also coping with the configuration of thinking based on nature. But if one thinks in the manner required by today's natural sciences, then one cannot combine the idea of human freedom with this thinking.

Some make life easy for themselves as regards human freedom and a human sense of responsibility. I know a criminal lawyer[40] who always began his lectures on criminal law by saying: 'Gentlemen, this lecture is about criminal law; let us begin by adopting the axiom that human freedom and human responsibility do exist; for if freedom and responsibility did not exist there could be no criminal law. But criminal law exists since that is what my lecture is about; thus responsibility and freedom exist.' This argumentation is somewhat simplistic, but it does indicate how difficult people today find the question: How can natural necessity be combined with freedom? This shows, in other words, that owing to developments during recent centuries human beings have increasingly become confronted with having to think about a degree of omnipotence in natural necessity. They do not say this in so many words. But they do bear in mind a degree of omnipotence in natural necessity. So what is this omnipotence of natural necessity?

It will help us to understand one another if I may remind you of something I have often mentioned. Thinkers today imagine that they are acting—or rather thinking—without prejudice and solely in a scientific manner when they claim that the human being consists of body and soul. It is so, is it not, that people, right up to the supposedly great—actually great only thanks to his publisher—philosopher Wilhelm Wundt,[41] think that the human being must consist of body and soul, if indeed even the soul still continues to be seen as valid. Only diffidently does the idea of the human being consisting of body, soul and spirit dare to show its face. Philosophers who nowadays believe unquestioningly that the human being consists of body and soul do not realize that this division is nothing other than the consequence of a historical event which was initiated by the eighth general Council of Constantinople[42] during which the Catholic Church abolished the spirit by declaring the dogma that a properly pious Christian must think of the human being as consisting of body and soul, with the soul possessing certain spiritual characteristics. This is what the Church decreed. And philosophers still teach this today without realizing that they are merely following the Church's dictates; they believe they are teaching philosophy impartially. This is today the situation with regard to a good many instances of what people call 'non-judgemental science'.

The situation is similar with regard to natural necessity. Overall, development from the fourth to the sixteenth century worked increasingly on a specific concept of the divine. If we look at the fine detail of intellectual development during those centuries we see, arising out of human thinking, a quite specific concept of God, a concept of God which culminated in the statement: God the Almighty. Only a few people know that prior to the fourth post-Christian century it would scarcely have been meaningful to speak of Almighty God. I'm not referring here to the truths propounded by the catechism which of course speaks of God the Almighty, God the All-Wise, God the All-Good, and so on. These are things that have nothing to do with the realities. Prior to the fourth century no one with any understanding of these things, who really followed these things, would have considered regarding almightiness as a fundamental characteristic of the divine being. In those days what still held sway were the residual effects of Greek concepts. When thinking of the being of God one would not, in the first place, have said [writing (Plate 8)] God the Almighty, one would have said God the All-Wise.

It was wisdom which was initially attributed to the divine being as his fundamental characteristic. Not until the fourth century did the idea of omnipotence gradually begin to enter into the concept of the divine being. And this then continued to develop. The concept of a personage was abandoned; it became increasingly an attribute of a merely natural, indeed a mechanical order. So the more recent concept of nature, the almightiness of nature [Plate 8], is nothing other than a further development of the concept of God [writing] from the fourth century and right on into the sixteenth century, except that the attribute of a personage was discarded so that the concept of God became instead an attribute of nature.

Today's genuine natural scientists would of course object strongly to such a statement. In the same way some philosophers believe they are without prejudice when contemplating the human being as consisting solely of a body and a soul although they are actually parroting the eighth Council of Constantinople of 869. Just as these philosophers have become dependent on a historical trend, so all those scientists, the Haeckelians, the Darwinians and all the others, right up to the physicists with their natural necessity, are merely dependents of a theological current which has been developing since Augustine[43] and right up to Calvin.[44]

We must begin to see through this. It is characteristic of every evolutionary current that it involves some kind of evolution, but also an involution or devolution. Thus while the concept of 'God the Almighty' was developing, an undercurrent also existed in the subconscious realm of the human soul which later became the 'over'-current: natural necessity [see drawing, red]. And since the sixteenth century a new undercurrent has been present which in our time is now preparing to become an 'over'-current [see drawing, white (Plate 8)].

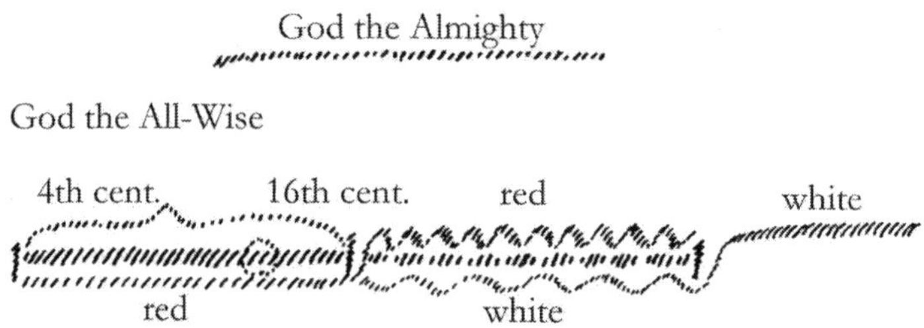

It is this which we have to cite as the characteristic feature of the Michael Age: the fact that something which was prepared in the form of an undercurrent of natural necessity must henceforth become an 'over'-current. One must comprehend the inner spirit of earthly evolution if one wants to reach any kind of serviceable concept regarding what is really being prepared.

As I pointed out the other day, earthly evolution, and specifically human evolution, is of its own accord moving in a downward direction. Earthly humanity, indeed earthly evolution itself is in decadence. I told you that even today it is a geological fact, which serious geologists admit,[45] that the earth's crust is in a process of decay. But more particularly it is humanity itself which is in a process of decay caused by sense-perceptible, earthly forces. So humanity must proceed in such a way that it will become capable of absorbing spiritual impulses which work against the decadence. That is why a conscious spiritual life must enter into humanity. We must make clear to ourselves the fact that we have already passed the highest point of earthly evolution. For earthly evolution to continue, spirituality must be taken up ever more clearly and distinctly.

This may sound like an abstraction. But for the spiritual researcher it is most certainly not an abstraction. As you know, through the Saturn, Sun and Moon stages, we can follow the development which has continued on to become the Earth stage. When speaking of modern humanity, we can also describe this development by saying that the Saturn, Sun and Moon periods were preparations, initial stages leading up to modern humanity. On the earth itself, the human being has only now attained his full humanity by taking in his 'I' through which he will bring ever further aspects into that humanity throughout subsequent development phases of the earth.

As you know, the beings whom we know as the Archai, today's Spirits of Personality or Spirits of Time, were, although with an entirely different appearance, at the same stage of development in the Saturn period as we human beings are here on earth. In my books I have expressed this by saying that the beings we now know as Archai, as Spirits of Personality, were human during the Saturn period; the Archangeloi were human during the Sun period and the Angeloi were human during the Moon period. And now, during the Earth period, *we* are the human beings.

Of course we always also joined in with our own preparatory form of development. By going back to the Moon stage we find that the Angeloi were human beings then. Of course they did not look like us for the conditions on the Moon were quite different. But apart from the Angeloi, those moon humans, we too were developing to quite a considerable degree towards a preliminary stage which was so advanced that even then we might have been mistaken for Angeloi. Especially when the Moon stage was already in decline we became quite a nuisance for the Angeloi. And now, in the Earth stage, we are in a similar situation, because as the Earth stage declines other beings are following on.

This is a significant and important result of spiritual research which must be taken very seriously indeed, namely that in the present stage of the Earth's development other beings are making themselves felt who will have reached their human stage on Jupiter—the next stage of earthly evolution. They will have reached the human stage in a form which, though different, will be comparable with the human form. We ourselves will be different beings on Jupiter. But those who are virtually Jupiter human beings are already here, just as we were already there at the Moon stage. They are here, even though they are not outwardly visible. I mentioned the other day what it means to be outwardly visible while also being a supersensible being. And supersensibly those beings are very much here.

Let me emphasize yet again: It is a most serious truth that certain beings, who already surround humanity, are beginning to assert themselves. They have been asserting themselves more and more ever since the middle of the fifteenth century. Initially, these beings have mainly been developing the stimulus for a force which is very akin to the human will force about which I said yesterday that it resides in the deeper layers of human consciousness. Those invisible beings, who are already asserting themselves strongly in the development of present-day humanity, are related to what as yet exists unconsciously in today's ordinary consciousness.

This amounts to a tremendous problem for those who take spiritual research entirely seriously. I was faced with it especially strongly—as I said at the time, in one way or another, to a number of our friends—I was faced with this problem especially strongly in 1914 when that catastrophe of the war broke out. One had to ask oneself: How could an event, immeasurable in its causes to a degree which would be incalculable with regard to any other event in history, come rushing in upon the humanity of Europe? For those who know that scarcely more than 30 or 40 individuals were involved in the decisions of 1914, for those who know what the soul constitution of most of those individuals was, the most significant of the problems was that most of the individuals involved, strange though this may sound now, were in a state of clouded, of darkened consciousness. In fact, in recent years a great deal has been taking place which was influenced by a dulled consciousness among human beings. We see at all the decisive points of time in 1914, and especially at the end of July and the beginning of August, how the most important decisions were taken in a state of darkened awareness, and this has been going on right up to our time.

This is a terrible problem. Looking at it through spiritual science we see that these darkened states of awareness were the portals through which those beings of will took hold of those human beings' consciousness—of that consciousness which was shrouded, enveloped in darkness—in order to work with *their own* consciousness instead. And those beings who took possession of our consciousness and who are as yet subhuman, what kind of being are they then? This is a question we must ask in all earnestness. What kind of beings are they?

Well, we have enquired after the origin of human intelligence, after the origin of intelligent human behaviour of which the tool—put simply—is the organization of our head. As we saw, this intelligent constitution of our soul originated in the deed of Michael, the Archangel, which is normally depicted symbolically as the fall, the casting out, of the dragon. This is actually a rather superficial symbol. If we properly imagine Michael with the dragon we should imagine the Being of Michael—and in addition the dragon, which is everything that enters into our so-called common sense, our intelligence. Michael casts the opposing hordes not into hell but into our human heads. [Drawing (Plate 9).] From then on this is where the

luciferic impulse has lived. I have already described human intelligence as actually being a luciferic impulse. So we can say that, in looking back over the coming into being of the Earth, we find the Michael Deed and, bound up with that Michael Deed, the illumination of the human being with his reason.

And what then arrives—those subhuman beings whose chief characteristic is an impulse which very strongly concords with the human will, with human will-power—these come up as it were from below, whereas the hordes or powers cast down by Michael came from above. And whereas the latter took hold of the human capacity to think, the former latch on to human will; they unite with it and are beings generated by the kingdom of Ahriman. [Plate 9.]

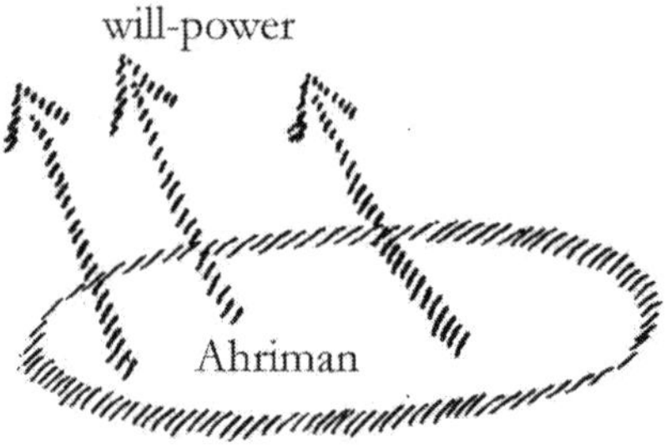

It was the ahrimanic influences which worked through those shrouded consciousnesses. Indeed, so long as these influences are not treated as objective forces in the same way as the forces present in the world, now known as magnetism, electricity and so on, are treated, so long will no insight be gained into that world of nature to which, according to Goethe's prose hymn *Die Natur*,[46] the human being also belongs. For, actually, nature as it is conceived of by present-day science does not dwell in the human being but only in his physical outer shell.

These beings, which represent a rising up of the ahrimanic essence analogous to the casting down of the luciferic essence at the beginning of earthly evolution, these beings, who also consist in a power which influences the human will—just as the other beings influence human thinking—must be recognized as having entered into human evolution. We must be clear about the fact that these beings are arriving and that we must reckon with a certain concept of nature which, however, initially only applies to the human being since the animal kingdom only entered into the earthly era later and can therefore not yet be influenced by them.

It will not be possible to comprehend the human race without taking these beings into account. These beings are being pushed as though from behind; the actual ahrimanic force which gives them their strong will-power and influences the direction of their actions and so on is what lies behind them. These beings which, in themselves, are subhuman beings are dominated en masse by higher ahrimanic spirits; and they therefore have within them something which reaches far beyond their own nature and essence. There is something in the way they manifest which, if it captures the human being, can work more strongly, even more strongly than is possible today for the weak human being unless he has gained strength through the spirit.

What is the goal of this horde? You see, just as the luciferic hordes which Michael cast down are pitched against human enlightenment, against human good sense, so are these other hordes focused on penetrating the human will to some extent. So what do they want? They rummage around in the deepest layers of consciousness where human beings today are still asleep even while they are awake. The human being does not notice them entering into his soul or into his body. But that is where they have the allure to attract everything which is still luciferic through not having taken in the Christ. This is what they are able to capture.

These things are extremely relevant today! I have already mentioned one phenomenon which is highly significant in the sense of cultural history. There are plenty of written justifications nowadays. All kinds of people, from Theobald Bethmann[47] to Jagow,[48] everyone actually, is busy writing. Clemenceau[49] and Wilson[50] will have their turn a little later, but they also will write; everyone is writing. We need only have a look, as examples, at two large volumes by Tirpitz[51] and Ludendorff.[52] It is highly interesting, for someone who thinks along with the spirit of his time, to examine the manner in which such individuals as Tirpitz and Ludendorff write. As regards content they differ greatly; they disliked each other profoundly and had very different views.

However, their points of view are not what interests us here, for what we want to examine is their spiritual configuration. Their books are written in the German of today, or what is very like the German of today. But, in the way they are expressed, their thought forms—one must have some understanding of such things, otherwise one would not notice what is going on and would place the books in the present time merely because they are dated 1919—their thought forms are written in a way which makes one ask: What exactly is it about this way of forming thoughts? I asked myself this question very seriously especially in connection with these two books because it is totally untrue, a real untruth, that they are written in German. Externally they are written in German, but actually they are translations because the thought forms stem from the age of Caesar. The way of thinking in the time of Caesar is present in these two writers.

Once one has gained an understanding of the metamorphosis of humanity in the way I described earlier one notices the backwardness of such souls, for they have remained untouched by the metamorphosis. The memoirs of Tirpitz and Ludendorff are only incidentally about present-day events; they might just as well be about Caesar's campaigns. This can be demonstrated clearly by someone who has the necessary methodology. In other words: Christianity has completely bypassed these two individuals; there is nothing Christian in them. There may be some expressions. Perhaps they prayed in Christian churches during their youth, but I don't know. I don't believe Tirpitz would have done, and I'm not sure about Ludendorff either. But that is not the point. There is no genuine Christ Impulse in their hearts, in their souls. They are caught in an earlier phase of human development.

These are the types of thought forms which can be touched by the spirits I mentioned just now. They can attract them and seize hold of them. It is on this that they want to base their dominion. This is the manner in which an alien element, an element from another world of spirit which is trying to gain ground, enters into human decision-making. In Ludendorff's case it is historically provable. Even though there is as yet no such thing as a historio-psychopathology—but there will be, soon enough—nevertheless in the case of Ludendorff this can be directly proven. It was on 6 August,[53] the capture of Liège. The whole army unit was jammed into one street with Ludendorff, still a colonel, in its midst. All the decision-making was up to him. What happened in Liège was entirely down to his rapid resolve. But his normal state of consciousness was lost at that moment. This brought his soul into a state resembling that of Caesar; his consciousness was dimmed and this brought about the clouding of consciousness which provides the portal for the ahrimanic world.

These problems are brought to us by the times we live in. We should no longer ignore such things. It is not easy to cope with them. What is easy is to think in a different way about human beings, namely not to think about them at all, not to encroach too closely upon them. This is not without danger in our present time when in many of its individuals humanity does not love the sense of truth which makes one speak in full truthfulness about these things, quite apart from the fact that a misunderstood sentimentality can make the soul feel dreadful about them.

However, what will result from an understanding like this is a thorough recognition of the need for the Christ Impulse. One must know where the Christ Impulse is absent. As I showed you yesterday, the Christ Impulse must gain a hold in the middle layer of our consciousness. So today we may add: When consciousness of the Christ Impulse takes hold in the middle layer of our consciousness, when the human being is truly filled with the Christ, then the ahrimanic forces will be unable to pass upwards through this middle layer and the forces of the intellect will be incapable of travelling downwards with their spiritual forces. Everything depends upon this being the case.

It is very necessary that we should today recognize that, while there are certain influences which are rooted solely in the human world, there are also influences which come from beings who are outside and beneath human beings and that it is upon these that certain other beings can exercise their influence. Last week I spoke about the Michael influence and I described this Michael influence to you. It is a very necessary influence. For just as much as it is true that the luciferic influence entered human intelligence through the Michael influence, so is it also true that the polar opposite is approaching through the rising up of certain ahrimanic beings from below. Only through the continued activity of Michael will the human being become forearmed against that which is rising up.

Already today it is physiologically quite dangerous to rely solely on natural necessity, on that kind of fatalism which is expressed by natural necessity. The human head is weakened by being taught in school and being taught by life to believe in ideas which are based solely on natural necessity, ideas which are rooted solely in the overall might of natural necessity. This will render human beings so passive with regard to their consciousness that other forces will be able to gain access there; and thereby the strength will be lacking which is needed to bring the Christ Impulse in its present configuration into the soul make-up of the human being.

It is my duty at this time to speak about what we have begun to discuss today, and I shall continue with this tomorrow, namely to speak about how certain ahrimanic beings enter into us, beings with whom we shall have to reckon. All kinds of people on our earth already know about what it is that is entering into our lives. But their interpretation of this is mistaken. Their interpretation is wrong because they do not know and do not wish to know about the true trinity of Christ, Lucifer and Ahriman in that they lump Ahriman and Lucifer together. They are then no longer able to make a distinction and can thus no longer properly recognize the true character of these ahrimanic beings who are beginning to rise up. It will only be when they can properly distinguish what is ahrimanic and how it contrasts with the luciferic that they will know what kind of supersensible influences are arising which constitute the reverse part of the fall of the dragon brought about by Michael. It is like a rising up out of ahrimanic depths, like a rising up of certain beings. And these beings will find certain points in the human being which are open to attack if human beings leave themselves open to unbridled instinctive impulses and fail to strive for clarity as to their impulses.

There exists today a method, or I might also say an anti-method, by means of which one can disguise what is instinctive through raising up a concept and then piling another one on top of it so that it is no longer possible to form a proper judgement about the matter.

Just think of the rallying cry of our more modern proletariat. As I have often said, this rallying cry is backed by some very justifiable demands for humanity. Yet it is not those demands for which the appeal is made. It is our idea about the threefolding of the social order[54] which constitutes the first genuine appeal. However, the rallying cry that is constantly articulated nowadays is: Workers of the world unite!

What does this mean? It constitutes a call for antagonism towards the other social classes. You proletarians should as individuals cultivate something akin to hatred: you should unite in your love for one another and in your hatred for others; seek the love of one class, let the love of your comrades arise out of your hatred. Love one another on the basis of your hatred. This is how one sets up two polar opposite concepts, thus causing people's perceptions to become so nebulous that their instincts are suppressed and they no longer know what is going on within themselves. This is indeed a kind of anti-method—if I may use this paradoxical expression. The purpose is to use present-day human thinking to cast a veil over the working of an instinct which provides strong points which are liable to attack by the ahrimanic beings I have described.

Lecture 6

DORNACH, 30 NOVEMBER 1919

In our descriptions over the last few days you have seen how, for a thorough understanding of the human being, it is necessary to enter into the matter of how the human being is organized, especially as regards the profound difference between the human head organization and what we might call the organization of the other parts. Of course you know that the rest of the human being is also sub-divided in a way which yields a division into three parts, but initially it is the differentiation between the head part and the rest of the organization.

From the point of view of spiritual science we speak about the human being as consisting of the head part of his nature and the rest of his nature. This division into the head and the rest amounts initially rather more to an image, a revelation created by nature, of the soul aspect and the spiritual aspect. The position of the human being within the whole of earthly human evolution can only be properly understood if one takes into account the difference between the position of the head organization and the position of the other parts of the organization. If we remain for the moment with the post-Atlantean evolution of humanity, we see that the head organization is bound up with the human being's life of thinking and that this reaches very far back into that post-Atlantean period.

Looking back to the time immediately following the great Atlantean catastrophe, the sixth, seventh or eighth millennium before Christ, we arrive in regions belonging to the civilized world of that time where the soul mood of humanity was such that it can scarcely be compared with that of our own time. What human beings in those times had in their consciousness, what characterized their conception of the world, can scarcely be compared with the way we today characterize the world on the basis of our sense perceptions and our thoughts. In my book *Occult Science* I termed this culture, which reaches back so far into the past, the primeval Indian culture. In the way in which the human organization of those times was linked primarily with the head, those ancient cultures differed to such a degree from our own that they entirely lacked our way of reckoning with both space and time. There was something like an overview of immeasurable widths of space, and it was as though various moments in time were viewed one within the other. The strong emphasis on space and time now present in our concept of the world did not exist in those ancient days.

The first inklings of this began in the fifth or fourth millennium, the period we describe as that of ancient Persia. The whole mood of the life of soul in those times can still, however, scarcely be compared with the mood of the human soul and of the world which exists now in our own time. In those ancient days human beings were constantly endeavouring to interpret everything in terms of a comparison between brightness and luminosity on the one hand and darkness and gloom on the other. The abstractions with which we live today were still entirely unfamiliar to those ancient peoples on the earth. They still possessed something of a universal view, an awareness of how everything visible is permeated with light or else shrouded in darkness.

This was also their way of looking at the world order. A person who was well-meaning and kind was experienced as being light, as being bright, whereas someone who was distrustful or selfish was felt to be dark. A person's moral individuality was seen as surrounding him as an aura. And if one had spoken to a person during that ancient Persian age about what we now call the natural order, he would not have understood anything at all. In his world of light and shade there was no such thing as what we now know as a natural order. For him the world consisted of light and shade and, for example with reference to sounds and notes, certain nuances were found to be bright while others were dark and shadowy. For him the world consisted of light and shade. And those things which found expression in this lightness and darkness were to him spiritual and also natural forces.

So to distinguish between what might be either natural necessity or human freedom would have seemed utter madness to him; for him the duality of human caprice and natural necessity did not exist. In his view everything could be encompassed within a spiritual-physical unity. To draw a picture for you—the meaning of which will become apparent in what follows—which characterizes that ancient Persian world-view, I would have to depict a line which somehow shows how the world serpent, the symbol of the All, uniformly encompasses the view of humanity {Plate 10}.

And then, approximately two millennia after that soul mood had existed, there came the time of which we still see the after-echoes in the Chaldean world-view, in the Egyptian world-view and in a specific form of a world-view the distant echo of which has been preserved for us in the Old Testament. Here something now appears which is a little closer to our present world-view. A nuance of a kind of natural necessity now appears in the ideas of humanity. But this natural necessity is still nowhere near what we might call a mechanical or even only a living natural order. In that age, natural events are still bound up with the will of the gods, with divine providence. Providence and natural events are still one and the same. When a human being moved his hand he knew that it was the divine in him which moved his hand or his arm. If a tree was swaying in the wind, looking at that swaying tree was no different from looking at his moving arm. He saw the same divine power as providence in his own movements and in the movements of the tree. There was, however, now a differentiation between the god without and the god within, although the god in nature and the god in man were still conceived of as being one and the same. It was clear in that period that there was something in the human being in which the providence outside in nature and the providence within the human being come into contact with one another.

This was what the process of breathing was felt to be. One said that when the tree sways, that is the external god, and when I move my arm, that is the internal god. When I breathe in the air, work on it inside myself and then expel it again it is the external god who enters into me and then departs again. This was how the same godly element was felt to be outside and inside: at one and the same time outside and inside. One said to oneself: As a being who breathes I am both a being of nature and my self.

Having shown you my characterization of the ancient Persian world-view with this line [previous drawing], I will now characterize the third age with this line [a lemniscate is drawn inside the oval (Plate 10)].

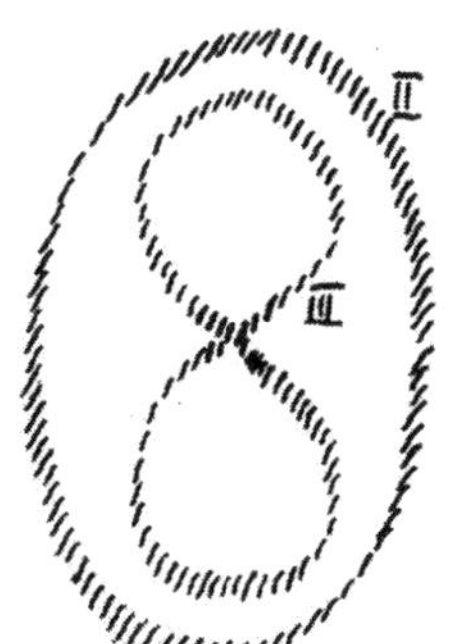

This line demonstrates the world of nature on the one hand and the world of human beings on the other, and it crosses over at a certain point, in the process of breathing.

Things change again in the fourth period, the Graeco-Roman age. Here humanity is tersely confronted with the contrast between outside and inside, between natural existence and human existence. Here the human being begins to feel the contradistinction between himself and nature. So if I wanted to characterize how the human being begins to feel in the Greek age I would have to draw it like this [drawing (Plate 10)]:

On the one side he feels what is external and on the other what is internal; and there is no longer the crossover point between the two.

That which the human being shares with nature remains in a certain sense outside his consciousness. It leaves his consciousness. In the yoga culture of India efforts are made to bring it back inside. That is why the Indian yoga culture represents an atavistic return to former developmental stages of humanity. It endeavours to bring the breathing process back into consciousness because in the third age it was natural to feel oneself both inside it and outside it. The fourth age begins in the eighth pre-Christian century. That is when those late-Indian yoga exercises commenced which sought to bring back atavistically what one had possessed earlier on, especially in the Indian culture, but which had meanwhile been lost.

Well, so awareness of the breathing process was lost. The question is why did the Indian yoga culture try to regain it. What did people think they would achieve by doing so? The answer is that one wanted to reach a true understanding of the external world. During the third cultural age the breathing process was understood in such a way that through it one understood something inwardly which was at the same time something external.

This is now something which must be achieved in a different way. The fourth age ended in the year 1413, or indeed in the middle of the fifteenth century, so we are today living in the aftermath of its culture which did indeed bring something of a duality into the soul-mood of human beings. Through our head organization we have an incomplete view of nature, of what we call the external world; and through our internal organization, the rest of our organization, we have an incomplete knowledge of our self. [Two separate shapes are drawn, see Plate 10, right-hand side.] Something is missing between these two, something in which we would discern a process in the world and a process belonging to our self.

So now it is a matter of regaining, of consciously regaining that which has been lost. That is to say, we must comprehend anew something which belongs both to the external world and to what is internal, something which once again overlaps. [A lemniscate is drawn around the two separate shapes, see Plate 10.]

It is for this that the fifth post-Atlantean epoch must strive. It must be the aim of the fifth post-Atlantean epoch to find, once more, something which is within the human being wherein at the same time an external process runs its course.

You will remember that I have already hinted at this important fact, namely in my last essay 'Culture, Law and Economics' in *The Renewal of the Social Organism*[55] where I firstly dealt with the significance of these things for our social life, but then also indicated clearly that something must be found wherein the human being takes hold of something within himself in which he also recognizes a process of the external world. As present-day human beings we cannot achieve this by harking back, for example, to the yoga culture. That belongs to the past for, as you know, the breathing process itself has changed. Of course this cannot be clinically proven. Nevertheless, the human breathing process has been different since the third post-Atlantean cultural epoch. Roughly speaking one could say: During the third post-Atlantean cultural epoch the human being breathed soul; now he breathes air. It is not only our ideas which have become materialistic; reality itself has lost its soul.

I would ask you, please, not to regard what I am now about to say as something unimportant. Consider the significance of the fact that the reality in which humanity lives has itself changed to the extent that the very air we breathe is different from what it was four millennia ago. It is not only the consciousness of human beings which has changed. No indeed! In those times there was soul in the earth's atmosphere. The air was the soul. This is not what it is today, or perhaps one should say it is still so but in a different way. The spiritual beings of elemental nature about which I spoke yesterday do enter into the air once more, and then one can breathe them by practising yoga-breathing. But that which could be achieved three thousand years ago through normal breathing is not something which can be brought back artificially. That this is possible is the great illusion of people in the Orient.

What I am saying now is most certainly a proper description of reality. The soul element of the air belonging to human beings is no longer there. That is why those beings, those anti-Michael beings about whom I spoke yesterday, enter into the air and through the air into human beings; and this is how they find their way into humanity as I described yesterday. We can only drive them out if we replace yoga practices with what is correct for today.

We must realize that it is necessary for us to strive for what is correct. And we can only strive for what is correct by becoming aware of a far more refined connection of the human being to the external world, thus enabling something to take place in connection with our ether body which can enter increasingly into our consciousness in a similar way to the breathing process. In the process of breathing we inhale fresh air containing oxygen and exhale useless carbon-dioxide air; and a similar process exists in all our processes of sense perception.

Imagine you are seeing something. Let's take a drastic example: you are watching a flame. As you do this something comes about which is comparable with but far more refined than inhaling air. Now you close your eyes—you can do something similar with any of your senses—and there you have an after-image of the flame which gradually changes, just as Goethe says: it fades.[56] Apart from the purely physiological aspect, the human ether body is very much involved in this process of taking in an impression of light and the subsequent fading away of the impression. And this process involves something exceedingly important. In it now is the soul element which three millennia ago was inhaled and exhaled together with the air. We must learn to comprehend similarly how the process of sense perception is filled with the soul element in the way that occurred three thousand years ago in the case of the breathing process.

This is linked with something else, namely that one can describe the human being as having lived in a kind of culture of the night three millennia ago. Yahweh made himself known through his prophets via night-time dreams. Now, however, we must fashion the fine details of our intercourse with the world in a way which ensures that our perceptions are not only sensual but also spiritual. We must ensure that with every beam of light, with every note or sound, with every sensation of temperature, as well as in the way these fade away again, we enter into an intercourse with the world which is of the soul, and this intercourse through the soul must become something meaningful for us. It is also possible for us to support ourselves in a way which will enable this to come about.

I have described to you how the Mystery of Golgotha came about in the fourth post-Atlantean period which, when we calculate this exactly [Plate 10], began with the year 747 before Christ and ended with the year 1413. The Mystery of Golgotha took place in the first third of that period. However, it was the lingering resonances of the old way of thinking, of the old culture, which initially enabled human beings to comprehend the Mystery of Golgotha. The manner in which the Mystery of Golgotha is comprehended must become utterly renewed. The old way of comprehending the Mystery of Golgotha is spent. It is no longer capable of coping with the Mystery of Golgotha. But meanwhile, many endeavours which have been undertaken to render human thinking capable of comprehending the Mystery of Golgotha have proved inadequate to reach up to the Mystery of Golgotha.

You see, all things which happen externally in material circumstances also have their spiritual and soul aspect. And all things which happen in the spirit and soul also have their physical, material side. The fact that the earth's air has become devoid of soul, so that human beings no longer inhale what was originally air filled with soul, has had a significant spiritual effect on the evolution of humanity. By taking into himself the soul through inhaling the living soul to which he had originally been akin, as we read at the beginning of the Old Testament—and God breathed into the human being the breath as the living soul[57]—the human being had a certain potential. He received an awareness of the pre-existence of the soul element, of the soul's existence, before descending in his physical body through birth or through conception. And in the same degree as the breathing process ceased to be ensouled, so did the human being lose his awareness of a previous existence of the soul element. Indeed, even when Aristotle appeared on the scene in this fourth post-Atlantean period, it was not possible any longer for the human capacity of comprehension to penetrate the mystery of the pre-existence of the soul.[58] There was no longer any possibility for this.

The curious historical fact is that the greatest event enters into earthly evolution, the Christ Event, and yet humanity first has to increase in maturity before becoming capable of comprehending it. At first, with what remains of their primeval powers of comprehension, human beings are still able to catch hold of what rays out from the Mystery of Golgotha. But then their capacity for comprehension fades, and dogma leads them ever further away from the Mystery of Golgotha. The Church banishes belief in pre-existence not because pre-existence cannot be reconciled with the Mystery of Golgotha but because the human capacity of comprehension, owing to the air having become void of the soul element, loses its ability to bring the force of consciousness into the soul, the consciousness of pre-existence. Pre-existence vanishes from whatever is left of head consciousness. When we regain the soul element in our sense impressions, then we shall once more have a crossover point [Plate 10], and in that point we shall be able to grasp hold of human will as it streams upwards out of the third layer of consciousness in the way I told you the other day. And at the same time we shall also have something which is subjective-and-objective, which is what Goethe so greatly craved.

And then we shall again also have the possibility of grasping, at first delicately, what is so remarkable about this sense process of the human being over against the external world. The idea that the external world merely has an effect on us and that we merely react to this is really rather unsubtle. All that stuff amounts to no more than a rough idea. In reality what happens is that a soul process goes from the outside to the inside where it is then taken hold of by the profoundly unconscious inner soul process in such a way that the two processes interact. World thoughts work their way into us from the outside, and human will works outwards from within. And at this crossing-point the human will and the world thoughts cross over, just as in breathing what was objective used to cross over with what was subjective. We must learn to feel how our will works through our eyes and how indeed the activity of the senses quietly mingles with the passivity which enables world thoughts to cross over with human will. It is this new yoga-will which we must develop. In this way something will be imparted to us, something resembling what was imparted to the human being through the breathing process three millennia ago. Our comprehension must become far more imbued with soul, far more imbued with spirit.

These are the things for which Goethe was seeking in his world-view.[59] He wanted to recognize the pure phenomenon—he called it the *ur*-phenomenon—in which he included solely what works on the human being from the outside, untainted by the luciferic thought which arises out of the human being's own head. That thought was intended only to serve the combination of the phenomena. Goethe was searching for the *ur*-phenomenon, not the law of nature. That is what is so special about him. So if we take the pure phenomenon, the *ur*-phenomenon, on its own, we then have externally something which enables us to feel the unfolding of our will as we observe the external world; and then we shall be able to rise up once again to something which is objective-and-subjective such as is described, for example, in ancient Hebrew teachings.

We should learn to stop speaking only about the antithesis of physical and spiritual. We must instead recognize, in our sense perceptions, the interplay between the physical and the spiritual as a union. We will experience today what was present in the Yahweh culture three millennia ago when we cease to see something material in nature, and also when we cease to conceive of some sort of fantasy soul in nature as did, for example, Gustav Theodor Fechner.[60] When we receive in relation to nature the soul element combined with the sense perception, then shall we have a Christ-filled relationship with external nature. And then this Christ-filled relationship with external nature will become something akin to a spiritual breathing process.

We can gain support in this by realizing ever more clearly, on the basis of our sound common sense, that pre-existence is something which lies at the foundation of our life of soul. So we must regard the purely egoistic idea of a post-existence—for it is purely egoistic since it arises from the longing to survive after death—we must complement this egoistic concept of a post-existence with the knowledge of the pre-existence of the soul. We must make a new kind of effort to reach the view that the soul is indeed eternal. It is this which we can describe as the Michael culture. When we make our way through the world with an awareness that together with everything we see, everything we hear there is soul and there is spirit flowing into us, and with the awareness that at the same time soul is flowing from us out into the world, then we shall have gained the awareness needed by humankind for the future.

Let me return once more to that picture. You see a flame. You close your eyes and see an after-image which fades. Is this nothing more than a subjective process? Physiologists today say it is. But this is not true. In the world ether it signifies an objective process, just as in the air the presence of the carbon dioxide you exhale signifies an objective process. You imprint on the world ether the image you experience solely as a fading after-image. This is not only subjective; it is also an objective process. Here you have what is objective. You have the possibility of recognizing how something taking place within you is in a subtle way also a world process when you become conscious of the fact: I see a flame, I close my eyes, I see it fade—of course it also fades when your eyes are open, only you don't notice this—and this is something which takes place not only within you but also in the world outside.

This is the case not only with a flame. If I meet someone and claim that what he has just said is true or untrue, this is a judgement, a moral or intellectual action within me. Just like the flame, it gradually fades. And this, too, is an objective world process. If you think well of a fellow human being, this too fades and becomes an objective process in the world ether. If you think ill of him, this also fades as an objective process. You cannot lock away in your secret chamber what you perceive or judge about the world. You seem to be doing it privately for yourself, but it is at the same time an objective world process. Just as the third age knew that the breathing process is both something taking place within the human being and at the same time an objective process, so must humanity in the future become aware that the soul process about which I have been speaking is also an objective world process.

This change of consciousness is something which calls for greater strength in the human being's mood of soul, greater than that to which we are accustomed nowadays. It is what is meant by taking in the Michael culture: permeating oneself with this consciousness. If we take light as the general representative of sense perception, we must make the effort of thinking about light as being filled with soul, just as it was a matter of course for people in the second and third pre-Christian millennia to think in this way, for light was indeed filled with soul. We must thoroughly break the habit of seeing in light only what our materialistic age is in the habit of seeing in it. We must thoroughly break the habit of believing that the sun merely emits those rays about which our physics and human consciousness in general are in the habit of speaking. We must come to realize that soul is penetrating space on the vibrations of light. And at the same time we must realize that this was not the case in the age which preceded our own. In the age preceding our own what reached humanity through air was that which now reaches humanity through light. You see, this is an objective difference in the earth's process. So thinking on the larger scale we can say: air soul process, light soul process [writing (Plate 11)]:

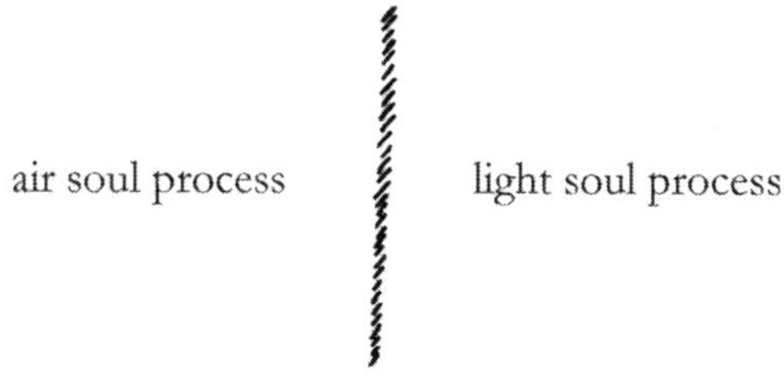

This is approximately what we can observe in the evolution of the earth. And in the middle between the two stands the Mystery of Golgotha, signifying the transition from the one to the other. Both for the present and for the future of humanity it will be insufficient merely to fantasize about the spirit in abstractions or fall into some kind of nebulous pantheism. What matters is to take what today's humanity experiences as merely some kind of physical process and begin to see that there is a soul element within it.

It is important that we now learn to say: There was a time before the Mystery of Golgotha when the earth had an atmosphere, and in that atmosphere there was the soul which was related to the soul element of the human being; now the earth has an atmosphere, but it is devoid of a soul element related to the human soul. Instead, the same soul element which was previously in the air has entered into the light; and this became possible because the Christ united himself with the earth. Thus both air and light have been transformed in their spirit and soul element during the course of earthly evolution.

It is silly to describe air and light purely materialistically in the same way throughout the millennia in which the earth's evolution has been taking place. Both air and light have changed inwardly. We live now in an atmosphere and in a light environment both of which have changed since our souls lived on the earth in former incarnations. Learning to recognize what is externally material as something which is of the soul and spirit is what is important now. Spiritual science will not be correct if people describe what is purely a physical existence on the one hand and then add, like a decoration, that by the way, oh yes, in this physical matter there is also something spiritual! People are peculiar nowadays in this respect; all they want is to withdraw into abstractions in such matters. Yet what is necessary instead is that they should in future not make an abstract distinction between what is physical and what is spiritual; they should seek the spiritual itself within the physical in order to recognize that what is spiritual is also the transition into the physical, into the way it works in the physical.

When we are able to understand this we shall be able to reach an understanding of the human being. 'Blood is a very special fluid.'[61] But what is talked of today in physiology is not a very special fluid but merely a substance one seeks to analyse chemically as is done with any other. There is nothing special about it. However, when we reach the starting point of being able to comprehend rightly the metamorphosis of air and light in the soul, then we shall gradually be able to advance to comprehending the human being himself as having spirit and soul in all his parts; no longer shall we have abstract physical matter and abstract spirit, for spirit, soul and body will be seen as working within one another. That will be the culture of Michael.

It is for this that our age is calling. It is something which must be grasped with every fibre of human soul life by those who wish to comprehend our present time. For a long while there has been resistance to everything seemingly unusual being included in our view of the world.

I have frequently quoted a droll example relating to something rather rough and ready. In 1835—not even a century ago—when the first railway line was about to be built from Fürth to Nuremberg, the learned faculty of medicine in Bavaria were asked whether such a thing would be healthy. The medical faculty declared—the document exists, this is no fairy tale[62]—that the railway line should not be built since it would make people nervous to travel across the face of the earth in that way. And they added that if certain individuals insisted on the building of railways, then high wooden fences should be erected on either side of the line to prevent passers-by from being concussed.

So you see: Passing judgements of this kind is one thing, but another thing is the evolutionary advancement of humanity. Today we smile at a document such as that issued by the Bavarian medical faculty in 1835. But have we any right to smile? Are we not faced with the very same reaction today? After all, the Bavarian medical faculty were not entirely wrong. If we compare the nervous condition of people today with that of two hundred years ago we do see that they are now more nervous. Perhaps the faculty were exaggerating somewhat, but people are indeed more nervous nowadays.

However, humanity's onward development is not a matter of things like this but rather one of ensuring that certain impulses which want to enter earthly development are indeed able to do so and are not rebuffed. It is easy to be complacent about what wants to enter human cultural development from time to time; one must not decide what is our duty with regard to human cultural evolution on the basis of complacency or even on the basis of an elevated form of complacency. I shall close today with these words because it is evident from all directions that an increasing battle will have to be fought between anthroposophical knowledge on the one hand and a variety of beliefs on the other. These beliefs, which want to continue on their own path and which have no wish to reach a new understanding of the Mystery of Golgotha, will adhere ever more strongly to the battle lines they have already drawn up, and we would be very reckless indeed if we did not take account of the battle ahead.

You see, of course, that I am not at all keen on fighting a battle, especially not one with the Catholic Church. It appears, though, that a battle of this kind is about to be foisted upon us. Someone who is familiar with the more profound historical impulses lying behind the modern beliefs will be most unwilling to do battle against something so venerable. But if a battle is being foisted upon one, then it cannot be avoided. And today's priesthood is utterly disinclined to open the door to that which must be granted entrance, namely matters of spiritual science. We can see that the necessary battle against the attitudes I read out to you the other day[63] is actually grotesque, since articles written against me state that the reader ought to inform himself about anthroposophical spiritual science even though my own writings have been forbidden to Catholics by the Pope. This is not laughable, it is profoundly serious!

A battle which comes about in this grotesque manner, by broadcasting judgements of this kind, cannot be taken lightly. And it can especially not be taken lightly if one is not at all keen to fight it. Take the example of the Catholic Church. And the Protestant Church is no different either, only the former is more powerful and its traditions are more venerable. One need only look at what the priest wears when he says mass, at every item of his apparel, and one need only understand every ancient, holy and venerable act performed during mass. These are things which are more ancient even than Christianity, for the sacrifice of the mass is nothing other than a

Christian version of an even more ancient mystery cultus. All this envelopes the priests who want to take up cudgels in this way!

So when one has on the one hand the deepest veneration both for the cultus and for its symbolism while seeing on the other hand the dreadful means employed in their defence and the dreadful means used to attack what should now enter into human evolution, it becomes clear how necessary it is to take a stance in these matters. This is most truly something which must be seriously studied and comprehended. Yet what we have come up against thus far is merely a beginning. Now is not the time to sleep through such things; now is the time for wide-open eyes! Thus far, throughout the two decades during which the anthroposophical movement has been making its way in central Europe, it has been possible for us to tolerate the sleepy sectarianism which has been so difficult to combat in our own ranks and which is still deeply entrenched in the souls of those who are involved in this movement. But it is now too late to continue with such sleepy sectarianism. What I have often emphasized here is profoundly true, namely that it is now necessary for us to focus clearly on how significant the anthroposophical movement is for world history and, while ignoring trivialities, how important it is to recognize the importance even of small impulses.[64]

Lecture 7

DORNACH, 6 DECEMBER 1919

YOU have often heard about how reaching a true understanding of the human being involves paying close attention to how this human being is organized in three parts. Within him the three parts are organized in a way which can be divided—roughly speaking, of course—into: the head, the organs of the breast, and the limbs, with the latter including a large part of what lies within the torso. You will also have gathered from my lectures and from what is written in *Riddles of the Soul* how everything connected with thinking and having ideas is connected with the head, how everything rhythmical, everything belonging to the sphere of feeling, is connected—roughly speaking, as I said—with the breast, and how the sphere of the will, which is actually the spiritual part of the human being, is connected with the limbs, with the organization of the limbs. These three systems of the human organism are relatively autonomous. And the life of ideas, the life of feeling and the life of will are also relatively autonomous, though of course they do work together.

You know, also, that the best way to grasp the distinction between the three systems from the spiritual point of view is to say: In ordinary waking life the human being is only fully awake in the system of his head, in everything involved with thinking and having ideas. In comparison, in everything connected with the life of feeling, with the rhythmic system, the human being is in a dream state even when he is fully awake. We know what is going on in our life of feeling indirectly through our ideas, but never directly through the actual feelings themselves. And our life of will is in even greater darkness, with all it involves being shrouded in sleep. We can thus explain more plainly than is usually the case that ordinary human consciousness is underpinned by other, less conscious states. Subconscious perceptions underpin the life of feeling, and comparatively even more subconscious perceptions underpin the life of will.

It is very important to realize, though, that thinking, feeling and will are actually present in all three systems of the human being. Feeling and will are also present in the head system, the system of thinking, although they are much weaker there than is the life of thinking and ideas. Similarly, thoughts are also present in the sphere of feeling where they come to consciousness only in a dreamlike way; they are weaker there than in the head sphere. What is, however, not normally taken into account in our age of abstract scientific thinking is the fact that these subconscious parts are as objective there in the same degree as they are subjective in our consciousness. What does this mean?

It means that the processes taking place in our life of thinking and ideas, in our life of the head, are processes which to a great degree take place within us. However, what we experience in our rhythmic system, in our breast system, in our sphere of feeling is not at all solely our individual possession. It takes place within us but at the same time it represents objective world processes. This means that when you have a feeling it is of course your feeling, but at the same time it is something which is taking place in the world, something of significance for the world. It is most interesting to observe upon what world processes our life of feeling is based. Let us assume that you experience something which generates very strong feelings in you either of joy or sorrow. You know that human life runs its course in seven-year periods. The first period [Plate 12] takes us from birth to the change of teeth, the second continues until puberty and the third to the beginning of our twenty-first year—of course all this is approximate—and so on. This is how the course of a human life is structured (the horizontal line with vertical divisions, over, and in Plate 12).

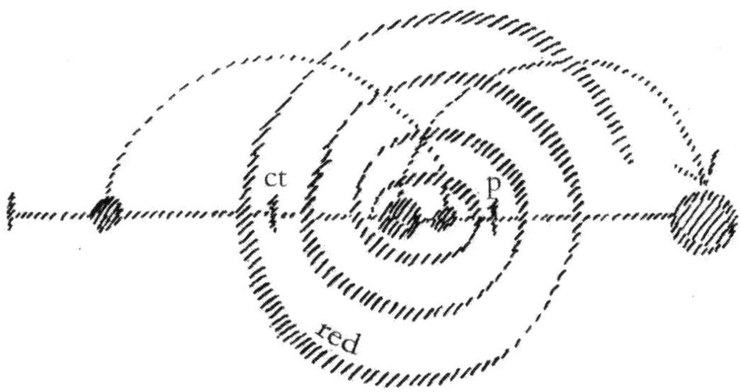

When we consider this structure we come to nodal points of human development which in early life are expressed quite clearly in the change of teeth and the arrival of puberty and which thereafter remain more or less hidden, although they are still quite clear later on for someone who knows how to observe them [the nodal points are marked]. What takes place in the body and the soul of the human being around his twenty-first year is just as obvious, for someone who knows what to look for, as are the change of teeth or puberty for external physiology. But on the whole less notice is taken of this.

This, then, is a more generalized structuring of human life. But when something occurs, some important event, for example between the change of teeth and puberty, something which is very arousing for the sphere of feeling [the spiral is drawn, red], then something specific takes place which is normally not noticed—because nowadays things are only crudely observed. The event, however, does take place and in a certain sense it makes an impression on the feelings. But when there is an impression on the feelings then—regardless of what is taking place in your consciousness, in your soul life as such—something occurs in the objective world. What occurs in the objective world can be compared to a kind of swinging-out which spreads into the world. But the remarkable thing is that it does not spread out endlessly; once it has spread out sufficiently, when its elasticity is extended to the full, it then swings back [the left-hand semicircle], and it then reappears in the next seven-year period as an impulse which enters into your soul life from outside. Since these things vary from one individual to the next, I shall not maintain that such an event occurs in every case after approximately seven years. But if it does occur it is not noticed by the individual.

We are constantly in the process in our soul life of going through such things which enter into our life of feeling and which are the reaction of the world to what we have experienced in our feeling sphere during the previous seven-year period. In other words, when an event has somehow stirred our feeling life it returns to our soul life during the next seven-year period. On the whole people do not notice such things. But if one makes some effort one can certainly notice them outwardly.

Surely we have all experienced a person who suddenly becomes anxious or ill-humoured without knowing why. The person changes from one minute to the next. If one is able to cast the eye of one's soul upon such behaviour, if one can sense what such a person is saying between the words, or even with the words, then one can look back to some former event by which feelings were aroused. During the whole intervening period something has been going on in the world which would not have been going on if that arousal of feelings had not occurred. Apart from the fact that the individual has had the experience, it also continues to take place outside him, objectively in the world. There are so very many opportunities for these things to take place objectively in the world, outside the individual, which have nevertheless been caused by that individual.

Mixed in with these objective processes in the world are those things which take place among the elemental beings, including those I mentioned the other day where I linked them to the breathing system, the rhythmic system. Here you see them working together with the rhythmic system via the arousal of the feelings. These things, if we understand them rightly, oblige us to say that the human being is constantly generating something around himself which resembles quite a large aura. Elemental beings mingle with the waves caused by the person and, depending on the person, these elemental beings can exert an influence upon what comes back. You can picture it like this: A feeling is aroused; you send it out in waves. When it returns to you it is not uninfluenced because the elemental beings have been busy with it in the meantime. So when it works back you receive the effect the elemental beings have had on it [the right-hand semicircle is drawn; the drawing is now complete (Plate 12)].

An interchange with elemental spirits arises through the spiritual atmosphere exuded by the human being. Everything arising from destiny in a person's life is linked to these things. Within our life we have a kind of fulfilment of our destiny. What we experience today is significant for something later on. This is how our destiny is built. And elemental beings who feel attracted to us by our own nature participate in building our destiny. They feel attracted to us and they join in working on us.

What you are seeing here is interaction between the human being and his environment and you are watching how spiritual beings play in our environment. And when you watch this interplay, much becomes apparent with regard to a person's destiny. Insight into these situations is, in our 'enlightened' times—'enlightened' nowadays always calls for quotation marks—very far away; only the traditions from earlier times, when humanity was more connected with an awareness of elemental beings, are present now. These traditions are beautifully expressed in early poetry where human destiny is more interwoven with intervention from elemental beings. One of the most beautiful poems still dealing with such intervention by elemental beings in our destiny is frequently shown in eurythmy where we see how those beings from the realm of the *Erlkönig* intervene in our lives:[65]

Erlkönig's Daughter

Count Olof rode full late and long
Bidding his friends to his bridal throng,

There danc'd the wood nymphs o'er verdant land,
Erlkönig's Daughter reached him her hand.

'O welcome, Count Olof! why haste ye from here?
Step thou in the ring and dance without fear.'

'O, I dare not dance, and I cannot stay,
For to-morrow is my wedding day.'

'Now hear me, Count Olof! dance thou with me,
And two golden spurs I will give to thee;

'And a shirt of silk most fine and white,
Which my mother bleached by pale moonlight.'

'O, I dare not dance, and I cannot stay,
For to-morrow is my wedding day.'

'Now hear me, Count Olof! dance thou with me,
And a heap of gold I'll give to thee.'

'A heap of gold I would take with glee,
But ere I dance, it may stay with thee.'

'If thou wilt not, Count Olof, dance with me,
Then sorrow and sickness will follow thee.'

Here you see the interweaving of the elemental world with human destiny in the way it influences the most conspicuous aspects of destiny: sickness and death.

She struck him a blow across the heart.

Please do take note of such things. In ancient poetry—Herder took this from folk poetry—things are not as they are in more modern poems. Of our modern poems we really can say that about 99 per cent are too much of a good thing. Poems emanating from ancient wisdom always correspond with the facts, with what is real. So they would never say 'She struck him a blow across the head', or on the mouth, or on the nose, but rather:

She struck him a blow across the heart.
Never before had he felt such smart.

It is necessary for there to be a connection with an organ of rhythm, hence the heart.

She raised him livid upon his steed:
'Ride home to thy lady dear with speed.'

And when he came before the door,
His mother saw him with anguish sore.

'Hear me, my son, quick tell thy tale,
O why is thy face so strangely pale?'

'Ah, well may my face be strangely pale,
Erlkönig's Daughter has wrought my bale.'

'Hear me, my son, so loved and dear,
What shall I say thy bride to cheer?'

'Tell her I went to the woods for an hour,
With horse and dog, to prove their power.'

On the morn, when day scarce shone in the west,
There came the bride and each wedding guest.

She poured them mead, she poured them wine:
'Now where is Count Olof, that bridegroom of mine?'

'Count Olof went to the woods for an hour,
With horse and dog, to prove their power.'

The bride raised up the robe so red,
There lay Count Olof, and he was dead.

What I want you to notice is the practical way in which the poem reports what goes on around a human being in such an hour of destiny. This is what always goes on around a human being, especially when events stimulating the feeling sphere are repeated periodically. They always return in a way which involves influencing our destiny not in the same way but after those elemental beings have influenced it. Just as we live in the external, physical air or under the influence of the mineral, plant and animal kingdoms, so do we also live with our initially subconscious parts, with our rhythmical system, in the spiritual sphere of the elemental beings. And that is where as much of our destiny is constructed as is capable of being constructed in our life between birth and death.

It is solely because we are fully awake in our head that we protrude from this interplay with the elemental beings. It is only in the wide-awake life of our head that we are not embedded in the kingdom of the elemental beings. That is where we protrude above the surface of the elemental ocean in which as human beings we constantly float.

What you see here is the repetition of the events, of the destiny events, already within ordinary life, through what takes place in our rhythmic system and in our limb system. This in its turn also enters into interplay with the surroundings, but it is more complicated, much, much more complicated, and this, too, swings back on itself but with a wider swing. These only return in the next life on earth, or in one of the next lives. There is thus no need for our destiny, our karma to be so very mysterious for us if only we observe that it is simply an enlargement of what we can study within a human life as regards the return of such events. They do not return unchanged; indeed, they are very much changed when they return.

Let me draw your attention to something. In my pedagogical lectures, wherever they have taken place, I have always pointed out that an important nodal point occurs round about the ninth year. A very great deal of attention should be paid in school to this important nodal point in human life. Up to that point, for example, nature studies should only be conducted by describing natural processes—in fables, in legends and so on—in connection with the moral life of human beings. Only after that should one make a beginning with simple, elementary scientific descriptions of nature, because it is now that the children will be ready for this. A proper curriculum arises entirely out of a real observation of the human being right down to every detail. I have already pointed this out in my essay on the pedagogical basis of the Waldorf School.[66]

There, too, I indicated the period of roughly the ninth year. That is when awareness of the ego reaches a new stage. The human being is now more capable of observing nature in a more objective way. Prior to that he merges whatever he sees in external nature with his own being. Consciousness of the ego has already been developing throughout the first seven-year period, even at the age of two or two-and-a-half. But now, in the second seven-year period, it returns again at around the age of nine. This is one of the most noticeable returns, this return of ego consciousness at around the ninth year. Ego consciousness now returns in a more spiritual form, whereas it was more in the soul during the second or third year. This is only one of the events which return in a more noticeable manner. But it can also be seen in connection with other, less significant events in life.

Understanding these intimate facts about the life of the human being will in future become increasingly urgent. Insight about such things will gradually have to become part of general knowledge. General understanding about such things does change from time to time. Nowadays we are unhappy if our children reach the age of ten without being able to cope with certain aspects of arithmetic. That was not the case in Roman times. The Romans were unhappy if a boy of ten still did not know the Law of the Twelve Tables,[67] whereas we do not mind if our children are not yet familiar with the legal system. Indeed, our soul constitution would be in a sorry state if this were still the case. So what is deemed to be necessary as general knowledge changes with the times, and we are now at a point in time when such intimate facts about the soul life of the human being must become a part of general knowledge. Human beings must get to know themselves more thoroughly than has been considered necessary until now. If this does not happen the consequences will be extremely unfavourable for the whole shape of human life.

The fact that we are unaware of the origin of something which disturbs us does not prevent it from happening in our life of soul. Things do return and they do influence our life of soul. We cannot explain them and we are indeed not even consciously aware of them. As a result, people begin to have all kinds of inner worries. They suffer greatly from this but have to accept them although of course they do not realize that they are the consequence of former earth lives. Matters of feeling always return in some form or other. For example, if you teach a child to pray, if the child develops a prayerful mood in his life of feeling, this, too, will swing back again at a later stage. It will swing back after a very long time, or even in between whiles as well. After a very long time prayerfulness will return as a soul mood of blessing. That is why I often say that no older person will be able to bless if he has not learned to pray during childhood. Prayer is transformed into blessing. This is the nature of such returns which swing back during life.

Such things must gradually come to be understood. The fact that they are not yet understood is the reason why the great significance of the Mystery of Golgotha cannot yet be fully comprehended by humanity. What does it mean to people bound up in present-day culture when one tells them that after passing through the Mystery of Golgotha the Christ became united with the life of earthly humanity? People do not want to develop ideas about the way in which they themselves are in interrelationship with what surrounds the Christ. For the understanding of our head the influence of the Christ Impulse is not very obvious. But when we look down into our unconscious, into the feeling sphere and the will sphere, that is when we enter the sphere of the elemental beings, and this is the sphere which for us is interwoven with the Christ Impulse.

Physiologically speaking, we submerge ourselves in our rhythmic system and then onward down into the region with which the Christ has united himself for our earthly existence. That is where one can say that the Christ is to be found objectively, rather than through tradition or some kind of subjective mysticism. We are now living in an epoch in which the events emanating from there—as I explained the other day—have a strongly objective significance with regard to human life. This is because they gradually begin to influence unconsciously the decisions people make when they are reluctant to accept such things. When we are willing to accept them we experience the influence consciously, which means that we can reckon with them, we can to some degree call upon those spiritual worlds, which are a part of our life, to collaborate with us.

It is also externally obvious that we are in this respect at a turning point of human evolution. I need only mention a certain fact about which I have often spoken in connection with one point of view or another. Looking at historical matters in the way they are often presented nowadays we have to say that historical accounts have not yet progressed to include the Mystery of Golgotha. You need only examine what ordinary world history presents you with. You read descriptions of the ancient Assyrians, the Babylonian kingdom, ancient Persia, the Egyptian kingdom, Greece, Rome. At this point mention is perhaps also made of the Mystery of Golgotha having taken place. But then the historical sequence continues with the migration of the barbarian peoples and so on, right up, on the one hand, to Louis XIV or the French Revolution or Poincaré and on the other to the downfall of the Hohenzollerns and so forth. But in the ordinary *fable convenue* known as 'history' you will find absolutely nothing about the continuing influence of the Christ Impulse.

As far as historical accounts are concerned it looks as though the Christ Impulse has been wiped out. How strange it is that, for example, a historian such as Ranke,[68] who was a devout Christian and who subjectively held the Christ Impulse in high esteem, should make no mention at all of the Christ Impulse in his historical writings. He is unable to make anything of it. The Christ Impulse has no standing in historical accounts. One has to say that as far as people's spiritual understanding is concerned Christianity does not yet exist in human history. Our anthroposophical spiritual science is the first to recognize it in a positive way in that it reveals the concrete historical development of the Event of Golgotha in its descriptions of the fourth post-Atlantean epoch. As you know, the Event of Golgotha is included in the way we present history. In fact we go even further. Not only do we present the evolution of humanity by including the Event of Golgotha in it; we also depict world evolution, cosmic evolution in such a way that the Mystery of Golgotha is central to it.

When you contemplate my book *An Outline of Occult Science*, you will see that it tells not only of past eclipses of the sun or past eclipses of the moon, or some explosions or eruptions in the cosmos, but also of the Christ Event as a cosmic event. The strange thing is that when one initially says that historians, so-called historians, do not find it possible to include the Christ Event in the course of history, official representatives of the faith go berserk. When they hear that something like anthroposophical spiritual science talks of the Christ Event, the official representatives of the faiths become enraged. This shows how little the faiths are inclined properly to fulfil the great demand of our time, which is to connect the Christ Event with world events in general. One cannot help concluding that people, even theologians, who frequently speak of the Christ, do so in a way which is no different from the way they speak of any divine being; it is no different, for example, from the way the Hebrews of old, or even Jewish people today, still speak of their Yahweh or Jehovah.

As I said the other day, you can take Harnack's book *What is Christianity?*[69] and cross out the name of Christ wherever he uses it and include the general name of God in its place. You will find that this does not alter the meaning at all since the author has no conception of what is specific about Christianity. In fact, page by page Harnack's book is a description of the opposite of what Christianity is; it deals not with Christianity but with the general teachings about Yahweh.

It is very important to point these things out since they are closely connected with the necessary requirements of our time. That which must stream into human cultural development is a human awareness of the presence not only of a general, abstract spiritual world but of a concrete spiritual world in which we live with our feeling and our will and from which only our thinking, our head, is separated. It is certainly the case that a new kind of world view is needed which involves a proper penetration of our feeling and thinking and doing with the Christ Impulse.

The fact that our astronomy, our doctrines of evolution, have unfolded in entirely abstract formulae in recent times is solely due to the Christ Impulse having not yet grasped hold inwardly of human beings. It has instead remained a tradition and has taken hold of human beings very subjectively and yet not inwardly in a way which would cause these inner experiences to become at the same time objective world experiences in which we would live in an interplay with what is taking place spiritually in all that surrounds us.

It is, however, possible to notice here and there the dawning of a strong awareness that new impulses are needed by humanity. But human beings find it so very hard to grasp a concrete life of the spirit. When they speak of the spirit they still yearn more or less strongly to live in the abstract.

Even our attitude to our thoughts needs to change in some way. I have often pointed out from one angle or another that what I mean by this is that the lectures on anthroposophical spiritual science given at the present time do not have the purpose of propagating a specific programme; they are not given with a specific aim in mind of generating enthusiasm for some kind of ideal. The reason for giving them is that they are needed by present-day humanity. So one must take as one's starting point certain soul conditions of earlier times which existed during epochs when we were as yet more closely connected with our true spiritual environment.

This was different in former times, but nowadays we ought to have a very strong feeling for it. I have often said that nothing further awaits humanity from the outside. It is from the inside, from our links with the spiritual world, that impulses for the progress of humanity must come, and we must develop a good eye for the fact that what we are encountering, without any fault on our part, are increasingly experiences of decline. We are to some extent already on the downward path of earthly evolution, and we must, as human beings, lift ourselves up in order to rise above the evolution of the Earth through our involvement with the spiritual world.

For this to come about, however, what we are striving for in the form of knowledge must be felt to be a force which will enable the whole of humanity to move on to the next phase of evolution if the earth were to die beneath our feet, just as we are able to pass over other, more minor, stages of evolution when our body dies and we pass through the portal of death. As individual human beings we pass through the portal of death into the spiritual world as our body dies away beneath us. That is what it will one day be like for humanity as a whole. The whole of humanity will one day beat a path across to the Jupiter existence, to what I call the Jupiter existence, and the earth will remain as a corpse. It is already in the process of dying. Individual human beings develop wrinkles and grey hair. And today, for geologists who are able to make proper observations, as I mentioned the other day,[70] the earth is showing clear signs of ageing. It is dying away from under us. So what we are searching for spiritually is indeed a way of working to counter the earth's ageing process. We really must fill ourselves entirely with an awareness of this.

From another point of view, earlier ages described their mystery knowledge as something akin to the power of healing, and also of physical healing. This awareness, too, must once again begin to permeate humanity. Our striving for knowledge must generate the awareness that with it one is making an effort towards the further development of mankind as a whole. We would naturally never reach this awareness if we were not to face up to what is concrete all around us in the manner I have described, for then we would regard the matter of what we feel and want and do as merely our own personal affair. We would not realize that this was going on outside of ourselves as well.

Another thing which will also be necessary—and here I must make a remark that may not be so readily understood in general—it will be necessary also to make an approach to the more exact aspects of human knowledge. These are, however, not yet at their best. One can still find the most impossible notions being put forward by the exact sciences.

Let me mention just one example which may be generally comprehensible. People imagine superficially [drawing (Plate 12, top left-hand)] that the sun is here somewhere. From it light emanates in all directions, as it would from any other source of light. All those who have a mathematical conception of this emanating light say: The light spreads out to infinity and then it somehow disappears; as it spreads out to infinity it then dies of its own weakness. But this is not true. Everything which spreads out reaches a limit and then it swings back

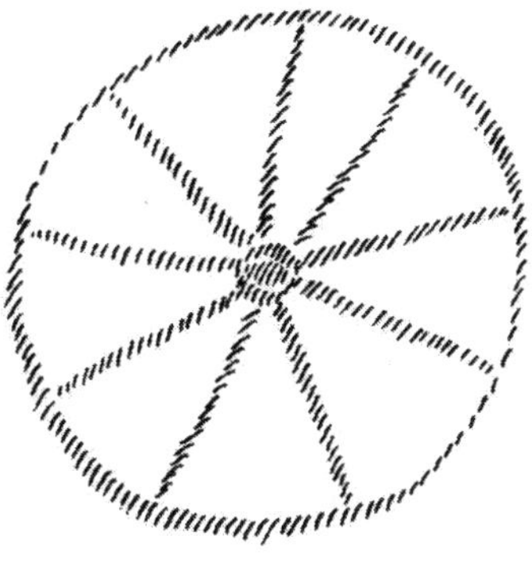

from that limit, reaching its original source in a different form [Plate 12]. The light of the sun does not spread out to infinity; it swings back upon itself not as light but now as something different.

This is also how it is with every kind of light. And this is basically how it is with all other effects. Every effect is subject to the law of elasticity, with a limit to that elasticity. Yet the idea previously described is everywhere to be found in our so-called exact sciences, and far too little account is taken of the reality. If you were a physicist I would point out to you how people in physics today reckon with distance travelled and with time taken. And then they make their calculation with the velocity, which is usually shown as c or v, a function of distance and time, and they depict it as a quotient [writing on the board: 'distance', 'time' and the formula (Plate 12)].

$$c = \frac{s}{t}$$

But this is completely incorrect. The velocity is not the result, the velocity is the primary quality which anything, whether physical or spiritual, has within it and we dissect the velocity into distance, or space, and time. We abstract those two things. Space and time as such are not real. Velocities, in the world, are something real, various velocities. This remark is directed solely to physicists. They will understand that even in all the things on which knowledge of time is theoretically based there are postulates which are flawed. These postulates are present everywhere only because we are not able to conceive of something spiritual as being something concrete.

This is what we are called upon to do in the Michael Age, that humanity may reach a situation in which it is possible to grasp what is spiritual in its concreteness, so that just as one speaks of air and water being in the environment, so can one also know that the various elemental and higher beings are in the environment. This is what matters, and this is something which must become human culture, just as it was human culture in olden times. But people are reluctant to admit this. They do not at all want to recognize the reversals in human evolution such as occurred, for example, in the middle of the fifteenth century. Yet there are details which prove that it did indeed occur.

Someone, a Swede or a Norwegian,[71] recently wrote a book in which he quoted a good deal from the alchemists. In particular he quoted a passage by an alchemist mentioning various substances, mercury, antimony and so on. And then that author of today who—as his book shows—is a very excellent modern chemist, says that he cannot imagine what the chemical recipe quoted by the alchemist is all about. Well, he cannot imagine what it is about for the simple reason that he, the modern-day chemist, talks about mercury, about quicksilver in that he imagines the mineral quicksilver. And when a modern chemist talks about antimony, well, for him this is antimony, the metal, and so on. In the book he quotes, however, something quite different is meant, not the external metal but certain processes which occur in the human organism. It is knowledge about the interior of the human body. Something based on the consciousness of the original author is quoted by that modern-day gentleman who assumes that the reference is to a laboratory experiment using retorts and so on. So he cannot help regarding what he is reading as nonsense. It is not nonsense, however, as soon as one realizes that the references to antimony, mercury and so on—even though there is also some connection to the actual metals—apply to processes within the human body. So someone reading that literature prior to the fifteenth century will find in it something entirely different from what comes to be understood later on.

Looking at such things could be yet another way of studying the transformations which take place in the constitution of the soul. Today we are living in an age when we should begin to pay close attention to things which, over centuries, humanity has persisted in ignoring.

Lecture 8

DORNACH, 7 DECEMBER 1919[72]

WHAT it has been my duty to tell you over these weeks culminates in the fact that we are about to experience how the spiritual world is beginning to enter into our present world, chiefly as a result of what first began in the middle of the fifteenth century. Everything changed round about the middle of the fifteenth century in what we know as the civilized world. What human beings were taking into their consciousness prior to the middle of that century was primarily connected with the internal part of the human organization. In whatever ancient writings we may still have—I mentioned them yesterday—you will find that expressions are used which very much resemble those used by today's chemists or physicists and so on. And yet today's chemists and physicists will be quite unable to understand what is written in those books for the simple reason that they believe the books refer to external processes. But it is internal processes, not external processes, which are described there, processes which take place within the human physical or etheric body.

Since the time of Galileo and Giordano Bruno people have begun to turn their attention more closely to the external world, so that now we have reached the stage of having an understanding of nature which influences all our thinking, and especially popular thinking and feeling. Our understanding of nature now speaks of many things in the mineral, plant and animal kingdoms which are unable to provide any elucidation about the human being, or even about his physical, bodily aspect. So the time has now come for us to ask ourselves: How do I myself, as a human being, relate to the external kingdoms of nature, to that which surrounds me in the animal, plant and mineral kingdom, in the external human kingdom and also in the kingdom of air and water, of fire and clouds, of sun, moon and stars? How, as a human being, do I relate to all this?

We shall be unable to find an exhaustive answer to this question without repeating our examination of the human being thus far. So let us begin with the human being of the senses and the understanding. Regarding our eyes, our ears and our other sense organs we can say that although they are connected with the other parts of our body, they are chiefly organs of the head and they perceive the external world. And we then work on what we perceive of this external world through those ideas and concepts which are the tools of our brain. We retain within us—since this is necessary for our internal integrity as human beings—whatever we have experienced through our senses and whatever we have thought about with our understanding and our memory. Whatever we have absorbed concerning the external world, whatever takes place within us as a part of the external world absorbed through our senses, whatever we understand through our intelligence about all that we have absorbed: that is what we retain as ideas in our memory. So, with regard to everything just mentioned, what are we as human beings when we encounter the world?

Let us take as our starting point the phenomenon of our sense perceptions. I have already mentioned this phenomenon during these lectures. Imagine you look at a flame with your eyes. Then you close your eyes and you have an after-image of the flame. This after-image of the flame which is within your eyes gradually disappears. Goethe,[73] who always spoke pictorially about such things, said: The impression of the after-image fades away. Then the original constitution of the eye and the nerves connected with it is reinstated after having been changed by the impression the light made on it.

What takes place in a sense organ is a simpler version of what goes on in your memory when you receive external impressions about which you think and which then remain in your memory. The difference is merely that when you take in the impression of a flame through your eyes the impression then fades after a short while. But when you take in something which fills your whole being and then think about it, you will later be able to remember the after-image, perhaps even for the whole remainder of your life. How does this come about? When the simple after-image you have in your eye fades away, perhaps after only a short time, this is because it does not pass through the whole of your organism but instead remains only in a part of it. Memory pictures, on the other hand, pass through the greater part of your overall organization and from there into your ether body and through the ether body into the world ether. When an image is not only an image in a single organ but one which passes through the greater part of the human organism and then on into the ether body and from there into the world outside, it can then remain as an after-image throughout the whole of a life. What matters is that the impression goes in sufficiently deeply and takes hold of the ether body, and that the ether body does not cling on to it but transfers it to the external ether of the world where it inscribes it.

Do not imagine that when you remember things it is merely a process within yourself. When you have an experience, you cannot always write it down in your notebook which you then refer to again in order to read about it, although in fact many individuals do in fact do just that with many of their experiences. What you do is write it into the world ether, and the world ether then recalls it for you like the imprint of a seal. Remembering is not merely a personal matter; remembering is an engagement with the universe. You cannot be alone when, as an inward human being, you want to remember your experiences. Not remembering an experience destroys a person's very being.

Consider the following example which I have often quoted. A man whom I knew very well and who occupied an important position suddenly felt the urge to go to the railway station, without any reason, and to purchase a ticket in order to travel long distances to places for no particular purpose. He did all this in a completely altered state of consciousness. While he was travelling he knew nothing of what he otherwise did, and he only came to his senses again when he found he had been taken in by an asylum for the poor in Berlin. The whole period after he had entered the train in Darmstadt was wiped out of his consciousness. Through reports from several sources it was discovered that he had been in Budapest and in Lemberg whence he had then travelled to Berlin before coming to his senses in the asylum. During that whole time his understanding was functioning normally; there was nothing wrong with it. Between the moment he left Darmstadt and his arrival at the asylum for the poor he was functioning perfectly normally. He knew how to buy a train ticket and how to find something to eat and so on. Yet while he was doing those things he had no memory of his normal life. He could remember his former life up to his departure from Darmstadt but had no memory of that whole journey.

This is one example but I could give you many others. I wanted to draw your attention to what our life would be like without any ongoing memory of all our experiences. Try and imagine as a human being what you would think about your self, your I, if you had no memory about a certain period of time—apart from when you were asleep of course, for you would anyway have no memory of that. What belongs to our capacity to receive sense impressions, to our intelligence, is entirely our personal affair. But as soon as this begins to be a matter of memory, then what the human being experiences in his soul life becomes an involvement with the universe. People of today do not yet know how strongly this is already a fact. But it will be a part of humanity's future which will lead to the etheric human being's memory becoming not merely a personal matter but a matter in which the human being is responsible to the universe.

When I began this series of lectures I spoke of how initially, in the age to which we can reach back historically, and even still for example in Greek times, there was a consciousness of one's country which did not cover great distances. I then told of how this consciousness was transformed into a consciousness of the earth, and that not until recent times would it be necessary for a universal consciousness to come about so that, just as he did in the far distant past, the human being would once again know himself to be a citizen of the whole cosmos. The path towards achieving this will be that we must clearly feel ourselves to be responsible for what we think, which can in turn lead to memory.

What I have just been describing refers to the greater part but not actually to the whole of the human being. I shall have to make a sketch to show you what I mean [Plate 13]. If this were to be the

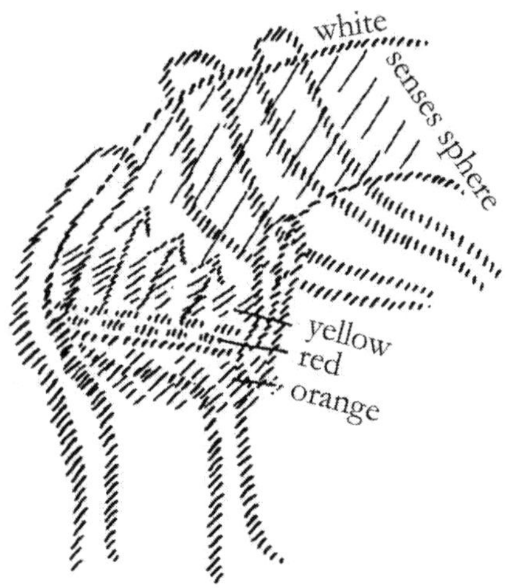

sphere of the senses [white]—in which I include all the senses as well as the region of understanding—then we would here reach that part of the human organism [red] which sends back our thoughts [arrows, red] so that they may become memories, that which in the human being collides with the objectivity of the cosmos. I have already a number of times indicated those parts of the human body in which he collides with the cosmos.

If you follow, let's say, a nerve going from some part of the body towards the spinal cord—I'll sketch this here—then for every such nerve you will also find another, more or less, which leads back again to another place. In the terminology of sensory physiology one would call the one a sensory nerve and the other a motor nerve.

[Plate 13]

Well, I have spoken before about the nonsense of there being sensory and motor nerves.[74] The important point is that every nerve pathway arises on the surface of the human body and returns to that surface while also being interrupted at some point. This resembles an electric wire emitting a spark; it is a kind of sensitive flowing-over from the so-called sensory nerve to the beginning of the so-called motor nerve. And at the point—there are countless, or perhaps very many, such points in our spinal column, for example, and in other parts of the body—at these points there are also the spatial points where the human being does not belong solely to himself because there he also belongs to the universe. When you connect all these points with one another, including the ganglia of the sympathetic nervous system, then you will come to this boundary, to this boundary which is also the physiological boundary of the body.

You could say that this is a way of observing the human being in two halves—this is rather more than a half, but let's say we are dividing him in half. So we are looking upon him as though he were a great sense organ. We see the way the senses take in impressions and then how the understanding, as a more delicate sense activity, works on these impressions resulting in memory images in the form of after-images. These remain for our life between birth and death because when a memory is formed it reaches up to the world ether. Our own ether reaches up to the world ether and encounters take place between us and the world ether.

The other part of the human being is the part which has the limbs as its final organ, everything belonging to the limbs. Just as this part has its final organ in the sense sphere [Plate 13] so does this other part of the human being have the limbs [additions to the drawing on

p. 120]: the feet are grown on, the arms are grown on. This is of course a very rough-and-ready diagram.

Whatever has the character of the will would have to be drawn going inwards, just as what belongs to the senses, to the intelligence, is attached to the other part of the human being. This will element is the other pole of the human being. Between the two lies the border, the inner border which arises when you join up all the nerve endings and all the ganglia. This borderline is like a sieve. You can go slightly across this borderline from the one side with the intelligence [see drawing on p. 120, yellow (Plate 13)] or, in the other direction the will can cross over from the other side [orange]. And there, in the middle, you find the sphere of feeling. Everything belonging to feeling is half will and half intelligence. Will presses up from below, intelligence presses down from above: the result is feeling. Feeling always consists, on the one hand, as in a dream, of intelligence, and on the other hand, as in sleep, of will.

We have now as it were dissected the human being from the point of view of spiritual science on the one hand into the pole of intelligence and on the other into the pole of the will; we have seen that the physical organs in an upward direction are an expression of the pole of intelligence. So having become familiar with the two poles, with the two aspects of the human being, we can ask ourselves: Is there something in the outside world which corresponds with what is present within the human being? There is, in reality, nothing corresponding with it. In the outer world there are the mineral, plant and animal kingdoms. But in what is within the human being, also physically, there is nothing which properly corresponds with those kingdoms.

You are now likely to object strongly, to express an objection which of course seems to be perfectly obvious. You will want to point out that of course we consist of the same substances as are present in the world outside us; we eat these substances and thus unite ourselves with them. The mineral kingdom is present in the salt and other substances we add to our food, and we also eat the plants; and meat-eaters unite with the substances which are in the animals, and so on. However, it is utterly erroneous to believe that in our body we are connected in any way with these substances from the external world.

What our bodily nature actually does is to react constantly against the influences of the outside world including those which enter into it through our food. It is indeed very difficult to persuade our fellow human beings today that what is essential in our body is not that we take in food but that we expel it again. Some substances are expelled rapidly and others only over the course of seven or eight years. Whatever you may eat today, nothing of it will still be within you in eight years' time. Everything is continually exchanged for something else; the activity of our body is to expel, not to absorb.

The fact of having to take something into your body is the same as needing the ground on which to walk. If you had no ground beneath your feet you would be unable to walk; as a human being the ground has no meaning for you except as something which gives you support. The activity of your body needs something against which it can react; you constantly have to come up against something, such as the food you eat, so that your body can actively react against it. Just as you would sink into the ground, so would the activity of your body sink into nothingness if it did not constantly come up against something. You do not eat in order to unite the food with your body; you eat so as to generate the activity needed in order once again to expel the food. Your essentiality as a human being consists in the activity of expelling the food. If you want to think what is true, you can as little regard the ground as being a part of the sole of your foot as you can regard what is in the food in its external aspect as being a part of your humanity. The human being is nothing other than a reaction against what exists in his environment. The human being is a reaction, an out-and-out reaction. Through and through, the human being is activity.

What I have just described takes place very differently on the one hand with regard to the organs of the sense and intelligence sphere and on the other with regard to the organs of the will sphere. In this way the human being is certainly a being of polarities. But what takes place in these two poles of the human being has little to do with whatever is present in the external world.

In the external world we have the mineral and the plant kingdom. This mineral kingdom and this plant kingdom, they are inwardly not closely related with our own being. If we want to search for something with which this mineral and plant kingdom is related we must look into the world through which we live before we are born, before we descend into the physical world from the spiritual world through birth or through conception. When we cast our glance upon the plant world and the mineral world we are obliged to say that before birth we lived in a spiritual world. I do not see this spiritual world through my physical senses and I do not think it by means of my physical understanding. This world, which is hidden from me as though by a haze when I am a human being possessing senses, reveals itself externally as the plant world and in its foundation as the mineral world. This mineral and plant world has much more to do with our life outside the world than with our life between birth and death. The plants we see around us by means of our senses, these plants are the impressions of those forces with which we are connected between death and a new birth. And the animal kingdom, too, does not have much to do with us as human beings here. It has more to do with the period immediately following our death; of that it is an external, polar-opposite revelation.

We can therefore say that we do not learn about what is within the human being by becoming familiar with it through the natural sciences. The situation is that present-day science, the science particularly appreciated nowadays, is a science which does not actually contain anything of the human being. You can know absolutely everything revealed today by the scientific method and yet learn nothing about the human being, since the human being cannot be found within natural scientific knowledge.

Over the past four hundred years all our popular ideas have arisen out of a popularizing of the natural scientific method. Even the peasant cultivating his land now thinks scientifically, though he may still describe it in his own words. Even Catholicism thinks scientifically in its dogmatic materialism. Natural scientific thinking dominates absolutely everything. But we have now arrived at a point in time when it has become necessary to establish the social order. A large part of today's civilized world—and this part will continue to grow until it has become the entire civilized world—has the urge today to build up a new social structure. People are thinking deeply about the structure of society. Social demands are today arising among civilized humanity. From what has this arisen? It has arisen out of deeply unconscious impulses within human nature. And what is assumed to be the means by which this might be satisfied? By the results of natural scientific thinking. These results of natural scientific thinking are considered in the widest circles to be 'social thinking', for that is what is applied in the matter of human social life.

Thus in Eastern Europe a new state-social-order is to be established based purely on the ideas of scientific materialism. The men whom Dr Helphand,[75] who called himself Parvus, has imported into Russia on the instructions of Ludendorff[76] and Hindenburg[77], so that they may there set up Bolshevism—these men are an embodiment of natural scientific methods par excellence. These men of Bolshevism are practical examples of what the natural scientific method becomes when it takes root in the heads of certain social revolutionaries. The embodiment of the natural scientific method now dwells in Russia thanks to Helphand's railway conductors on the sealed train which travelled across Germany bringing the men of Bolshevism to Russia under the aegis of Ludendorff and Hindenburg.

On no account must we overlook the consequences resulting from that embodiment of natural scientific methods! I have already drawn your attention to certain facts. There are two philosophers, two very petit-bourgeois philosophers. One of these, Avenarius,[78] taught at Zurich University; he certainly paid great attention to developing a petit-bourgeois attitude of mind. The other is Ernst Mach,[79] who taught in Prague and Vienna. I myself heard him lecture in 1882 at the Austrian Academy of Sciences.[80] Ernst Mach always appeared to me to be the very incarnation of bourgeois narrow-mindedness and rectitude. When we talk of the 'state philosophy' of Bolshevism today we realize it is no coincidence but rather an inner necessity that the philosophy of Avenarius and Mach represents this 'state philosophy', for these things are related: taking natural scientific methods to their extreme results in their metamorphosis into social thinking. That is why this matter must be taken very seriously. Natural scientific thinking initially developed its social flowering in the East. But the flowering will continue to increase if the matter is not tackled at its root, namely at its origin in natural scientific thinking.

Today something like a wave of thinking and feeling is running through the world. This wave has its origin in the materialistic thinking of the social sciences. And as it spreads, this wave takes hold of the social thinking called for and thereby becomes a power capable of destroying humanity. It is absolutely destructive to humanity. The leading, foremost circles lacked the power and strength with which to pour into human thinking a truly sustaining spiritual wave. That is why the materialistic wave came to the fore in the social thinking of the proletarian masses. Marxist thinking, which has been flourishing so grotesquely over the last four to five years, represents the social flower and fruit of materialistic natural scientific methods when applied to social life. And we dare not forget that this is how our civilized world is configured at present. By not noticing this we are sleeping through the most important phenomena and symptoms of life. At the present time one is not a full human being if one sleeps through these phenomena.

Some individuals do rise above this general view. They sense already today to some extent that if we continue to think and feel as we have done up to the present, then we shall be unable to continue. We are becoming increasingly embroiled in chaos. Wake-up calls like the following are rare as yet, but they do exist. I should like to read one such wake-up call here.

Issue 31/32 of the socialist weekly magazine on culture, *Neue Erde*,[81] contained an interesting essay by Karl Polanyi under the heading 'A Crisis of Ideology'. He explains that a general antipathy towards capitalism is beginning to appear in tandem with a rejection of Marxist socialism.

> The amalgamation of Marxism and socialism prevailing today remains the bugbear of all modern thought. Every intellectual attempt to address the most urgent social problems of our time becomes bogged down in this intellectual swamp ...
>
> ... The outbreak of the world war brought the turning point for all capitalist, and therefore Marxist, thinking. The leaders of humanity have recognized clearly, while the masses have sensed vaguely, that so-called vital interests will no longer dominate the world, but forces of quite another kind and type. The ever-present economic interests sought after by the imperialists and fought against by the socialists have proved to be not only utterly unrealistic and abstract to the extent of being nothing but rhetorical phrases but also nothing more than superstitions and empty flights of fancy. It has become entirely obvious that it is not the actual situation but the *mere idea* of the situation which is the driving force leading the masses on ... This utterly paradoxical age has actually been *believing in* egoism. It was no longer denied and nor was it whitewashed as idealism; on the contrary! Humanity set out for its doom in the sacred name of economic vital interests, surrounding it with the halo of glory and of *sacro egoismo* which of its own accord had raised itself to heaven. *Materialism had declared itself to be the one and only ideal, thus bringing the materialistic world to the culmination of its journey.* This idealizing of the material as the only reality has been termed *Fatherland* by the capitalists and, by the Marxists quite openly: socialism!
>
> The result: Utilitarian ethics, materialistic conceptions of history, positivist epistemology, deterministic philosophy: these are no longer viable in the new ambience. But Marxism, as an ideology, is built upon this basis. Its time is over.

This is the wake-up call of a soul who is capable of at least perceiving what it is that is leading into the negative aspects, the chaotic aspects of our age. And then comes the question, the terrible question of destiny: 'What shall take its place?'

This is the question asked by the man who wrote what I have just read to you. He then continues: 'The answer to this question has no relevance for Marxism, which would be a matter of lesser importance for upright spirits in their search of clarity. If the sun were to be extinguished one would have to find one's way about in darkness rather than set up a will-o'-the-wisp to replace it.'

> But what is darkening the sun for the human race is a new and even brighter sun coming up over the horizon. Having freed ourselves from the nightmare of an evolutionary theory which would have condemned us, without peace and without a home, to a meaningless existence on a treadmill of eternal collaboration; having awoken from the hallucination of a false view of history; having escaped the clutches of a fixed idea of a ridiculous determinism which represented the freedom of our will as a game of chance played by forces at work behind the scenes; having at last, in place of a belief in dead mass, been reborn into our own self, we shall find within ourselves the strength and the calling to make real for humankind the demands of socialism for justice, for freedom and for love.

Here is a soul full of yearning who sees how we are heading for chaos and therefore asks the destiny question: 'What shall take its place?'—and who then continues with an answer which serves up all the old catchphrases that have become no more than the husks of words: Justice, Freedom, Love. They have been preached for such a long time. But they most certainly do not represent the concrete path.

'Today Marxist socialism merely obscures the destiny question confronting humanity; it inhibits the free forces of a radical solution, it fixes thinking in the semi-darkness of an outdated world of dogma, it acts by means of enigmatic auguries, obscure authorities and mystical symbols. It blocks the clear view for humanity.'

Correct: 'It blocks the clear view for humanity'—but catchphrases do not open up the view! And then the writer continues: 'The Church has outlived its calling by a thousand years. Marxism may perhaps outlive us, but the new spirit which has been born out of the misery of this Great War is sure to outlive Marxism.'

But where is the new spirit?—asks this writer who does appear to possess a sense for the nullity of our time which will lead into chaos. Well, a friend of ours, who has long been connected with our world-view, has added a few lines to what I have just read out to you. What I read to you was written by someone who sees that something new is needed, but who then merely brings forth all the old catchphrases.

What our friend says is this: 'We see here a world-view which realizes that Marxism, the most logical form of which is today's Bolshevism, belongs to the old way of thinking. It is nothing other than a counteraction to the old world of capitalism and, just as with capitalism, it is its spiritual life which is sick. Although it is anti-capitalist in economic matters it nevertheless rests on the same basis spiritually. What ought to take its place and also the place of the modern natural scientific world-view is the anthroposophical world-view arising out of a "philosophy of freedom".'

These are a few lines added by a friend of our movement. They show clearly that because things are as they are the spiritual science of anthroposophy is what needs to come about. Not until people admit that the sickness of our present time can only be cured by an anthroposophically oriented spiritual research, not until people realize this will it be possible to evade the chaos.

Without being presumptuous it therefore has to be said that it will only be possible to evade the chaos if a sufficient number of individuals can be found who are able to give Karl Polanyi the same answer to his question 'What shall take its place?' as was given by Dr Kolisko[82] in Vienna. So long as people continue to believe that the health of our movement is to be found in any kind of sectarianism, so long will they remain incapable of recognizing its significance. Its significance will only be recognized once people realize that it is a matter of worldwide importance.

Only those who not only recognize the significance of this world-view but also make of it the inmost impulse of their will can become its true bearers. I do not wish to gloss over with many words what I wanted to tell you in this lecture. It will not be long before we meet again for similar discussions. There is no need to take our leave, for the interval this time will not last so long.

But I do want to say that a most heartfelt wish would be fulfilled for me if many of you were to take profoundly to heart over the next few weeks what I have been describing as a most important aspect of the current state of world affairs.

We have spoken of various damaging influences emanating from the elemental world in our present time. You know that an old and true perception, if one comprehends it rightly, describes the end of the worldly year, as Christmas approaches, as a time during which the most spiritual influence possible within the earthly sphere of human beings is at its most intensive.

Let us, perhaps especially in this season, which has for centuries been so important and essential for human beings—although at present it has come to mean little more than giving 'appropriate gifts'—let us, during this period, in accordance with an old custom of the soul, endeavour to seek refuge with those ancient spiritual powers who continue to influence our human destiny, by allowing their whole earnestness to work upon our soul in the way it stands in its relationship between the spiritual world and the human world!

This is all I intended to say to you today.

The date of my next lecture here will be announced in due course.

LECTURE 9

DORNACH, 12 DECEMBER 1919

SINCE our trip has been delayed by a few days,[83] I am able to speak to you here today, tomorrow and the next day. I am especially pleased about this because a number of friends have arrived from England to whom I shall now be able to speak before leaving.

These friends will have noticed that the building of the Goetheanum has made some headway even in difficult times. Thus far, though, it has not been possible to complete the building work and there is as yet no certainty as to when this will be. Nevertheless, what has been completed hitherto will show you what the spiritual background is out of which this building has grown, and how it is bound up with the spiritual movement represented here. So since it is possible to speak to a larger gathering of our English friends after quite a long interval, I'm sure you will agree with my basing our considerations today on the building itself. In the next two days it will then be possible, in connection with what can be said about the building itself, to add certain points which I feel sure it will be important to mention at the present time.

Since at least the idea of our building is now becoming visible, anyone looking at it will notice the special way in which it is linked with our spiritual movement while also gaining an impression, perhaps especially from this building in the way it represents our spiritual movement, as to what the nature of our movement is intended to be.

Consider the situation of any sectarian movement, however widespread, finding it necessary to build a house like this for its gatherings. What would have brought this about? Well, depending on the requirements of the society or association, it would have been built on a larger or smaller scale in one architectural style or another and you would have found, inside it, in one or another emblematic sign an indication of what was going to be taught or presented within it. None of this, you will have noticed, has been applicable to this Goetheanum building. This building is not intended to be merely for the external use of the anthroposophical movement or the Anthroposophical Society. As it stands before you, in all its detail, it has been born out of what our movement intends to give to the world with regard to the spirit. It would not have been sufficient for this movement to erect a building in some random architectural style.

When the moment came when it was possible to discuss building a house of our own, this movement felt the urge to find a style which would emerge from the foundations of our spiritual science, a style which would express in every detail the spiritual substance flowing through our movement. It would have been unthinkable to have a house built arbitrarily in any arbitrary style for our movement. This should enable anyone to infer immediately how far this movement is removed from any sectarian or similar movement however widespread it might be. We needed not only to build a house but also to find an architectural style[84] which expressed in every detail all that is spoken by our anthroposophical spiritual science in every word and in every sentence.

Indeed, I am convinced that when someone is able to enter sufficiently into what can truly be sensed in the forms of this building—please note that I said sensed, not idly fancied—it will also be possible for that person to discover in these forms, to read in these forms whatever is also expressed here in words.

This is no external matter. It is something which is inwardly bound up with the whole intention of this spiritual movement, a movement quite different from those spiritual movements which have gradually been emerging in human life since the beginning of the fifth post-Atlantean cultural period, or, we could say, since the middle of the fifteenth century. This is founded on the conviction that in the present time it is necessary to place something into human evolution which is different from what has hitherto been placed into human evolution since the middle of the fifteenth century.

All the developments among civilized humanity over the past four to five centuries seem to me to have one specific characteristic in common, which is that external life in the widest sense has become heavily mechanized to the extent of becoming a kingdom in its own right. It forms a kingdom in its own right which is monopolized by those who consider themselves to be practitioners of living. And in addition to this external mode of living, which has spread over all areas of so-called practical life, there is also an amalgam of spiritual views, world-views or philosophies or whatever you want to call them, which have over the years, but especially over the last three to four centuries, become estranged from life. In the feelings and sensations they give to human beings they hover as it were above real practical life.

The difference between these two streams has become so blatant that one cannot help saying: In our present age a time has arrived when these two streams are incapable of understanding one another; or perhaps one should say that they can no longer find any points of contact through which they might be able to have any effect on one another. We manage our factories, we set our trains on their railway lines and we send our steamships across the oceans; we let our telegraphs and telephones come into play. And we do all this by allowing the mechanisms of life to run automatically and completely take us over.

And side by side with this we preach. We preach a great deal. The ancient ecclesiastical denominations preach in the churches, the politicians preach in the parliaments, the various aspirations preach on all kinds of subjects, about the demands of the proletariat, about the demands of women. Such a great amount of preaching goes on, and the content of this preaching is surely something which is clearly desired in humanity's present state of consciousness. And yet were we to ask where we can find the bridge between what we preach and what our external life is bringing about all around us we would, if we were honest with ourselves, be unable to find a satisfactory answer on the basis of the way our times are going.

I mention the following phenomenon simply because it is the best example of what I have been describing. As you know, in addition to all the other opportunities we have today which allow us to preach, a good number of secret societies also exist. Among these, let us examine the ordinary lodges of Freemasonry including those which have the highest and the lowest degrees. In these lodges we find symbols: triangle, circle, set square and compasses, and others. We even find in this context a much-used phrase: the Master Builder of all Worlds.

What is all this? Well, when we go back to the ninth, tenth, eleventh century and look at the civilized world in which all those secret societies, those lodges of Freemasons, spread out like a froth across civilization, we find that all those instruments which nowadays are laid as symbols upon the altars of those lodges were once tools of the trade for the building of houses and churches. There were set squares, there were circles—I mean compasses—there were water levels, plumb-lines; all these things were put to use in ordinary external life. In the lodges of Freemasonry talks are now given with reference to these things which no longer have any connection with everyday life, talks about all kinds of beautiful matters which, however beautiful they may be, are completely foreign to ordinary life and ordinary practicalities. Ideas have come into being, thought constructs which have no practical relevance whatever for daily life.

We have gradually arrived at a situation in which people go to work from Monday to Saturday and then listen to sermons on Sunday. These two things have nothing to do with one another. And in preaching we frequently refer to those things which in bygone times had a lively connection with external life as symbols of what is beautiful, what is true, even of what is virtuous. Yet these things are out of touch with everyday life. We have even come to believe that the more out of touch with everyday life our sermons are, the greater is their capacity to raise us up to spiritual heights.

The everyday profane world has become something inferior. We see how today all kinds of demands emerging from the depths of the human being are not properly comprehended for what they are. What, often, is the connection between those sermons put forth in grand houses about how virtuous we all are, how we all love others regardless of race, nation, colour? What is the connection between such sermons and what really happens, what we really foster, by cutting out our coupons and letting ourselves be paid pensions by the banks in order to ensure the safe continuation of our external lives on the basis of principles which have absolutely nothing to do with what those virtuous individuals talk of in their elegant apartments? We found, for example, theosophical societies in which everyone talks of brotherliness, yet we do not have the least influence over what happens when we cut out our coupons. By cutting out those coupons we set off a whole sequence of economic matters.

Our life has fragmented into these two entirely separate streams. For example—and this is no theoretical example but one from life—it can happen, and has indeed happened, that a lady approached me saying: I've been asked for a contribution intended to assist people, but they drink alcohol; surely as a theosophist I cannot agree to this! That is what she said. All I could say in reply was: Well, you hold stocks and shares; how many breweries do you imagine are supported by your assets?

With regard to what is important it is not a matter on the one hand of preaching in a way which voluptuously gratifies our soul while on the other hand adopting an attitude to life based on a way of living which has come down to us over the past three to four hundred years. Few people have any inclination to enter thoroughly into this fundamental problem of our time. Why is this? It is because this dualism has entered into our life—most strongly during the course of the last three to four centuries—a dualism between external life and our so-called spiritual strivings. When people today speak of spiritual striving they are on the whole referring to something entirely abstract, something unworldly, and not to something capable of being involved in everyday life.

The question, the problem this points to will have to be tackled at its very roots. If we here on this hill had been acting in accordance with the endeavours of the past three to four centuries, we might very well have sought the services of any architect, of some famous architect, in order to put up a beautiful building in whatever style of architecture we might have chosen. But this could never have been what we would have done. In that case we would have entered this building, we would have been surrounded by everything beautiful belonging to some style or other, and we would have uttered words in keeping with the building, just like all those beautiful sermons spoken in keeping with the external lifestyle chosen by people nowadays.

Such a thing was not possible, for this is not what is meant by the spiritual science oriented in accordance with anthroposophy. Its intention has from the outset been entirely something else. It was not intended to set up that old false contradistinction between spirit and matter where the spirit is dealt with *in abstracto* and where it is impossible for it to submerge itself in the essence and being of matter.

When is it appropriate to talk of spirit? When does one speak truthfully about spirit? One speaks truthfully about spirit only when one is referring to spirit as the creator of matter. The worst possible way of speaking about spirit—which is today often regarded as the most beautiful way—is to refer to it as a cloud-cuckoo-land never to be by touched by matter. One must speak about spirit in a way which refers to it as having the strength to immerse itself directly in matter. When speaking about spiritual science one must think of it not as being something which rises up above nature but rather as being a fully-fledged science of nature itself. When speaking about spirit one must think of spirit with which the human being can unite in such a way that this spirit can also mingle with social life through the mediation of the human being. A spirit about which one speaks only in the parlour, a spirit which one wants to please by being virtuous and by loving one's fellow human beings, a spirit which will do its best to abstain from immersing itself in ordinary life, such a spirit is not genuinely spiritual. A spirit of that kind is a human abstraction. To rise up towards it is not a rising up to the true spirit but rather the ultimate outpouring of materialism.

That is the reason why we had to erect a building which in every detail is thought of as being, and is seen as being, something which arises out of what lives in our anthroposophically oriented spiritual science. And linked with this, too, is the reason why, in these difficult times, there has arisen an approach to the social question which does not want to remain enclosed within cloud-cuckoo-land but would instead prefer to be a matter of real life from the outset of its activity, the very opposite of sectarianism in any form, by reading what is written in the demands of our time and doing justice to them.

Of course there is much that has not turned out so well in this building. But surely in all honesty one cannot nowadays expect to be immediately successful in every detail. What is important is that a beginning is undertaken, a necessary beginning in certain matters. And it seems to me that such a beginning has been made with this building. So one day, when this building is complete—just as the nutshell fits the nut—we shall within these walls, which are not foreign to us, bring into it what flows through our spiritual movement and assorts well with every line, with every form and colour.

It is so essential at the present time for at least some individuals to be aware of this will, for it is this will which is all important.

Let me now return once again to a number of characteristics which have come to the fore among civilized humanity over the past three to four centuries. There are in this evolution of civilized humanity some phenomena which characterize for us the deeper foundations of what in human life just now is developing *ad absurdum*. It is indeed a development *ad absurdum*.

The fact is that a large proportion of humanity, of human souls, is asleep, actually asleep. When one is somewhere where certain things are taking place which are what I would call genuine counter-images, antitheses of all civilized life, when one is somewhere where these counter-images are not immediately obvious but which nevertheless are taking place in numerous regions of today's civilized world and which are symptomatic of what will continue to gain more and more ground, then one notices that human beings are indeed outside themselves with their souls, that they are outside the most important events of the times. They live in the everyday, without paying any attention to what is actually happening at the present time unless they are directly affected by those processes. Admittedly, however, the actual impulses for those processes do lie in the unconscious depths, in the unconscious soul life of those people.

At the foundation of the dualism I have already mentioned is another dualism, the dualism expressed, for example, in Milton's *Paradise Lost*, which is a characteristic example of it. But this is merely an external symptom of something which fills the whole of modern thinking, sensitivity, feeling and will. In more recent human consciousness we have a sense of the antithesis between heaven and hell or, as others describe it, between spirit and matter. Actually the modern difference between the heaven and hell of the peasant out in his field and the matter and spirit of so-called enlightened philosophers is merely one of degrees. The thought impulses on which both are founded are identical.

The contradistinction is between God and the devil, between paradise and hell. People are convinced that paradise is good and that it is frightful that human beings have been banished from it. Paradise is something which has been lost and waits to be found again. And the devil is seen as a terrible adversary who opposes all powers linked with the concept of paradise. Those who have no understanding of the contradistinctions of soul which hold sway even in the most superficial strands of our social differences, our social demands, cannot imagine the magnitude of this dualism between heaven and hell, or between that lost paradise and the earth. Speaking the truth nowadays often involves speaking in paradoxes; indeed, to explain some things truthfully one often sounds crazy to ones' contemporaries. But as in the Pauline sense of human wisdom being foolishness before God,[85] so might today's human wisdom, or human madness, also appear as madness to human beings of the future.

Human beings have gradually dreamed their way into these contradistinctions between earth and paradise. They confuse paradise with what ought to be striven for, which is the divine in the human being; they do not realize that striving for paradise as they understand it would be just as bad for them as striving for the opposite. If one imagines the structure of the world in the way it is presented in Milton's *Paradise Lost*, then one is renaming a power which is inimical to humanity—if it is striven for in a one-sided way—as one which is divine and good. The result of this is to find oneself striving for something which is an opponent of what is good in the human being.

Our protest against such a view will be shown in the sculpture which is to be set up in the eastern part of our building, a nine-and-a-half metre group sculpted in wood[86] which will depict, as a replacement for the luciferic contradistinction between God and the devil, what must be the foundation of human consciousness in the future: the trinity of the luciferic, that which belongs to the Christ, and the ahrimanic.

Modern civilization is so little aware of this underlying secret that one must also say the following. For certain reasons which I may yet speak about here, we have named this building the Goetheanum because it accords with Goethe's views with regard to art and knowledge. However, it must also be said that the contradistinction between the powers of good and Mephistopheles, which Goethe has set up in his *Faust*, embodies the same error as that put forward in Milton's *Paradise Lost*. Goethe shows the good powers on the one hand and the bad power, as Mephistopheles, on the other. In his Mephistopheles Goethe has confused higgledy-piggledy what is luciferic on the one hand with what is ahrimanic on the other hand. As a result, for those who understand these things, Goethe's Mephistopheles figure represents a mixture of two spiritual individualities.

We, though, must recognize that the true human being can only be depicted as an image of balance. When one endeavours on the one hand to rise up above one's head, as it were, into fantasy and ecstasy, into what is a false mysticism, into everything fantastical, that is the one power. The other power is the one which seeks, as it were, to drag the human being down into materialism, into what is prosaic and dry-as-dust. We understand the human being rightly only when we see him striving for balance between on the one hand the ahrimanic and on the other the luciferic {Plate 14}.

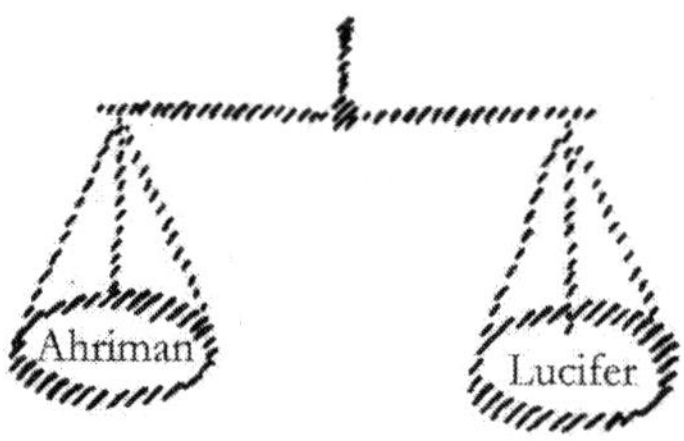

The human being has the task of perpetually striving for balance between what wants to lead him upwards out of himself and what wants to lead him downwards out of himself. More recent spiritual civilization, however, has confused the fantastical nature of the luciferic with that which is divine. So now descriptions of paradise are in fact descriptions of the luciferic and there is that dreadful confusion between what is luciferic and what is divine because people do not realize that the most important task is to hold the balance between the two powers which seek to drag the human being in the one direction or in the other direction.

What was necessary initially was to uncover this fact. If the human being is to strive towards something Christian—something which is nowadays often interpreted in rather odd ways—then he must realize that what he should be striving for is a balance between the luciferic and the ahrimanic. He has to realize that over the past three to four centuries true knowledge about the human being has been by-passed to such an extent that little is known about this balance, so that in *Paradise Lost* the luciferic has been renamed the divine, to which the contrast has become the ahrimanic, which is no longer Ahriman but the modern devil, or modern materialism or something similar. This dualism, which in reality is the duality between Lucifer and Ahriman, this dualism is still spooking about in modern consciousness as the contradistinction between God and the devil. So the 'paradise which has been lost' should really be comprehended as a description of the misnamed lost kingdom of Lucifer.

One has to speak so pointedly about more recent civilization because it is necessary for human beings to reach the realization that they are on a slippery slope—this is a historical necessity, but necessities also exist so that they may be comprehended—they are on a slippery slope, and only the most radical cure can set them back on to an upward path. Very frequently these days descriptions of the spiritual world are taken to refer to something supersensible which does not live here on our earth. In seeing something spiritual people want to flee from what surrounds us here on our earth. But they do not realize that by fleeing into an abstract spiritual realm what they find is not the spirit but the region of Lucifer. A good deal of what is nowadays termed mysticism, or what is termed theosophy, denotes a search for the luciferic region. Today's striving for the spirit cannot involve merely knowing about the spirit; what is appropriate for the present striving, for today's striving for the spirit is to have an understanding of the connection between the spiritual world and the world into which we have been born and in which we live between birth and death.

Here is the question we should be asking above all others if we want to turn our attention towards spiritual worlds: Why are we born out of those spiritual worlds into this physical world? Well, the reason why we are born into this physical world—and tomorrow and the next day I will enter in more detail into what I am only sketching now—is because on this earth we can experience things which cannot be experienced in the spiritual worlds. In order to experience these things one has to descend to the physical world, and thereafter one has to carry results of these experiences back up into the spiritual worlds. In order to achieve this one has to immerse oneself in this physical world, one must immerse oneself knowingly with one's spirit in this physical world. One must immerse oneself in this physical world for the sake of the spiritual world.

Fundamentally speaking, let us look at a normal human being who takes in sufficient nourishment, who sleeps the necessary number of hours, has breakfast, lunch and dinner and so on, who also has intellectual interests, who has indeed advanced spiritual interests and therefore becomes a member of a theosophical society and who does what he can to find out what goes on in the spiritual world. Let us look at a person like this, someone who has, as it were, even in his little finger everything which some literature or other of a theosophical nature has told him in this present age, but who otherwise leads an ordinary life. Let us look at this human being!

What is the meaning of all the knowledge he acquires through his advanced spiritual interests? What it means to him is some inner pleasure of soul, some genuine luciferic enjoyment of a rather refined kind. But nothing of all this will be carried through the portal of death, nothing at all. Among people like this—and there are a good many—there are those who, despite having even in their little finger knowledge about what an astral body is, what an ether body is, and so on, have not the faintest idea what is happening when a candle burns. They have not the faintest idea what magical feats are pulled off whenever a tram runs along the street outside. They may ride in the tram, but they know nothing about it. And there is more. They may have knowledge even in their little finger about the astral body, the ether body, about karma and reincarnation, but they have not the faintest idea what goes on nowadays, for example, in a gathering of proletarian people. They are not interested. All that interests them is what the ether body looks like, what the astral body looks like; but they are not interested in the journeys made by financial capital since it became the ruling power at the beginning of the nineteenth century.

Knowledge about the ether body, about the astral body is of no use once such people have died. This is something which can indeed be said on the basis of a true understanding of the spiritual world.

But it can only be meaningful once this spiritual knowledge becomes the instrument by means of which one is able to immerse oneself in physical, material life and there absorb whatever cannot be absorbed in the spiritual world but must then be carried into that world.

The natural sciences are today taught in our universities covering very many subjects. Experiments are carried out, research is done, and so on. And all this leads to the natural sciences with which we feed our technology, or even cure people, and do all kinds of other things. And side by side with this there are the ecclesiastical confessions. But I ask you: Have you ever taken note of the content of those ordinary Sunday-afternoon sermons where there is talk of the kingdom of Christ and so on? What connection is there between the natural sciences and what is said in church? On the whole, none at all. The two things carry on side by side.

On the one hand there are those who believe they have the strength with which to speak about God, about the Holy Spirit and all kinds of other things. But even if they say they have feelings about all this, they still talk in abstract concepts, in abstract viewpoints. And the others talk about a nature in which there is no spirit. Nothing is done to form a bridge between them! And then in more recent times we have also developed all kinds of theosophical views, mystical views. These mystical views talk of many things which are far away from real life, but they do not talk about the life of human beings.

Let me ask you: Is it right to speak about the Creator of the universe in such a way that He appears to be a very beautiful and interesting spirit even though He would never be capable of creating the world? The spiritual beings who are so often spoken about today would never have been capable of creating the world; if they were as we imagine them they would not even be capable of becoming involved in our knowledge about nature or about human social life.

Without being presumptuous, perhaps I may be permitted to use an example to show what I mean. In one of my more recent books—*Riddles of the Soul*—I drew attention, as I have also done in my lectures, to the nonsense which is taught in one of today's sciences, physiology, namely that the human being has two types of nerve, the motor nerves which underlie the will and the sensory nerves which underlie perceptions, sensations. Well, since the invention of telegraphy we have had an image of how telegraphy works [Plate 14, right]. A nerve goes from the eye to the central organ and then from the central organ to one limb or another. We see something, a limb, moving; the telegraph wire passes from this organ, from the eye to the central organ and that activates the motor nerve so that the movement is carried out.

Science is appointed to teach this kind of nonsense. It has to be allowed to teach it because one speaks in the abstract about what one sees spiritually with regard to all sorts of things without developing thoughts capable of intervening positively in the way nature works. One lacks the strength to discover, in what one sees spiritually, some knowledge about nature itself. There is, namely, no difference between motor and sensory nerves; what we call will nerves are also sensory nerves; their purpose is to enable us to perceive our own limbs when they are expected to make movements. The classic example of tabes dorsalis[87] proves the opposite of what ought to be proven. I shall not enter into this any further here as you do not have the necessary background knowledge. But I would certainly very much like to discuss this one day with people knowledgeable about physiology and biology.

All I want to point out here is that we have natural science on the one hand and on the other hand there is much speaking and preaching about spiritual worlds which fails to touch on any real worlds surrounding us in nature. This is something we need, however. We need knowledge of the spirit which is at the same time strong enough to become a science of nature. But we shall only succeed in this if we take into account the will about which I wanted to speak to you today. If we had intended to set up a sectarian movement which had some dogmatic ideas regarding the divine and the spiritual and which simply had need of a building, then we could have erected or caused to be erected any kind of building.

But that was not what we wanted. Since we wanted to demonstrate even through this external action that it is our will to immerse ourselves in real life, we were obliged to create this building ourselves out of the will of spiritual science. The details of this building will one day show that important principles, which have been caused by those two dualisms to appear in a very false light, can be established on a healthy basis.

There is one more point I would like to make today. Please look at the sequence of seven columns which will stand on either side of our main building [drawing (Plate 15)]. At the top are the capitals, and

at the bottom the plinths. They are not identical, for each is a further development of the previous one. In this way you may gain a view of the second capital if you enter in a living way into the forms of the first and bring to life the idea of a metamorphosis as something organic; you now have a thought which is so full of life that it is not abstract but instead follows the laws of growth. In this way you can see how the second capital develops out of the first, the third out of the second, the fourth out of the third and so on up to the seventh. This is how we have endeavoured to develop a capital in a living way—and similarly with the architraves—one out of the other in imitation of the creativity, the spiritual creativity which lives in nature itself where one form, there also, emerges from the previous one. I have the feeling that now not one of the capitals could be different in any way.

And something very remarkable has come to light in all this. Normally when people speak of evolution they often say development, development, evolution on and on, first the less complex, then the somewhat more complex, the somewhat more differentiated and so on; the greater the perfection, the greater the complexity. But I found myself unable to put this into practice when I tried to let the seven capitals metamorphose from one to the next. When I reached the fourth I thought I would have to make the fifth even more perfect, even more complex. But since I was not following an abstract route, as would have been the case with Haeckel or Darwin, I had to make the next form evolve once again out of the previous one, just as in nature one form arises from another in accordance with the vital forces. So with the fifth capital, although its surfaces were more artistic than those of the fourth, the overall form became simpler rather than yet more complex. And the sixth became simpler still, and the seventh even more so. In this way I discovered that evolution is not a matter of becoming ever more and more differentiated [the straight line is drawn on the blackboard (Plate 15)] but rather of a rise to a climax followed by a downward movement to something ever more simple.

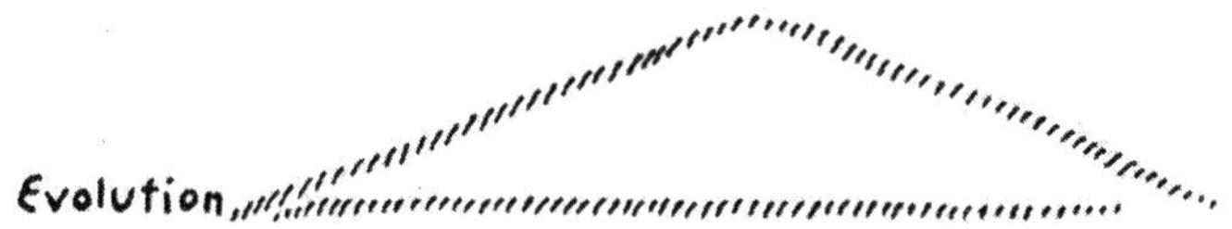

This arose quite simply out of the work as it was being done. I was able to see that the principle of evolution as it became manifest during the process of working artistically was the same as the principle of evolution in nature.

If you look at the human eye you will see that it is certainly more perfect than the eyes of a good many animals. And yet the eyes of many animals are much more complicated than human eyes. They have inside them, for example, certain structures which are no longer present in human eyes for human eyes have, as it were, once again become less complicated than many animal eyes. If we trace the evolution of the eye we find: at first it is primitive, simple; then it becomes ever more complicated; then it becomes simpler again; and the most perfect is not the most complex; it is simpler than the middle stage.

One was constrained to do the same in creating artistically what became an inner necessity. It was not a matter of aspiring to research something; it was a matter of aspiring to make contact with the forces of vitality. And here in our building the endeavour was to imbue the forms with the same forces as those which the spirit of nature had created as the foundation of nature. There was a search for a spirit which is creative and which lives in the productions of the world rather than merely in preaching. That is what is essential. It is also the reason why a good deal was rejected with regard to those who wanted to decorate our building with all kinds of symbols and suchlike. There is not a single symbol in this building; everywhere there are forms taken from the creative activity of the spirit in nature.

This in turn reveals the initial stage of a will which will have to find a way of continuing. What is to be hoped is that people will understand this view of the matter, that they will actually understand how access to the original sources of human intentions, of human creativity is needed in all realms by more recent humanity. All kinds of demands are made on us today. All these demands are separate from one another; they derive from the various fields of life. So what we need is something which brings everything together. This cannot come from anything which merely floats about in the surroundings of external, visible existence, for everything visible is founded on something invisible, and this is what we have to grasp hold of today. Let me put it like this: We should listen carefully to what is going on today, and if we do we will find that it is not at all absurd to notice that everything old is falling to pieces. So something must be set up to take its place. However, one needs a degree of courage in order to become acquainted with this thought, and this courage cannot be found in external life; it must be developed by an entirely inward effort.

I should like to characterize this courage as follows. Today's sleeping souls would surely be delighted if someone were to turn up in one place or another with the ability to paint like Raphael or Leonardo. This would be quite understandable. But what we should have the courage to say today is that only those have the right to admire Raphael and Leonardo who know that today one cannot and one should not be creative in the way Raphael and Leonardo were in their time. Something quite prosaic can be said to illustrate this. Only someone has the right today to recognize the importance of the theorem of Pythagoras who realizes that this Pythagorean theorem is not waiting to be discovered now. Everything has its own time, and matters must be grasped on the concrete basis of their own time.

More is required of us today than might be expected of those who attach themselves to some sort of spiritual movement. Today we need to recognize that we must face up to a renewal within the evolution of humanity. It is easy to claim that we are living in a time of transition. Every age is a time of transition; what matters is to understand what it is that is undergoing the transition. I do not want to make that trivial claim that our time is a time of transition. What I do want to say is this: People keep claiming that neither nature nor life leap forward disjointedly.[88] People are considered wise and clever when they state: Sequential development, no leaping! Well, actually nature does constantly move forward in leaps {drawing (Plate 14)}. Step by step nature forms first the green leaf of the foliage, then remoulds this into sepals, then into colourful petals, then into stamens and pistils.

{Plate 14}

Nature makes leap after leap, each time shaping a form. And in wider life there is one turnaround after another. In the life of a human being new circumstances arise at the change of teeth, and yet others at puberty. And if our powers of observation were less crude than they are today, one would also observe the beginning of a third phase around the twentieth year, and later yet again as life proceeds.

History, too, is an organism in which such leaps take place. Yet we now pass them by unnoticed. People are entirely unaware of the significant leap which occurred around the turn of the fourteenth to the fifteenth century, or rather in the middle of the fifteenth century. Yet what was initiated at that time wants to reach its fulfilment now, in the middle of our century. And it is definitely not a matter of idle fantasy but rather a statement of the exact truth when one points out that events which have moved human beings so greatly, and which have recently reached such a culmination, are tending towards something which can truly be observed to be a preparation for what is going to irrupt into human evolution during the middle part of this century. These are the things of which one must be aware if one does not intend to set up arbitrary ideals for human evolution but strives to discover spiritual science together with the creative forces of the world so that these can then also enter into life.

LECTURE 10

DORNACH, 13 DECEMBER 1919

YESTERDAY I spoke to you about the relationships between anthroposophical spiritual science and the forms present in our building. I wanted especially to point out that the relationship this building has with our science of the spirit is not an external one but that what has flowed into these forms is the spirit which holds sway in our spiritual science. It is especially important to be able to claim that a genuine feeling and understanding of these forms amounts to a reading of the inner meaning present in our movement. Today I intend to mention some other aspects regarding the building in order then, either still today or else tomorrow, to follow this up with some important points emerging from anthroposophy.

When you look at the ground plan of the building you will notice that it has the form of two overlapping circles, one smaller and one larger, which I can draw like this [the ground plan is drawn (Plate 16)].

The building as a whole is oriented east to west [the east-west line is drawn (Plate 16)]. As you can see, this east-west line is the only symmetrical axis; everything relates symmetrically to this axis.

For the rest, there is here no mechanical repetition of the forms such as is otherwise found in architecture, for example with matching capitals and so on; rather, as I said yesterday, there is an evolution of the forms so that subsequent forms evolve out of previous ones.

Rounding off the outer ambulatory you can see seven columns on

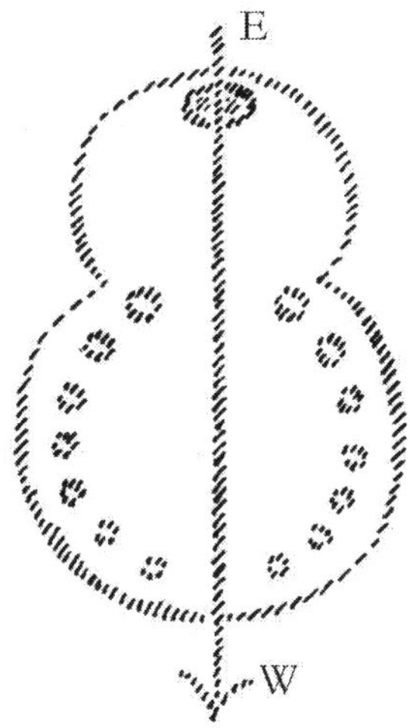

the left and seven on the right [the columns are indicated (Plate 16)]. And, as I mentioned yesterday, the seven columns have capitals and plinths, and between them architraves, all of which develop their forms sequentially.

If you can have a sense of this ground plan, then, simply in these two interlocking circles—by grasping this through your feelings—you will find something which points to the evolution of humanity. As I said yesterday, a significant caesura occurred in the evolution of humanity approximately in the middle of the fifteenth century. What we call 'history' in the external academic sense is no more than a *fable convenue*, for it gives us only external information. History in this sense gives us the impression that the human beings of the eighth or ninth century were no different from those of the eighteenth or nineteenth century. Actually, some more recent historians, for example Lamprecht,[89] do say that this is nonsense and that actually the soul constitution and the soul mood of human beings was quite different before and after the stated date. In the present time we find ourselves in the midst of a development we can only comprehend if we become aware of how we are developing towards the future with certain specific soul forces of our own. These soul forces, which continued to develop until the fifteenth century, are in the process of fading away—although they do to some extent still haunt human souls. They belong to that which is dying out, that which is doomed to fall away from human evolution. If one wants to become capable of making a contribution to the affairs of humanity in the present time and in the near future, one must develop an awareness of this important turnabout in human evolution.

Such things find an expression especially where human beings are trying, in a meaningful way, to indicate what they feel and sense. Let us remind ourselves of the architectural development discussed here yesterday and which I now want to mention again, using an example which demonstrates how human evolution progresses.

Let us look at the forms present in a Greek temple. What do these forms of a Greek temple tell us? We can only understand what they are telling us by realizing that the whole architectural concept of this Greek temple is oriented towards creating a dwelling place for the god or goddess whose statue is present there. All the forms of the Greek temple would amount to an absurdity if they were not conceived of as a dwelling which enwraps the god or goddess who is to stand within it.

When we now proceed from the forms of the Greek temple to those of the next significant architectural buildings we come to the Gothic cathedral. If one enters a Gothic cathedral and sees it as something complete in itself then one is failing to understand its forms just as one fails to understand the forms of a Greek temple if one does not include in it the statue of the god or goddess. A Greek temple which lacks the image of a god or goddess is impossible for us to comprehend in a feeling way. Similarly, a Gothic cathedral which is empty is also impossible to imagine in a feeling way. A Gothic cathedral is only complete when it is full of a congregation, or rather when it is filled with people who are being addressed by someone so that the spirit of the word holds sway in the hearts of the congregation. That is when a Gothic cathedral is complete. The congregation is part of it, for without that its forms are incomprehensible.

What is it that evolves, for us, from the Greek temple to the

Gothic cathedral? There are, also, other developments between these two: intermediate forms about which other erroneous interpretations are made. But what is the significance of this evolution for us? In Greek culture, that flowering of the fourth post-Atlantic period, we see that something still lived there, some way in which the divine-spiritual powers lived among human beings, a way which made those people, who could only imagine them in images, want to build dwellings for them. The Greek temple is the dwelling of the god or goddess of whom people were still aware; the gods still moved about among human beings. The presence of the Greek temple in the midst of Greek culture would be inconceivable without that awareness of the divine-spiritual powers.

If we now move on from the flowering of Greek culture towards its gradual conclusion in the age of the fourth post-Atlantean period, that is towards the time of the eighth, ninth, tenth centuries after Christ, we arrive at the forms of Gothic architecture in the way it calls for there to be a congregation. It entirely fits in with the feeling life of people in those times. The mood of soul of human beings was now of course different from what it had been in the time of Greek thinking. There was no longer an immediate awareness of the presence of the divine-spiritual powers; they had moved far away into the beyond.

The earthly realm was often bemoaned as having fallen away from the divine-spiritual powers. The physical earth was seen as something to be avoided, something from which one must avert one's gaze; it was the spiritual powers to whom one ought to turn. So one person after another sought the company of others in the congregation—in a way searching for the group spirit of humanity—whereby the workings of the spirit gained a degree of abstractness. That is also why the forms in Gothic architecture make a rather abstract, mathematical impression in comparison with the more dynamic forms of Greek architecture with their gesture of forming a domicile around the god or goddess. In the Gothic forms everything soars upwards, aspiring to attain the spiritual distances for which the soul is searching. For the Greeks, their god and their goddess were present. With the ears of their soul they heard them murmuring. In the uprising forms of Gothic times, however, the yearning soul could only sense the divine.

Thus, with regard to a mood of soul, humanity came to yearn, to live in yearning and seeking, relying on yearning and seeking in community, feeling that searching in community would be more felicitous, while at the same time becoming ever more convinced that the spiritual and the divine, rather than living in direct contact with human beings, was something to be sought where it lay mysteriously hidden in underground regions. In order to find a way of expressing what was yearningly striven for, yearningly sought after, all one could do was somehow seek a connection with something mysterious. And the expression for a soul mood of this kind was the cathedral, especially in its typical form of the Gothic cathedral. However, in yearning for what was the highest and most mysterious when endeavouring to rise from the natural to the supernatural, it was necessary to move from what was merely Gothic to something else which, one could say, did not merely unite the members of the physical congregation but rather the overall spirit of humanity, or all the soul-spirits of humanity striving together towards a central point, a mysterious central point.

Imagine the totality of all human souls streaming together from every point of the compass. Here worldwide humanity meets as though in a great cathedral, not Gothic in appearance but with the same intention as a Gothic cathedral. In medieval times such things were connected with the Bible. Imagine how the 72 disciples—one need not think of physical history but this was the spirit which flowed through the world at that time—imagine how in the spirit of the times the 72 disciples of Christ spread out to all quarters of the compass in order to plant into souls the spirit which was to unite in the Mystery of Christ. Then, in what streams back into the centre from the Christ Spirit which the disciples carried out to the souls, in what streams back from every direction of the compass you have, in the most all-embracing way, in the most universal way what people of the early Middle Ages thought of as that which strives towards the Mystery.

There is perhaps no need for me to draw all 72 of them, but I can suggest them here [drawing (Plate 16 right-hand side)]. This signifies the 72 pillars. From these 72 pillars the rays would emanate which flow from humanity as a whole towards the Mystery of Christ. If you were to surround the whole with some sort of wall—as I have already explained, one cannot remain fixed at the Gothic stage—with some sort of wall with a circular ground-plan and imagine the 72 pillars here, then you would have the cathedral which embraces as it were the whole of humanity. If you were then also to imagine its orientation from east to west you would find a ground-plan quite different from that of our building which is a combination of two partial circles. This ground-plan here would give you an entirely different feeling, a feeling which I have tried to describe to you. The main lines of orientation in such a building would have the form of a cross so that one would have to imagine the main aisles also being arranged in the form of a cross [Plate 16].

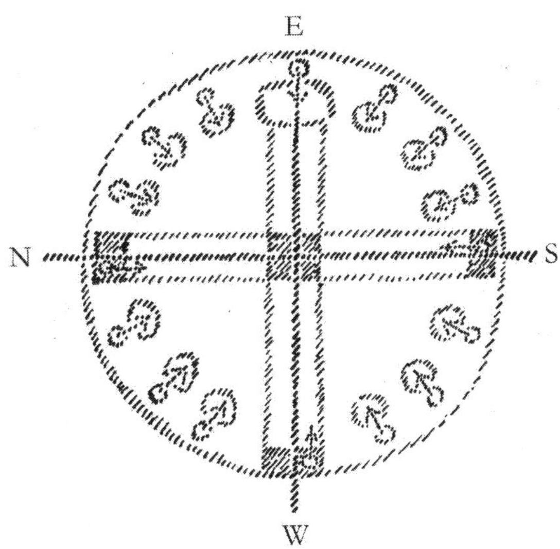

For medieval human beings this represented the ideal cathedral. If this [drawing continues (Plate 16)] is the east and this the west, then north and south are here. In the north, south and west there would be three portals and here in the east would be a kind of main altar;

and where each arrow is there would be a kind of side altar. And here, where the arms of the cross intersect, the temple within the temple would have to be situated: this would then be the summing-up of the whole, a repetition in miniature of that which is represented by the whole [Plate 16]. In the abstract language of today we would describe this as a miniature domicile for the sacrament in the shape of the building as a whole.

Try to imagine what I have sketched here in an architectural style resembling the Gothic but with a good deal also of forms from the Romanesque style, with the whole picture oriented in the way I have shown. What I have given you is a sketch of the Grail Temple as imagined by human beings in the Middle Ages, that Grail Temple which represented an architectural ideal in the latter period of the fourth post-Atlantean epoch. This was a cathedral into which would flow all the yearnings of a humanity oriented towards Christ in the same way as the yearnings of a congregation would flow into an individual cathedral or, furthermore, in the way human beings in a Greek temple, in a specific region, would feel themselves to be united with their god or their goddess—even though they themselves would not have been inside the temple since the temple was a dwelling solely for the god or goddess and not for human beings.

Another way of expressing this would be to say that a Greek, in describing his relationship with the temple, would say the same as he would with reference to a person's relationship with his house. He would say Pericles[90] dwells in this house. He would not mean by this that the person in question had any relationship such as ownership with the house; he would simply be expressing his feelings about the relationship of Pericles with the house. And he would have been expressing exactly the same nuance of his feeling regarding the architectural style of the temple when he said: Athene dwells in this house, this is the dwelling place of the goddess Athene; or Apollo dwells in this house.

This is not something which could have been said by the medieval congregation of a cathedral. A cathedral was not a house in which the divine-spiritual being dwelt; it was a house which expressed in every architectural nuance that it was a meeting place in which one oriented one's soul towards the mysteriously divine. Thus, within the '*ur*-temple' of the later part of the fourth post-Atlantean culture there was the temple of the temple, the cathedral of the cathedral. So of the whole structure one could say: Once I have entered here, I shall be able to raise myself up to the mysteries of the universe! In the case of the cathedral one had to enter into it. In the case of the Greek temple one only had to say: This is the house of Apollo, this is the house of Pallas Athene. And the central point of that '*ur*-temple', where the arms of the cross intersected one another, there was the central point which harboured the Holy Grail.

So you see, this is the manner in which one must follow up the moods which characterize the different historical periods; if one does not do so one cannot get to know what really happened. And above all one cannot, without such considerations, discover the soul forces now beginning to evolve in our own present time.

Well then, the Greek temple enveloped the god or the goddess and one knew that they were present there among the human beings. But medieval people did not feel this. They felt that within the earthly world they had been deserted by the divine. They yearned to find a way to the gods or to the god.

We meanwhile are still at the outset of this, for only a few centuries have thus far passed since the great turnaround in the middle of the fifteenth century. Most people are barely able to discern what is coming about, but it will come about, and things will change within the souls of human beings. So what now flows into the (architectural) forms, that within which the consciousness of our time will be embodied, this will once again have to change. However, these things cannot be brought about through reason, through intellectual fantasy. They can only be sensed and felt and observed artistically. Anyone wanting to approach them by means of abstract concepts does not, in fact, understand them.

Nevertheless one can point to these things by characterizing them in various ways. So the Greeks felt in some way that the gods or goddesses were their contemporaries, their fellow inhabitants. And medieval people had their cathedral which was not God's dwelling place but which served in a way as an entry portal to the path which leads to the divine. People gathered in the cathedral where they sought, as it were, to find their path by means of humanity's group soul. This quality of the group soul is what characterizes medieval humanity. Prior to the middle of the fifteenth century the human individuality was less prominent than it is now. Since that time it has been the essential characteristic of the human being to strive for individuality, to strive for the forces of personality in order to discover the centre of one's own being.

One cannot reach an understanding of what is rising to the surface in the many social demands of our time unless one recognizes the individual spirit in every human being, the desire of every individual human being to stand upon the foundation of his own being.

Something especially important for the human being will arise out of this age which began in the middle of the fifteenth century and will come to its conclusion near the fourth millennium. Something very important for this period will arise. You see, to say that every human being is striving for his own personal individuality is rather a vague way of expressing something. The group spirit, even that of quite a small group of individuals, is much easier to comprehend than that which is being sought by every individual out of his own original source. It is for this reason that it has become especially important in recent times for every modern human being to comprehend what is meant by seeking the balance between opposite poles.

In the one direction one wants to rise up from the head. Everything that makes us into daydreamers, fantasists, hallucinators, what gives us vague mystical urges for an indefinable future, or what fills us when we become pantheists, or theists or something similar, belongs to the one pole. And the other pole is sobriety, aridness of mind or, put trivially while not being at all untrue with respect to the spirit of our time, philistinism, bourgeois narrow-mindedness, anything that drags us down to earth and into materialism. These two polar forces exist within the human being, and he stands between them with the duty to seek for balance. How many ways are there by means of which one can search for balance?

You can discover this by once again looking at the image of the scales [drawing (Plate 17)]. How many ways are there by means of which one can search for balance between two poles which pull in opposite directions? As you can see, if one pan of the scales carries 50 grams, or 50 kilograms and the other the same, then there is equilibrium. And if one pan carries one kilogram and the other also one kilogram, once again there is balance. And if there are one thousand here and one thousand here, yet again there is balance.

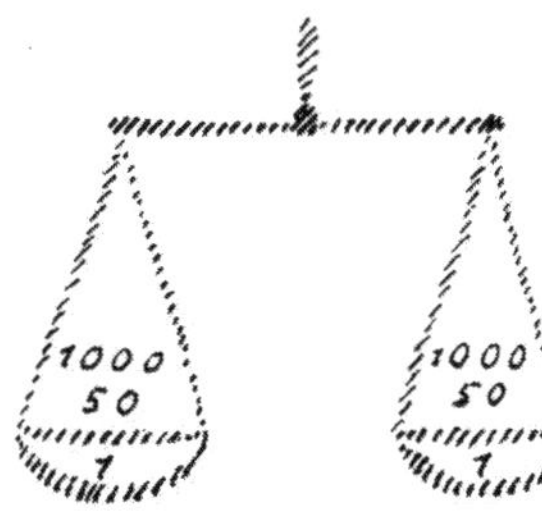

[Plate 17]

Balance can be sought in countless ways. And this corresponds with the countless ways in which one can be a human being. That is why it is so essential for present-day human beings to be aware of how their very being exists in the striving for balance between the two opposing poles. As I have just said, the search for balance cannot be defined specifically. The human being of the present time will only cope with his search if he links it with the striving for balance.

Just as important as it was for Greeks to feel that Pallas Athene or Apollo were working in their community because here was the house of Pallas Athene or here was the house of Apollo, just as important as it was for medieval human beings to feel that there was a place where they could gather which harboured something—whether it was the relic of a saint or even the Holy Grail itself—a place where they could gather and into which the longing of their souls for something indefinable could flow, so is it now important for the modern human being to develop a sense of who he is as an individual, a sense that as an individual he is a seeker for balance between two polar opposite forces. From the point of view of the soul one could also say that on the one hand there exists everything which one is looking for beyond the head, everything effusive, everything fantastical, everything which wants to develop passion and which cannot be bothered with real situations in life. That is the one extreme of the soul, and the other is what drags the soul down to the earth, to everything prosaic and dry-as-dust, any humourless intellectualism and so on.

This can also be expressed physiologically. The one pole involves the rushing of the blood, the boiling of the blood to fever pitch. The one pole, physiologically speaking, involves everything connected with the forces of the blood, while the other is everything associated with bony rigidity, with whatever is petrified right up to the physiological extreme leading to sclerosis in its various forms. So here too, between sclerosis and fever as the radical extremes, the human being must seek physiologically to retain his balance. Basically, life consists in the search for balance between what is prosaic and dry-as-dust and what is effusive and fantastical. In our soul we are healthy when we have found the balance between what is effusive and fantastical and what is prosaic and dry-as-dust. And in our body we are healthy when we can live in an equilibrium between fever and sclerosis. This can be attained in infinitely many ways, and it is this in which the individuality can come alive.

It is in this sense that the human being, especially now in our modern times, must find the meaning of Apollo's ancient dictum 'Know yourself'—but not in a disconnected kind of way. What it means is 'Know yourself in your striving for balance.' It is for this reason that we shall place in the eastern part of our building the sculpture which will give people a sense of this striving for balance. This is what will be expressed in the carved wooden group I mentioned yesterday. In the centre will be the figure of Christ. In this figure the endeavour is made to represent the Christ in a way which will show: this is indeed how the Christ walked upon the earth in Palestine within the human being Jesus of Nazareth at the outset of the Christian era. Conventional images of a bearded Christ were not created until the fifth or sixth century, and they are most certainly not, if I may say so, true portraits. Our endeavour here has been to create a true portrait of the Christ who at the same time represents the human being in his striving for balance [drawing (Plate 17)].

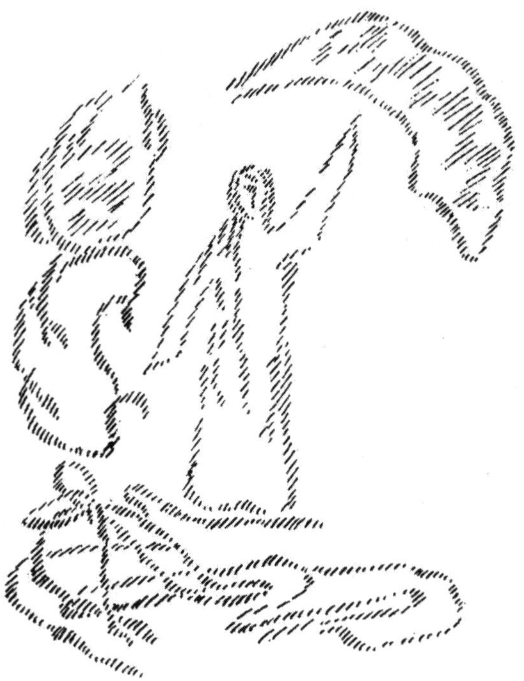

You will also see two other figures in this group. Here is the plunging Lucifer and here the aspiring Lucifer. And here, down below, is an ahrimanic figure linked to Lucifer, and here a second ahrimanic figure. And the representative of mankind stands between the ahrimanic figure—everything that is philistine, dry-as-dust and materialistic—and the Lucifer figure—everything that is effusive and fantastical. The Ahriman figure: all that leads the human being to petrifaction and sclerosis. The Lucifer figure: all that brings about feverishness beyond what the ordinary health of a human being can tolerate.

Having first had in the centre of the Gothic cathedral something which contained not an image like this but perhaps the relic of a saint or even the Holy Grail—anyway, something which had no direct connection with those in its vicinity—so now we shall have an all-enveloping building, a building which embraces the human being in his striving for balance.

If destiny will permit this building one day to be fully completed, then those seated within it will have before them something which, at the sight of the Being who renders earthly evolution meaningful, will enable them to say: The Being of the Christ. The intention is that this should be sensed in an artistic way. There must be no intellectual fantasizing about the Christ; a true feeling and sensing is what must arise. The whole concept is an artistic one, and the most important aspect is what comes to expression artistically. Solely the aspect of feeling and sensing is what matters, without anything intellectual being used as a ladder by which to attain feeling. It is the feeling and sensing which should lead the individual to look eastwards while saying, 'That is you yourself,' without this denoting an abstract definition of the human being; for balance can be attained in an infinite number of ways. It is not the image of God which is to be enveloped, for Christians, too, are not supposed to make an image of God. What is to be enveloped is that which has arisen out of the group-soul nature of the human being and become the powerful individuality of every human being. The forms here bear witness to the working and weaving of impulses for individuality.

If you can approach what I have just said not through your intellect, which is often the favourite method nowadays, but through your feeling life, and if you can consider that nothing here is intended to be symbolic or intellectual—for our endeavour has been to allow everything to flow out through artistic forms—then you will have grasped the underlying principle which this Goetheanum building is intended to express. And you will also have grasped how anthroposophical spiritual science is intended to connect with the inner spirit of human evolution. These days it is not possible to find meaning in anthroposophical spiritual science without following the path which arises out of the great challenges facing humanity both now and in the near future. It is utterly essential to learn how to speak in a different way about what is actually carrying humanity towards the future.

A good many haughty secret societies exist today which actually offer no more than what still stems from the age preceding the great turnaround in the fifteenth century. And this also often shows in a remarkably superficial manner. We ourselves have often found the same endeavours within our own circle, too. How very often have we not been told, when trying to point out the special value of occult striving, that this is a very ancient matter. For example a man once approached us who was presenting himself as something of a Rosicrucian. Whenever he had something to say—which was usually no more than his very own superficial opinion—he made a point of saying: As the Rosicrucians 'of old' would have said. He never omitted to say 'of old'. Many of today's secret societies like to emphasize the antiquity of what they represent. Some do indeed stem from the Rosicrucians—in their own way, of course—while others reach far further back, especially to ancient Egypt. Anyone wanting to peddle Egyptian temple wisdom can easily hoodwink the majority of today's population merely by announcing his intention.

Most of our friends do understand that our anthroposophical spiritual science does not aspire to return to antiquity. What it aspires to is the direct revelation now coming down to the physical world out of the world of spirit. It therefore has many other matters to discuss rather than taking seriously those secret societies which rely on antiquated ideas and which still play a considerable role in human events. When you hear what these people who are initiated into certain mysteries belonging to the secret societies have to say—and they do open their mouth occasionally on their own initiative—they chiefly speak about three things.

Firstly they speak about what the genuine seeker finds in the spiritual world when he has crossed the threshold to that world. What he finds is that as soon as he has crossed the threshold to the spiritual world he encounters powers which are the actual enemies of mankind, the true, real, spiritual enemies of human beings here on the physical earth. Such people claim to know that something, which is hidden from ordinary consciousness, is interwoven with those powers which can, with some justification, be called the spiritual causes of sickness and death and is also interwoven with everything connected with human birth. And you will then hear from such people who are knowledgeable about these things that one ought to remain silent about them. They say 'ought' because they mean that one should not tell ordinary folk, by which they mean immature souls—in other words the majority of humankind—about what exists beyond normal consciousness.

The second experience people have when they come to know the truth—one can only know the truth once one has grasped the mysteries of the supersensible world—the second experience is the degree to which everything they observe with their senses is illusion; the more things have been researched, the more they are a deceit. Losing the ground under one's feet in this way, the ground which human beings of today need more than ever, losing this ground comes to an end once one has stepped across the threshold. Then they can say: It is a fact, for I have seen it.

The third experience is that as soon as we begin to work in the world, whether we use tools or till the earth, whatever work we do as human beings becomes woven into the fabric of the social organism; we are then doing something which is relevant not only to us as human beings but to the universe as a totality. Nowadays when people construct a locomotive, or when they manufacture a telephone, or a lightning conductor, or a table, or when they heal a sick person, or do not heal him but allow him to remain sick—in doing all this they take it for granted that this is going on solely as a part of human evolution on the earth. But they are wrong. I hinted at this in my Mystery Drama *The Portal of Initiation*, namely that when something takes place here on earth events come into play all over the universe. You will remember the scene with Strader and Capesius;[91] this shows a profound truth.

These are the three experiences people latch on to if they know about such things. But in those societies they are preserved in a form befitting the middle of the fifteenth century and are therefore often completely misunderstood. People latch on to these things by pointing: firstly to the mysteries of sickness, health, birth and death;

secondly to the mystery of the great illusion in the sense world; and thirdly to the mystery of the universal significance of what human beings do in the world. And they have a certain way of talking about these things. But the time has come for all these things—especially for all these most important things—to be talked about in a different way than was habitual in the past.

What I want to do is give you an idea of how differently such things were talked of in the past and of the way in which such talk flowed out into popular consciousness, penetrating everyday scientific thinking, everyday social thinking and so on. And I want to show you how one will have to speak in future when one is really telling the truth, and what then must flow out from the mystery sources of knowledge and into outer natural ideas and outer social views and so on.

It is this tremendous metamorphosis, this historical metamorphosis—which must be comprehended today through the awakening of human beings out of their group consciousness and into their individual consciousness—it is this tremendous metamorphosis about which I still intend to speak to you.

LECTURE 11

DORNACH, 14 DECEMBER 1919

IN what I intend to say today I shall refer, to some extent in a more general way, to what I spoke about yesterday and the day before. From those two previous lectures you will have gathered that spiritual science, in the sense referred to here, is to be born from the most profound and earnest requirements of human evolution in our time and in the near future. I have often mentioned that we are here dealing not with those ideals which stem from subjectivity but with those which may be gleaned from the spiritual history of human evolution. One can most definitely glean from this spiritual history of human evolution that the science of initiation—the science which derives its knowledge from beyond the threshold to the spiritual world—is most urgently needed for the further evolution of humanity.

The powers representing what comes from the past are those which object to everything that can possibly be of value for a true knowledge of the spiritual world. It is such objections from those individuals in whom outdated powers live which must be overcome. The claim that relearning and rethinking regarding the most important affairs of human evolution are needed must be thoroughly and earnestly comprehended. So I do beg you to work towards overcoming anything that might tend towards a sectarian attitude, such as is still somewhat rampant within the soul of anthroposophy, and truly to see how significant anthroposophical spiritual science is for the world and for humanity.

Humanity is today still a long way from awakening from that sleep in which it became enveloped by the developments—I have already described certain aspects to you—commencing round about the middle of the fifteenth century. Everything incorporated into humanity at that time, external science with its great triumphs, the materialistic concept of universal laws, and the erroneous social ideas appearing so obviously as a result, all these things which have enshrouded humanity in sleep are still mightily at work. No fruitful progress will be possible until humanity has been shaken awake.

Let us not forget that knowledge of the spirit has mighty enemies in all those who above all want to continue thinking along their habitual lines out of sheer complacency. It would be wrong to assume that the more such enmity and opposition stemming from those quarters comes to the fore, the more will spiritual science become known, so that surely there is no need to bother about such obstacles. Well, ignoring such opposition might be one way of looking at the matter. But it would be the wrong way of tackling things. After all, if noxious pests attack us we do not ignore them, we seek to rid ourselves of them, and this cannot always be done in a gentle way. But of course every case is different and must be treated as such.

These things must be understood on the basis of what is necessary today. From this point of view we should be especially pleased if, in these increasingly difficult times, there are still individuals who have the will needed to espouse our cause. But there are as yet unfortunately far too few of those who are able fully to comprehend the seriousness of what is at stake with regard to the evolution of humanity. On the one hand there are those who do not want to forsake the comfortable ways of thought to which they have been accustomed for so long. But on the other hand there will have to be those who are willing to ward off that which is anyway doomed to perish. We must not believe that we should be prevented from acting by any leniency towards that which is anyway doomed to perish. Over the last five to six years we have been able to learn how something belonging to olden times can be reduced to absurdity.

And those who have not yet learnt this will soon have ample opportunity to do so. Meanwhile, that which is new for human evolution must be fired up in us.

So I was filled with a degree of satisfaction when a letter was presented to me the main content of which I shall communicate to you today. That same professor has once again made an appearance, this time at Reutlingen, near Stuttgart, in order to rant about what is intended by anthroposophical spiritual science with all the same reasoning as that contained in his absurd pamphlet[92] which I mentioned here recently. Well, no doubt that professor, one of the adornments of Tübingen University—for that is what adornments are like in that camp, and they are similar at other universities as well—that adornment of Tübingen University no doubt spoke in the same vein as he had written in his pamphlet. On this occasion he was faced down—a letter tells me—by our friend Dr Walter Stein[93] with the true panache needed today, when one seriously takes into account what is at stake.

The discussion, which took place there a few days ago, is described by our friend Dr Stein in a letter to his wife:

> I was at Reutlingen yesterday where Professor Traub was speaking against Steiner. I took part in the discussion. It was a life and death battle. I presented Traub as an unscrupulous man completely ignorant about the subject on which he was speaking. He was only able to stammer his final words. He was broken. The town pastor, who had opened the meeting, was completely trounced by me to the extent that when mention was made of the passage where Christ speaks of reincarnation he said: Christ is *mistaken* here—imagine, the town pastor of Reutlingen! I rose and shouted: Listen, everybody! That's today's religion for you, a god who is mistaken!—The audience went wild. Initially an attempt was made to interrupt me and prevent me from speaking. Somebody shouted: Keep to the point! There was shuffling and stamping. But I continued to speak, quite calmly, pointing at Professor Traub, saying: Here's

your authority! Well, I was the one who was applauded. I won. That man is finished. And I'm still half dead today.

It has, of course, been possible to foresee that powerful hatred would irrupt against the anthroposophical spiritual science which has been carrying on in Europe now for two decades. Anyone could foresee this who knew and knows how intimately linked this anthroposophical spiritual science is with the powers who are called upon to bring about the progress of humanity at the present time and in the near future. This anthroposophical spiritual science must not be confused by lethargy, by that attitude which likes the soul to luxuriate in spiritual ideas and concepts. And if Dr Stein feels this is a matter of life and death, well, there is indeed something quite correct in this.

We are at the beginning. The battle to destroy us has been joined. In so far as we have understood the right impulse of our spiritual science we have never made any moves towards aggression. But we may not avoid what must necessarily be done to counter the aggression which will increasingly assail us from without. We must not lose courage and we must not be lethargic. Bringing truth into human evolution will not be comfortable, and we must certainly not gird ourselves with forbearance in certain matters. In fact we appear to have achieved a good deal if the gentlemen who officially represent Christianity are stuck for an answer and are ready to say: Christ is mistaken here! The town pastor, of course, cannot be mistaken! If what the town pastor has to say disagrees with what the Bible says, then it is Christ who is in the wrong, not the town pastor! This is the attitude we now encounter everywhere, only we don't want to see it because it is uncomfortable to see it. But this attitude is visible everywhere if only one were willing to notice it.

Those, however, who clearly see the correlations in life know full well that the European misfortune of recent years, even though it might appear to have run its course externally, is intimately bound up with the way of thinking to which people have become accustomed as they gloat voluptuously over the great progress humanity is supposed to have made.

What is now needed is that we should become inwardly realistic. But, under the influence of recent culture people have lost the capacity to be realistic. Everywhere it is one's personal wishes that count. If one day the history of the past five or six years is written, it will only be possible to do so on the basis of spiritual science. Those chapters of world history will have much to tell about what part the personal aspect played in the great events of world history. As I just said, it will be impossible to speak about the events of the past five to six years except on the basis of spiritual science.

I need only mention something I have often said here. Of the 30 to 40 individuals who were in leading positions when they participated in what was termed the outbreak of the world war—imprecise language is favoured here, because it helps to disguise the truth; it was neither an outbreak, for it was something quite different, nor was it a world war, for it was something different which will not be over for a long time—of those 30 to 40 individuals who were involved at the time a large number were not fully alert, the forces of their souls and their spirits were not all there. And wherever consciousness is clouded, that is where there are portals through which the ahrimanic powers can find easy entry to the decisions and the will of human beings.

The ahrimanic powers played an essential role at the beginning of the events which took place in 1914. Even today, if one wished, one would already be able to discern entirely externally, on the basis of the facts, how necessary it is for spiritual knowledge to be involved in human evolution. But we are so very far in our thinking, in our feeling and in our will from taking such things seriously. On the one hand there is the fact, and even more the coming fact, that the time is ripe for the arrival of individuals who are able to bring a fit and capable soul to bear on the spiritual impulses which have been breaking in upon our physical world since the final third of the nineteenth century.

But in addition to our having entered into a materialistic age there is also that other fact, namely that the portals leading from the spiritual world to our own world have been open since the final third of the nineteenth century, so that individuals who bring their open souls and their open consciousness to bear upon these spiritual impulses are able to have relationships with the spiritual world. Of course, the number is still small of those in whose consciousness the spiritual world already plays a part. But the fact is that the spiritual world does already enter into the soul and spirit of certain individuals. We can say that the next 10, 20, 30 years up to the middle of this century will be such that more and ever more human beings will have learned to listen quietly to their inner being in order to bring to this inner being the impulses of the spiritual world which want to enter there.

Those who are already able to receive such impulses from the spiritual world, those who know about the truths and knowledge which must be allowed to enter into human evolution, these individuals know that if their ability for working through the science of initiation is not used to make fruitful what we call natural science or also what we call art, then humanity will find itself heading for a rapid decline, a dreadful deterioration. If the teaching at our universities continues as it is now for the next 30 years, if for another 30 years our thinking about social questions continues as before, then in 30 years' time Europe will be devastated. You can set up countless ideals in one field or another, you can rail till you are blue in the face about individual demands emanating from one group or another, you can say whatever you like about your belief that something must be done about the urgent needs of humanity for its future, but all this will be in vain if the transformation does not come out of the depths of human souls, out of thoughts concerning the relationship of this world with the spiritual world. If we do not change our view, if we do not change what we think, then a moral deluge will engulf Europe!

We must come to realize what it would mean if a number of individuals, in comprehending the knowledge which lies beyond the threshold, were obliged to say: The confusion, the materialistic tendencies, the social errors will continue while human beings fail to rethink or relearn; what if those few who are in possession of initiation science have to look on while humanity continues to go downhill as a consequence of complacency in thinking and feeling! We should not delude ourselves as to the amount of reasons why such impulsions might arise in today's so-called civilized world. Many such impulsions hold sway now, for is it not actually more natural to expect today's humanity, in its arrogance, to reject whatever arises out of the science of initiation? Humanity is so infinitely clever in every one of its individuals! Humanity tends so strongly to deride whatever can be attained through working on the progress of one's own soul. Humanity thinks it knows everything without the need to learn anything.

Neither natural nor social problems can be solved today without the enlivening of human thinking, feeling and will from out of the spiritual world. Yet many today consider it fantastical to talk of a science of initiation or of something which is described as being the threshold to the spiritual world. Of course it is not yet possible for every individual to cross the threshold to the spiritual world; but surely it is not forbidden to recognize the truth of what is meant by those who are capable of crossing that threshold. People are wrong when they insist on saying, from one point of view or another: Why should I accept what somebody or other says about initiation science if I myself cannot look into the spiritual world? This is not right. Ordinary common sense, if it is not misled by today's erroneous natural or social ideas, is perfectly capable of making up its own mind as to whether there is truth in what someone is saying. When a person talks about spiritual worlds one need only observe his manner of speaking, the seriousness which is brought to bear on what he is saying, the logic of the description and so on, and one can then form one's own judgement as to whether what he is saying about the spiritual world shows that he is a charlatan or whether it is founded on fact.

This is something one can decide for oneself, and no one is prevented from making something bear fruit in natural and in social thinking if it has been brought forth from the source of spiritual life by those who are eligible to speak about the principle of initiation.

The powers of human evolution which have been guiding the human being unawares to enable him to make progress, these powers are now exhausted and will be utterly exhausted around the middle of the century. New powers must therefore be called up out of the depths of souls. Human beings must come to accept that in the depths of their souls they are linked with the roots of spiritual life.

Of course not everyone is as yet capable of stepping across the threshold. Over the course of the past few centuries human beings have become accustomed to experiencing whatever they encounter as taking place in time. But the first thing they will experience after crossing the threshold is that there is a realm in which time, as we know it, has no meaning. One must extricate oneself from one's idea of time. That is why it is so useful, as regards understanding the spiritual world, to begin by imagining things backwards. Take a play at the theatre which outwardly begins with the first act and then proceeds to the fifth, and then imagine it backwards until you arrive at the beginning of the first act; or imagine and experience a piece of music not as it is played, but backwards note by note; or go through your day's experiences not from morning to evening but backwards from evening to morning.

This is how we can seriously accustom our thinking to do away with time. In everyday life we are used to imagining events happening one after another, after the first comes the second, after the second the third, after the third the fourth and so on [the numbers are added in Plate 18]; we always imagine that our thinking is a reproduction of external events. But now let us begin to imagine that we are thinking backwards from the end to the beginning, that we are feeling backwards from the end to the beginning. To do this we

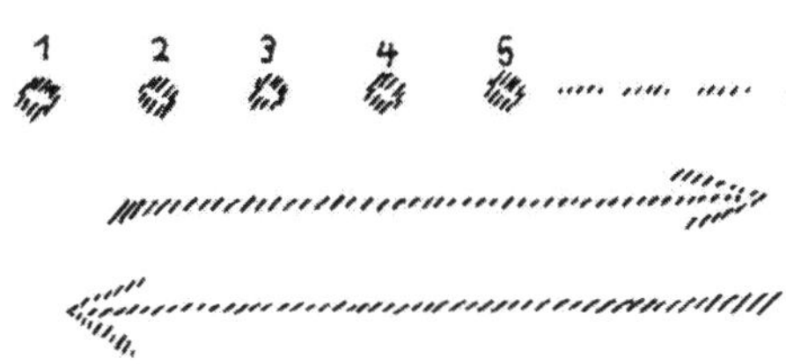

need to exercise a degree of inner coercion; and this coercion is good because it coerces us to move out of the ordinary world of sense. Time runs from one, two, three, four and so on in this direction [arrow to the right]. But if we think backwards from evening to morning we are thinking counter to time [arrow to the left]. We do away with time.

If we are able to proceed in this way with our thinking, going as far backwards over our life as we can manage, then we shall have made a great deal of progress. Those who are unable to step out of time are unable to enter the spiritual world.

We describe how the human being is subdivided into the physical body, the ether body, the astral body and the I [see Plate 19, left]. Initially, only the physical body and the ether body come into consideration as regards the physical world, the sense-perceptible world. The ether body has some earthly relevance in time; the astral body can only be found if one steps outside time. The physical body exists in space. The I, the true I can only be found once one has stepped out of space; the world which is inhabited by the true I is devoid of space.

So our first experiences are twofold: stepping out of time and stepping out of space as we cross the threshold to the spiritual world. I have often pointed out various aspects of what can lead to imagining the absence of space[94] by drawing your attention to the dimensions, although not in the infantile manner of the spiritualists—who often talk of four-dimensional space and suchlike—but in a more serious manner. Consider how much you will have lost of the content of your consciousness once you are no longer in space and no longer in time. The whole of your life is adapted to space and time, as is also your soul life. You enter a world to which you are not adapted. And not being adapted to a world involves sensations of pain and suffering. So it is not possible to enter the spiritual world without overcoming pain and suffering. People are not aware of this, but the reason why they shy away from the spiritual world is because they do not want to enter a world which resembles an abyss in which there is neither space nor time.

Now that I have thus placed before your spiritual eyes what is experienced on the other side of the threshold you will realize vividly that there are few individuals nowadays who possess inwardly the strong courage with which to experience being without firm ground and without time. Nevertheless, there are some individuals whose destiny obliges them to step across the threshold. But without the wisdom which can come from beyond the threshold it is not possible to proceed. This shows you what is necessary, namely that in future the mutual trust between human beings must be enhanced. This would be a social virtue, a fundamental social virtue. But in this day and age of social demands this is a virtue which is rare; people demand that one should live for the community and yet they do not trust one another. The most unsocial instincts prevail in our age of social demands.

For overall human progress, it will become necessary for human beings to grow into the spiritual world, it will become necessary to have confidence in the one who is justified in speaking about the science of initiation, not out of a blind trust but on the basis of sound common sense. One can always accept what is brought across from the other side of the threshold if one truly endeavours to apply sound common sense.

With sound common sense we must always look on the one hand to the one who is justified in speaking but then also to what we ourselves encounter. Not everyone, perhaps, speaks of Christ being mistaken, but there is something in the way such people speak which represents the prevailing logic in our life today. If someone comes along and says he cannot distinguish between what is brought over from the spiritual world with true inner logic and what is claimed by the university professors, then he is not applying sound common sense, or at least he does not have the will to apply sound common sense. Surely out of one's own sound common sense one must be able, when someone speaks of Christ being mistaken, to realize that one cannot count on that person in these matters.

We have lost a true science of the soul. We have no such thing any longer. I have even mentioned in public lectures, quite recently also in Basel[95] and other places, why we have lost a true science of the soul. The Catholic Church, for example, became uneasy about the spirit as long ago as the ninth century. That is why, as I have often pointed out, the spirit was abolished during the eighth Ecumenical Council of Constantinople[96] in the year 869. The dogma promulgated at that time was that a true Christian should believe not that the human being consisted of body, soul and spirit but of body and soul only, whereby the soul had some spiritual characteristics. And the teachings of psychology today are still based on this; they merely repeat the dogma of AD 869. The confessing churches, too, monopolized the soul in their dogma. All knowledge about the soul was monopolized by the confessing congregations. True knowledge, free knowledge was taken to belong only to nature.

So it is not surprising that today we lack a science of the soul. Secular scholarship refers only to natural science, since knowledge of the soul has become monopolized and knowledge of the spirit has been abolished. There is no science of the soul. If we base what we have to say on today's foremost scientific thinking we cannot progress any further. If we base what we have to say on the empty phrases of psychology—for that is chiefly what they are—we cannot reach a genuine understanding of what goes on in the soul. You know from my description in *Knowledge of the Higher Worlds* that, when we step across the threshold into the spiritual world, thinking, feeling and will separate. In today's normal consciousness, thinking, feeling and will combine in a kind of chaos; they are intertwined. At the moment when one steps across the threshold to the spiritual world, at the moment when one intends to gain experience of initiation science, that is the moment when thinking, feeling and will become autonomous powers within one's consciousness. They become autonomous. Then one gets to know them. Then one learns to distinguish thinking from feeling and from will.

In particular one learns to distinguish between thinking and will. The thinking which is at work within us, when we refrain from looking at its content but see it as a power, when we see thinking as a power within us, then this power of thinking is a kind of illumination of what we experienced in spiritual worlds before birth, or before conception. And the being of will in us is something embryonic, something incipient which will only be fully developed after our death. Thus we can say: If this [drawing (Plate 19)] is the course of a human being's life between birth and death, then here is thinking during the course of life in the way it lives in the human being, merely as a semblance, for its true nature lies before birth or before conception; and the will is no more than a seed, for that which is to develop out of this seed only develops after death. Thinking and will are profoundly different within human nature.

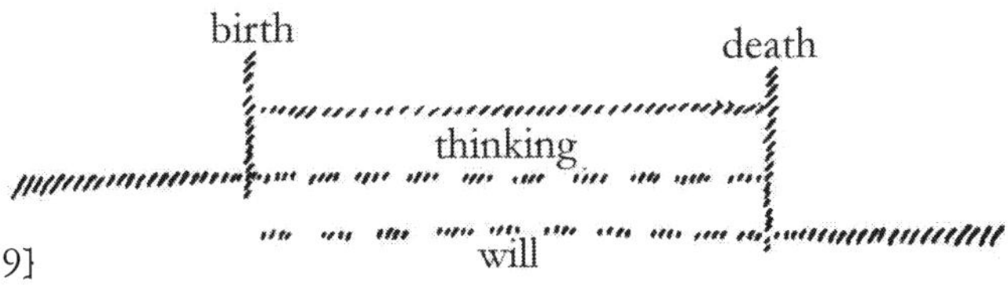

[Plate 19]

If someone now applies to this the logic of our present time, which likes to put everything tidily in its place and construct systems, then he might say: We were told today that thinking is the power which plays into existence from our life before birth and that will is the power which points towards the life after death. This would be a nice separating out of thinking and will by means of definition. But definitions do not serve our purpose. Some definitions, especially those which are supposed to be scientific, are very shrewd but they all have a snag somewhere, like that in the example from ancient Greece[97] in which the question is asked: What is the human being? The human being is a two-legged creature with no feathers. So next day a pupil brings a plucked cockerel and says: This is a human being, for it is a two-legged creature with no feathers.

Well, things are not so simple that one can deal with them by means of the ordinary tools of our intellect. It is all very well to say: What we experience as thinking has its true existence before birth and what plays into us here is only something like a mirror image of thinking. This presents us with a certain problem, but you will be able to overcome it by exerting your thinking somewhat.

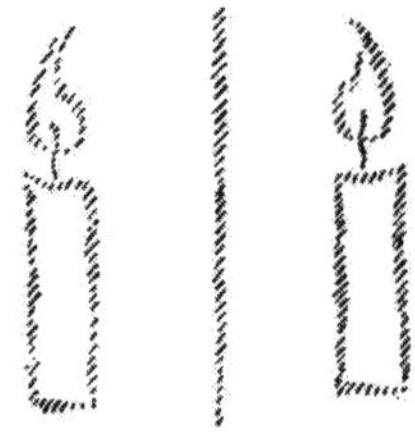

[Plate 19]

Think of a mirror with an object in front of it, for example a candle, so that the mirror image is here [Plate 19]. It is easy to differentiate between the two. You are not likely to mistake one for the other. And if you screen the candle with something, you will see only its mirror image. The image will do whatever the candle is doing. Whatever happens in the mirror image will show you exactly what the candle is doing. Since you are accustomed to thinking spatially you will easily be able to imagine what the candle itself is doing. That which is within us, however, is the power of thought as a mirror image, and the reality lies before our birth. The actual power, of which we have the image in our life, lies before birth. Hence the axiom of human consciousness: I think, therefore I am *not*.[98] Cogito ergo *non* sum! This is the fundamental principle we have to comprehend, that we think in images, whereas the power of thinking lies before birth. In recent times the opposite has been set up as the fundamental axiom of philosophy: cogito ergo sum, which is a nonsense. So you see how recent humanity is having to pass its test. But we are at the parting of the ways. It is up to us to learn how to think about the basic tenets of soul life.

Having thus in a way arrived at the nature of thinking, we can now make similar claims with regard to will. Will is not like an image with a mirror image; in relation to its manifestation between birth and death and what comes after death, will is like a seed with its fulfilment. The arrangement by means of which we have the image of thinking and the embryo of will is the only thing which makes it possible for us to be free between birth and death. You can read about this in my books *Riddles of Man*, *Riddles of the Soul* and *The Philosophy of Freedom* where these things are also discussed philosophically.

We now come to the specific point which will show you how inadequate ordinary, everyday thinking is for a comprehension of reality. Having grasped the essence of thinking, we at the same time have to say: This thinking is no mere thinking, for it has within it also some power of will. Within that inner part of ourselves which thinks we also exercise will. Thinking is the main aspect, but it also has an undertone of will, just as our will has an undertone of thinking. There is something twofold in us: something which is mainly thinking but with an undertone of will [in the drawing on p. 180 'will' is written in brackets beside 'thinking']; and something which is mainly will but has an undertone of thinking [beside the word 'will', 'thinking' is added in brackets].

When you consider reality, you do not arrive at tidy concepts which can be packaged into systems; one aspect is always at the same time the other to a certain extent. Not until you penetrate these things fully will you arrive at an overall view of how the human being is connected with worlds which lie outside what we can see with our eyes and hear with our ears but which we nevertheless inhabit just as much as we do our world of senses. We cannot claim that worlds other than that of the senses are not relevant to us, for we exist in the midst of them. We must realize fully that as we walk about here on this earth, as we make our way through the sense-perceptible air, we are also at the same time going about in spiritual worlds.

What I am saying is that affinities with the spiritual worlds appear when we look into these intricacies of human soul life. Through that which is more thinking, with only an undertone of will, we are linked with a certain aspect of the life of the spiritual worlds. And we are linked with a different aspect through that which is more will and less thinking. There is profound significance in this. What we discover in this way expresses itself in human life, and the nuances which are present in the world derive from the way either one power or the other in human nature develops more in the one or more in the other direction. Those powers which are present in the will with an undertone of thinking were developed more prominently in ancient Hebrew culture. And those powers of human soul life based chiefly in

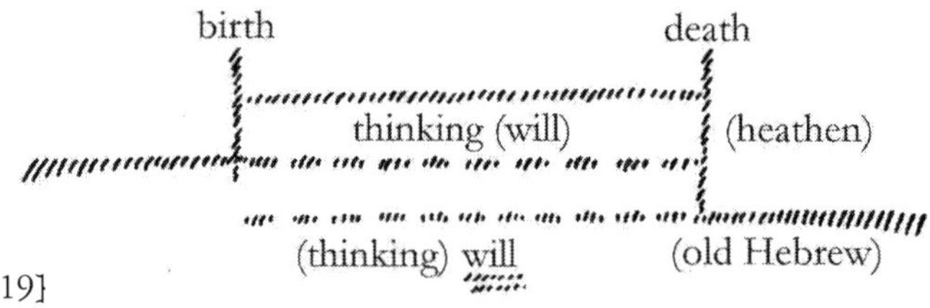

[Plate 19]

thinking with an undertone of will were developed in what one terms the ancient heathen culture. [To the drawing on p. 180 the words 'heathen' and 'old Hebrew' are added.] And now, in the present time, we have two streams running side by side. In the civilized world of the present time we have, mingled with one another, one stream, which is a continuation of ancient heathen times in our view of nature, and the other stream, which is a continuation of ancient Hebrew times, in the social view of our present time, in our ethical and our religious concepts.

This dualism is alive in the individual human being. On the one hand he worships nature in a heathen manner, and on the other hand, apart from taking his habits of thought into the social sciences or sociology, his thoughts are concerned with the social, indeed the ethical, life. And as he philosophizes he says that in the one field he finds freedom and in the other the imperative of nature. And then he finds himself in an eerie region amidst freedom and natural imperatives between which there is no bridge, and so on; the bewilderment is immense.

And this bewilderment is in many ways the content of life today, the content of life as it withers away. For what is it that our present life lacks? We have a view of nature which is no more than a continuation of ancient heathen thinking. And we have a moral, social view which is merely a continuation of the Old Testament. Christianity is an episode which was initially comprehended historically, but which has meanwhile trickled away through the sieve of culture. Strictly speaking Christianity is not here. With regard to those who repeatedly speak of Christ you can do as I recommended in connection with Harnack's *What is Christianity?*[99] You can treat Adolf

Harnack's *What is Christianity?* in such a way that you cross out 'Christ' wherever this is written and substitute 'God the Father', or even perhaps some pantheistic 'god', and this will not alter his meaning at all.

These are all things which one must say today, for it is on the basis of such considerations that we have to recognize the content of our future consciousness. In a similar vein, today's theory of evolution talks of the human being having evolved from lower forms of life and so on, or of those lower forms of life having evolved upwards and become human. Of course if you consult my book *Occult Science, An Outline* you will see that from a certain point of view we, too, have to say this. But the matter is such that we have to add the fact of the human head at present on our shoulders being once more in a process of decline. If our organism as a whole—please do understand what I am saying—if our organism as a whole were to have the same organization as our head, then we would constantly be involved in the process of dying, whereas actually we live through the way the vital forces present in the other parts of our organism are constantly being sent up to our head. The forces which in the end bring about our death are those which hold sway in our head. Our head is an entity which is constantly dying, it is in decline. That is why it is in our head that what belongs to the soul and spirit can be developed.

If you make a diagram of the head, you have to imagine the upward development having already become a reverse development; there is an emptiness here [drawing, see below (Plate 18)]. And it is into this emptiness, into what is constantly being destroyed, that soul and spirit enter. This is literally the case. Basically we bear soul and spirit through our head because our head is already in the process of dying. We are constantly dying in our head. And the undertone of

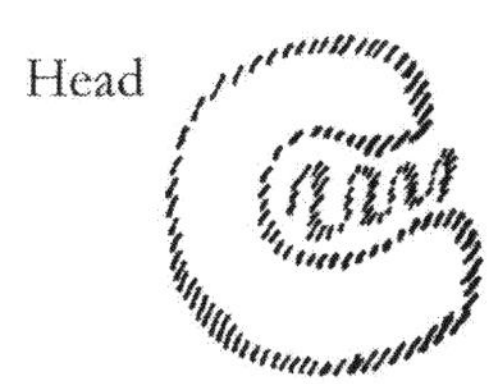

[Plate 18]

will which is in our thinking is what lies in our head. This undertone of will is a constant urge, a constant impetus towards dying, towards overcoming matter.

When we then actually die this will takes over. When our body is committed to the earth that which has been taking place in our head from birth to death continues on, quite physically, in our whole body. You carry your head on your shoulders. In it, quite independently, the process—constantly refreshed and thus preventing what wants to rise up from the rest of the organism—takes place which is then committed to the earth either through cremation or through decomposition. What you have within your skin between birth and death thus continues.

It continues in the earth. According to the same principle as you think with your human head the earth thinks too, because you are dissolving into it through your corpse having been buried in it. By passing through the portal of death we bring into the physical earth through our dissolving body what we otherwise confiscate from it during our life between birth and death. This a truth of natural science. And the human beings of the future must comprehend such truths. Today's natural science is infantile with regard to such things for it never reaches the point of thinking about them or conducting research into them.

And conversely, the destructive element of what is in our head is the continuation of what was already present before birth or before conception. The destruction only begins once we are born and receive our head; prior to that it was not destruction. With this we are definitely touching on an extraordinarily significant mystery of world existence. That which lives in our head, through which we enter into a relationship with other human beings and with external nature, is a continuation of what takes place in the spiritual worlds before we enter into the physical body. By gaining a thorough understanding of this we arrive at being able to recognize how the forces from the spiritual worlds play into this physical world. This is most vivid when we examine these things concretely rather than abstractly.

Here is an example [the figures are written on the board]: Goethe

[Plate 19]

1832
1865 }
1898 } – I.
1931 – II.
1964

died in 1832. The age belonging to the first generation after his death, up to 1865, was not such that many forces played into it from his spirit. This is merely one example; of course the forces from other individuals also play into life. Until the year 1865 someone paying attention to Goethe's soul would have noticed little of any forces playing in from there. But then, after the first 33 years, something from him does begin to enter from the spiritual world into our earthly development. This became ever stronger and stronger until the year 1898. If we then continue to follow this up beyond that time, we find that the first period in which Goethe's supersensible forces played into our earthly culture runs from 1865 to 1898. From 1865 there was nothing significant, but then it begins. After 33 years we then arrive in 1931 at a further period; this would be the second. And in 1964 the third period would take place.

So we can say that an example such as this can teach us how, relatively soon after an individual has passed through the portal of death, the forces he then develops play into what is going on here on the earth. What we need to know is how this takes place. Someone who truly works spiritually knows how the forces of the spiritual worlds play into those with which he is working. I said the day before yesterday that the middle of our present century marks an important point in time. Observations such as those made in the example I have just given are the basis on which such observations can be made as to how forces from the spiritual worlds play into the physical world.

The middle of our present century coincides with the end of the period in which what might be termed the atavistically remaining forces which led up to the middle of the fifteenth century will enter into their strongest decadence. Before the middle of this century humanity will have to decide to turn towards the spirit. Many people are still inclined to say: Why does misfortune come upon us? Why don't the gods help? Well, we are now in an epoch of human evolution in which the gods do help if human beings make an approach to them; but the gods are obliged, in accordance with their own laws, to work with free individuals, and not with puppets.

I have now reached the point I mentioned yesterday. If a knowledgeable person, even still in the times of ancient Greece, indeed in the times leading up to the middle of the fifteenth century, pointed to phenomena, to manifestations relevant to the birth and death of a human being, he was able to point to the world of the gods and how that world wove the destiny of the human being through birth and death. Today, however, one has to speak differently. Today one has to say that an individual's destiny is determined by his previous lives and by the manner in which, through this, he himself creates the forces in accordance with which the divine worlds can approach him. We must now learn to think in reverse as regards the relationship of the human being with the divine, spiritual worlds; we must learn to seek in the human being himself the source from which the forces arise through which one or another spiritual being can approach him.

This is the important moment in earthly evolution which we have now reached. What happens outwardly must now be understood as an expression of inner occurrences which can only be comprehended through the insights of spiritual science. Every human being has today, I would say, the possibility of observing the final outcomes of events. More than enough human beings have been murdered over the past four to five years; at least ten to twelve million in the civilized world, and three to four times as many have been crippled for life in various countries. Such are the immense achievements of our civilization! But we shall gradually have to realize that these are the outcomes. The source, on the other hand, will have to be sought in what plays in human souls when they oppose what wants to enter from the spiritual world in order to uphold the human being in the future. It is from this point of view that all things must be viewed and deepened, profoundly deepened.

Perhaps one should say that some of what has been happening could better be described from a different point of view. Broadly speaking, I shall now mention something which will bring this lecture to an up-to-date conclusion, especially since a number of our English friends have been present at all these three lectures, which has given us much pleasure. What I want to mention now is that one can speak today of victors and vanquished. It is an obvious point of view, but perhaps there is an even more important viewpoint which might perhaps be drawn from the following.

Here at this very place I once read out some observations by Fercher von Steinwand,[100] that German-Austrian poet who, in the 1850s, had been speaking about the future of the German people. His lecture is the more remarkable for having been given in the presence of the then King of Saxony and his ministers. Those of you who were present when I read the passage will remember that Fercher von Steinwand was speaking in the 1850s about the German people being predestined to become in future something similar to what Gypsies represented at that time. Fercher von Steinwand had been contemplating the evolution of humanity most profoundly. Such things can indeed be observed with full objectivity. And when one does observe such things with full objectivity one may perhaps reach a view which differs from that more ordinarily held. One will ask: What is it that has changed with regard to the so-called vanquished and with regard to the so-called victors?

Well, the actual victor is the Anglo-American being. And this Anglo-American being is predestined, by the powers I have often described here,[101] to dominate the world in the future.

One must ask whether this means that the German people will be excluded from experiencing the things by which the external world will be ruled in the future. What is actually going on? The responsibility for human events—not that of the individual, of course, but the responsibility of a nation—ceases to exist. The responsibility not of the individual but of the nation ceases to exist in the case of those who are downtrodden, and they are indeed downtrodden. They cannot regain their strength. All claims that are made in this matter are based on short-sightedness. The responsibility ceases to exist. So all the greater does the responsibility on the other side become. That is where the responsibility will lie. External dominance will be easily won. It will be won by means of forces which they themselves have not earned. Outwardly the transfer of external dominance will come about with the force of an absolute necessity. But the responsibility will be profoundly significant for the souls. The question is already recorded in the book of human destiny: Among those who come into possession of external dominance as though through external necessity—and do not be mistaken, it will indeed be a purely external dominance—will there be a sufficient number of individuals who can bring it about that into this purely external, materialistic dominance, into this culmination of materialistic dominance are planted the impulses needed for spiritual life? And this cannot be permitted to come about too slowly, either!

The middle of this century represents a highly significant point in time. One must be able to sense the full weight of this responsibility if one has been chosen as it were by external natural destiny to establish the dominance of materialism—and it will indeed be the dominance of materialism—in the outer earthly world. For it is also this dominance of materialism which carries within it the seed of destruction. The destruction has already commenced, and it will not cease. Becoming the bearer of external dominance at this time amounts to taking on and living within the forces of destruction, the forces of human sickness. That which human beings are going to carry over into the future is what will be born out of the new seed of the spirit. It will be necessary to take great care of this. And responsibility for this will lie on the side of those to whom it falls to take on world domination.

One must avoid not being serious about these things. One must consider them very thoroughly; one must not be seemingly spiritual while actually being materialistic. Two statements are heard very frequently. One is the way people say: What is the point of talking about social ideas? Ideas never get transformed into bread! This is a cheap objection which is frequently heard nowadays. The other statement is: Once people can find work again everything will be all right; the social question will look quite different. Both these objections amount to materialism in disguise. Both have the result of denying spiritual life.

In what way are we different from the animal world? The animals set out to find food so long as there is some which fits in with their instincts. If there is insufficient they starve. What advantage does the human being have? He works at producing food. And the moment he begins to work he also begins to think. And when he thinks the social question arises. And if human beings are to work they need incentives to work. The incentives which have hitherto existed will cease to exist in the future. New incentives are needed for work. It is wrong to state that everything will be all right once people have work. No, when people have thoughts which arise out of a sense of responsibility for the world which carries their soul, then the forces which arise from these thoughts will lead over into their hands and their will, and work will arise. Everything depends on the thought. And our thinking itself depends on how we open our hearts to the impulses of the spiritual world.

One must today converse a great deal about responsibility and about the significance of the thought. That is why I wanted to draw attention to this nuance in today's lecture.

Destiny being what it is, it turns out that one cannot set out on a journey whenever one wants to go, and so it has come about that we shall still be here tomorrow.[102] I will therefore speak tomorrow at eight o'clock specifically about the anthroposophical basis, the spiritual and occult basis of the social question.

LECTURE 12

DORNACH, 15 DECEMBER 1919

THE tasks facing humanity now and in the near future are incisive, significant and weighty. Powerful courage of soul will be needed to master them. Those who examine these tasks in an endeavour to gain an insight into what is needed by mankind will frequently come up against the superficial facileness with which public, so-called public matters are handled. People waffle on about policies of one sort or another. They base their view of life on a few emotional titbits, on a few of their own or their country's egoistical views on life, instead of truly yearning to find an actual foundation on which to base a healthy judgement which would be appropriate for the serious situation now prevailing. Over recent months, or even years, I have been giving lectures here on many aspects[103] of current history and current requirements, always with the aim of furnishing the facts upon which people might base their judgements, though not of course in order to present them with finished solutions. What is needed today is the strong desire to gain an ever-increasing understanding of the facts of life in order to build a true foundation for one's judgements.

I am obliged to say this especially because it is obvious that the various statements I have made, also in writing, concerning the social question and the threefold nature of the social organism[104] have simply been taken too superficially; far too few questions are asked with reference to the actual principles involved. People nowadays find it so difficult to reach these actual principles because they are—though they would not agree with this—theoreticians with regard to every aspect of life. Those who most strongly imagine themselves to be practically inclined are in fact those who are theoreticians in the strongest sense because they usually settle for a few ideas, a few ideas about life and then form judgements about life based on those few ideas. Yet what is needed today is a truly universal and all-embracing examination of life in order to find a practical judgement concerning what is really necessary. It really is an intellectual frivolity to waffle on about policies or fantasize about life while still lacking an adequate foundation. If only a seriousness about life were to be found in the depths of people's souls!

When the other aspect, the practical aspect of our efforts in spiritual science, namely the threefolding of the social organism, is presented to the world, what happens is that our whole way of thinking and working on this threefolding of the social organism is met with prejudice and feelings of intolerance. What is the source of this prejudice and these feelings of intolerance? Well, people form ideas about what is true—I mean with reference to the social life. They form ideas about what is good, what is right, what is useful and so on. And once they have formed these ideas they are of the opinion that these ideas have absolute validity for everywhere and forever.

Let us take the example of a person from western or central Europe who tends towards socialism. His ideals have a specifically socialistic formulation. But what are these ideals founded on in their socialistic formulation? The foundation of his ideals is that if they satisfy him then they must also satisfy everyone else on earth for ever and ever as long as the earth continues to exist. There is little comprehension of the fact that all thoughts about social life must be born out of the underlying character of a time and a place. It thus does not easily occur to people that there must be a variety of nuances in the way one introduces the threefolding of the social organism into our present European culture together with its American companion. Once it has been introduced the nuances will come about of their own accord as far as the aspect of place is concerned, namely the location of the various peoples in their regions. And as for the aspect of time, once the ideas put forward in *Towards Social Renewal* have become outdated as human evolution moves forward, then other variations will have to be found.

What I have put forward are not absolute ideas but ideas for the present time and the near future of humanity. In order to comprehend the full necessity of a threefolding of the social organism into an independent life of culture, an independent life of rights and state and an independent economic life, one will be obliged to examine in an unbiased way how the intermingling of culture, state and economy has come about in our European-American civilization. This intermingling of the strands, the strand of culture, the strand of rights and the state, and the strand of economic affairs is not a simple matter. Our culture, our civilization is an entanglement in which three strands are enmeshed which have entirely different origins. The origin of our life of spirit and culture is entirely different from the origin of our life of rights and the state and entirely different again from that of our economic life. And these three currents from different sources are chaotically intermingled. I can today only give you a brief sketch by following these three currents back to their sources.

Our cultural and spiritual life as it is seen today physically and through the senses is a continuation of ancient Greek and Roman culture which has now streamed on down to our higher schools and universities. All of our humanistic education right down to our primary schools emanates from what has streamed down to us from the Greek element [drawing, yellow, see p. 199 (Plate 20)]. Our European cultural life is, in the first instance, of Greek origin which has merely passed through the Roman phase. The Roman phase is a phase of transition. Other things, too, have mingled in most recent times with the cultural life stemming from Greece, such things as the technology of various fields which was not yet attainable by the Greeks: the technology of mechanics, the technology of commerce and so on. One could say that the technical colleges, the commercial colleges and so on have joined our universities, adding more modern elements to the humanistic ways of thinking which hark back to

Greece. Such things flow into our souls, and I do not mean only the souls of the co-called educated classes. Today's socialist theories, as they hover in the minds of proletarians, are also nothing other than a derivation of what stems from Greek cultural life. They have merely undergone various metamorphoses.

And these cultural elements reach even further back, namely to the Orient. What we find in Plato, what we find in Heraclitus, in Pythagoras, in Empedocles, and especially in Anaxagoras, all this reaches back to the Orient. What we find in Aeschylus, in Sophocles, in Euripides reaches back to the Orient, what we find in Phidias reaches back to the Orient. Greek culture itself reaches back to the Orient although it underwent significant changes on its way from the Orient to Greece. Over in the Orient culture was much more spiritual than it was in ancient Greece; in the Orient it was an emanation from the Mysteries of Spirit, or one could call them the Mysteries of Light [drawing continues, see p. 199]. Greek cultural life was a filtered, a diluted spiritual life compared with that of its oriental origin which rested on very special spiritual experiences. To describe those spiritual experiences I should have to characterize them in the following way.

We shall have to go back to prehistorical times since the Mysteries of Light or the Mysteries of Spirit are most definitely phenomena belonging to prehistory. I shall endeavour to describe to you the character of that spiritual life. As we know, when we go very far back in human evolution we increasingly reach ancient times when human beings possessed an atavistic clairvoyance, a dreamlike clairvoyance through which the mysteries of the universe revealed themselves to them. It is perfectly correct to say that human beings lived all over the civilized earth of Asia during the third, fourth, fifth, sixth, seventh centuries before the Mystery of Golgotha, and that spiritual truths revealed themselves to those human beings who possessed this clairvoyance which was bound naturally to their blood, to the bodily organs. This was the population who were spread over furthest distances, but their clairvoyance was on the decrease, it was growing ever more decadent. And this descent into decadence of that atavistic clairvoyance is not only a phenomenon of cultural history, for it is at the same time also a phenomenon of the social life of humanity.

Why is this so? It is because out of the broad masses of that earthly population, coming from various centres, although chiefly from one centre in Asia, there arose a specific kind of human being, a type of human being who possessed special aptitudes. Apart from that atavistic clairvoyance which they still retained, those human beings also had in their inmost life of soul a dreamlike comprehension of the mysteries of the world, and in addition to that dreamlike comprehension they also possessed—and they were the very first to have this—they also possessed what we now describe as the power of thought. They were the first to have this dawning of intelligence.

It was a momentous social happening for those ancient human beings, who possessed only the dreamlike view of the mysteries of the world, to find arriving in their territories immigrants whom they could not yet understand because although they also possessed spiritual insights these were different from their own, namely the power of thought. They were a different type of human being. The Indians regarded the caste whom they named the Brahmans as the descendents of those who had united the power of thought with the old atavistic clairvoyance. When those people moved into the more southerly region of the northern highlands of Asia they were named Aryans. They were the Aryan population. Their basic characteristic was—if I may make use of some later terminology—that they united the plebeian capacity of atavistic clairvoyance with the power of thought.

And the mysteries which we call the Mysteries of Spirit or the Mysteries of Light were founded by the human beings who were able to combine atavistic clairvoyance with that first kindling of intelligence, that inner light of the human being. And our spiritual development is an adjunct of that early spark of enlightenment, definitely an adjunct.

Something of what had been revealed did remain for humanity. But one must take into account that the Greeks, especially the more cultured ones, experienced the dying away of the old gift of atavistic clairvoyance and that what remained was the power of thought. And then the Romans retained solely the power of thought. The Greeks still retained an awareness that the power of thought had arisen out of the same source as had the old atavistic clairvoyance. That is why Socrates still experienced something which he named his daemon[105] who inspired him, although only with dialectical, intelligent truths.

The Greeks also produced significant artistic depictions of the intelligent human being as he rises up out of the rest of humanity. If you study their sculptures you will notice three strongly differentiated types. There is the Aryan type as in the head of Apollo, of Pallas Athene, of Zeus, of Hera. If you compare the ears of an Apollo with those of a Mercury head, or the nose of an Apollo with that of a Mercury head, you will see how different the types are. The Greeks wanted to show in the Mercury type how in ancient Greek culture there had been a confluence of intelligence with the ancient, past clairvoyance which was still present as a superstition, as a lower form of culture, on the basis of which the Aryan type had risen up, represented in sculpture by the head of Zeus, by the head of Pallas Athene and so on. And the lowest of all, the races still possessing the remains of ancient clairvoyance and still living in the periphery of Greece, were represented in sculpture of as yet another type: the Satyr type, which was entirely different from the Mercury type. Compare the Satyr nose with the Mercury nose, or Satyr ears with Mercury ears. The ancient Greeks combined in their art the confluence of what they bore in their consciousness concerning their coming into being.

That which gradually emerged in modern times, having gradually filtered through the Mysteries of Spirit or of Light in ancient Greece, possessed some specific cultural and spiritual characteristics. These characteristics were filled with an inner force which enabled them to create the foundation of humanity's life of rights. Out of the revelations from the gods in the mysteries came the external social organism, the theocracies. Everything harks back to the theocracies. And those theocracies were not only capable of bringing into themselves the life of rights, the life of politics out of the mysteries;

they were also able to bring order into the economic life out of the spirit. The priests in the Mysteries of Light were at the same time also the economic, the commercial administrators of their domains. They ruled economically in accordance with the mysteries. They built houses, they built canals, they built bridges, they organized the cultivation of the land, and so on.

In primeval times this is what developed through the spiritual, cultural life. But this culture gradually became abstract. Spiritual life became increasingly a sum of ideas. In the Middle Ages, theology became an aggregate of concepts in place of the ancient spiritual life. There was no longer a proper connection with the spiritual life which thus became abstract, curial. If we look back to the ancient theocracies we find in the ruler the one who has received his mandate from the gods in the mysteries. His latter-day heir is the western ruler who is no longer recognizable as the heir finally descended from the theocratic ruler who received his mandate from the gods in the mysteries. All that remains now is the crown and the coronation mantel. These are outer insignia which later became more like medals. If one has an eye for such things one can still recognize in some aristocratic titles their origin in mystery times. But everything is now externalized.

Hardly less superficial is also the culture now in vogue in our schools and universities as the final echo of what were divine communications in the mysteries. The spiritual life has flowed into our life, but it is utterly abstract, it is now no more than a life of ideas. It has become what in the end is termed in socialist circles an ideology; it is a conglomeration of thoughts which are *mere* thoughts. This really is what our spiritual life has become.

The social chaos of today is what has evolved under the auspices of this spiritual, cultural life which has become so watered down and so abstract that it has lost all its vigour. It is up to us to put this spiritual, cultural life back on to its own foundation, for only then will it flourish. We must find our way back from the merely abstract spirit to the creative spirit. And we can only achieve this by endeavouring to develop the cultural life of officialdom once more into the free life of the spirit which will then once again be alive. Neither the spiritual life patronized by the Church nor the spiritual life maintained and protected by the state, nor the spiritual life gasping under the burden of commerce and industry can be fruitful for humanity. Only an independent spiritual life can do this.

The time has now come for us to muster the courage in our souls to show the world openly and in freedom that the spiritual, cultural life must stand on its own ground. Many people are asking: How can we do this? First of all it is important that we explain to people what is necessary. We shall have to win as many people as possible who realize the necessity, for example, of providing the spiritual, cultural life with its own foundations, and who understand what the pedagogy of the nineteenth century has become for our schools and universities, namely that it can no longer do any good for humanity unless it is rebuilt out of a free spiritual life. There is as yet little courage in people's souls out of which such truly radical demands can be made. It will only be possible to make these demands if we can win sufficient individuals who understand this situation. All our other social work is purely tentative today. The most important thing is to ensure and to work towards bringing ever more and more individuals to an insight regarding what is socially necessary, one aspect of this being what I have just described. We must seek to enlighten people by every means at our disposal; that is what is important today.

We are not yet productive with regard to the spiritual, cultural life; we are only in the process of becoming productive in this. There are a few beginnings of which I shall speak in a moment, but we are not yet productive with regard to the spiritual, cultural life. We must become productive by means of helping the spiritual, cultural life to become independent.

Whatever occurs on the earth leaves residues. In today's oriental culture, in oriental spiritual life, the Mysteries of Light are less watered down than they are in the West although they are by no means what they were in the times I have been describing. Nevertheless, if one looks into these things, one can discover that what the

Hindu people still have today, what the oriental Buddhists have, is much closer to an echo of what we also have in our spiritual life, only it has come to a halt at a different stage. But we are not productive, we are highly unproductive. When tidings of the Mystery of Golgotha arrived in the West—whence did the Greek and Roman scholars take the concepts with which to comprehend it? They took them from oriental wisdom. The West did not bring forth Christianity; it stems from the Orient.

And something else: When spiritual culture was felt to be rather unfruitful in English-speaking regions and people were sighing for something more fruitful, the theosophists went to the downtrodden Indians and sought there the source of their modern theosophy.[106] They found no fruitful source in their own surroundings by which to improve their spiritual life and thus turned to the Orient. Apart from this telling fact, you can also find many other instances of the West's unfruitfulness for spiritual life. And every instance of western unfruitfulness for spiritual life is at the same time an indication of how necessary it is to establish an independent spiritual and cultural life in the threefold social organism.

A second strand in the entanglement of streams is that of the life of rights and the state. That is the cudgel in our culture, the second stream. Looked at externally, we observe how the honourable judges sit upon their judgement benches together with the jurors and pronounce judgement on crimes and misdemeanours, or we observe the civil servants in their bureaucracy presiding over our civilian world, to the despair of those who are thus ruled. Everything we speak about under the name of jurisprudence or the state, and everything which arises out of this jurisprudence and this state by way of politics, all of it is this stream here [drawing, p. 199 white (Plate 20)]. Just as I term this [orange] the stream of the spiritual life, so is this [white] the stream of the life of rights, of the state.

Where does all this come from? This, too, harks back to mystery cultures. It harks back to the mystery culture of ancient Egypt which migrated through the southern regions of Europe and then moved through the mundane, unimaginative nature of the Romans and in this unimaginative nature of the Romans joined up with a side-branch of oriental nature where it became catholic Christianity or the Catholic Church [see drawing, Plate 20]. Put rather drastically, this Catholic Church is in its essence also a kind of jurisprudence. From its various dogmas and right up to that great and mighty judgement portrayed throughout the Middle Ages as the 'Last Judgement', it transformed the entirely different spiritual life of the Orient with its Egyptian element of the Mysteries of Space into what became a society of world judges pronouncing world judgements and world punishments, with sinners and good and bad people. It is indeed a form of jurisprudence.

In our entanglement of spiritual streams, to which we give the name of civilization, this is the second element, and it has not linked up with the others in any organic way. That it has not linked up becomes obvious to anyone entering a university to attend, let's say, first a lecture on jurisprudence or constitutional law and subsequently a theological lecture on, perhaps, canonical law. These things lie side by side. And they have shaped human thinking and society. Even in later times, where the origins have been forgotten they still continue to shape people's inner life. The life of rights has made subsequent cultural life more abstract, and in external life it has influenced the shaping of customs and habits and how institutions are set up. And as the spiritual streams of the Orient became more decadent, what was their final social offshoot? It was the feudal aristocracy [see Plate 20]. When meeting an aristocrat one can no longer recognize his origins in oriental theocratic cultural life for he has shed all that, and what remains is mere social convention.

And as for the intelligentsia of journalism, they sometimes suffer from some form of nightmare! In more recent times this incubus has invented a curious expression of which they are inordinately proud: 'cultural aristocracy'. One hears this from time to time. That which passed through the Roman ecclesiastical constitution, through theocratic jurisprudence and then became worldly in medieval township culture, what is this in its final manifestation? It is the bourgeoisie [see Plate 20]. Thus have these spiritual and cultural forces in their final manifestation become thoroughly jumbled up together.

And there is also a third stream connected with all this. Looking in from outside today [drawing, orange], where is this third stream especially obvious? For Central Europe there has been a method which demonstrates where these final manifestations of something which was formerly different have been developed. This took place when a man in central Europe sent his son to a counting house in London or New York to learn the customs of commercial life. In the customs of commercial life which originated in the commercial procedures of the Anglo-American world we find the final manifestation of what originated in the Mysteries of Earth, of which the Druids, for example, represented a specific variation.

In the ancient days of Europe's population the Mysteries of Earth still retained a specific form in the life of wisdom. That European population which knew nothing, which was entirely barbaric as regards the revelations of oriental wisdom, the Mysteries of Space, and then as regards Catholicism, that European population, which was met by Christianity as it spread, possessed a specific form of the life of wisdom which amounted to an entirely physical form of wisdom. Historically only the most external customs can still be studied, such as how the festivals were celebrated out of which the usages and habits of England and America have emerged. The festivals here were related to quite different matters than were those of ancient Egypt where the harvest was connected with the stars. Here the harvest itself *was* the festival, and the highest festivals of the year were linked with the economic life. In this region the economic life was the foundation. Looking at the spirit of these things as a whole one notices that, coming over from Asia and up from the south, human beings bring a life of culture and a life of rights which they receive from above and then lead down to the earth.

But here, in the third stream, the economic life springs up, its tendrils climb upwards in such a way that what was formerly customary in the life of rights and in the life of spirit and culture now becomes purely a matter of the economic life. This developed to such an extreme that, for example, the insemination of the herds was a special annual celebration in honour of the gods. And there were other such festivals as well, all based on the economic life. If we go to regions in northern Russia, in central Russia, Sweden, Norway, or to regions which until recently were a part of Germany, or to France, at least northern France, and to what is today Great Britain, if we go to all these regions we find that even before Christianity spread to them they had a clearly pronounced form of economic culture. And whatever of the old customs still exists in the festivals of the rights life or in the festivals for the gods, all of this is an echo of that ancient economic culture. [The drawing (Plate 20) is now complete.]

This economic culture encounters what comes from the other side. To begin with this economic culture failed to develop an independent life of rights or of culture. The original customs of the life of rights were discarded because Roman law had flowed in. And the original customs of the life of culture were discarded because Greek culture

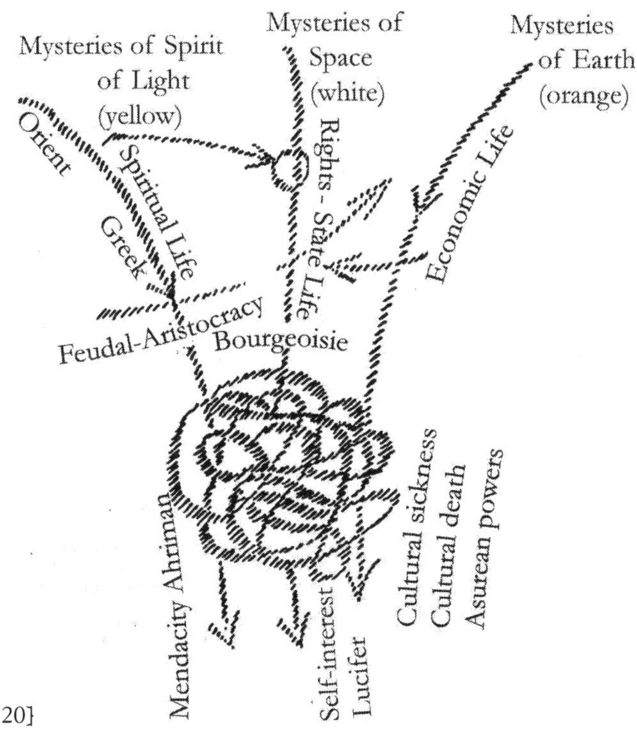

[Plate 20]

had flowed in. Initially this economic life is sterile, but it gradually works its way up, although this is only possible by overcoming the chaos arising from the alien life of culture and rights. Take today's Anglo-American cultural life. This Anglo-American cultural life contains two elements which are starkly differentiated.

Firstly there exist in the Anglo-American cultural life, more than elsewhere on the earth, the so-called secret societies which are fairly influential, indeed much more so than is realized. They do certainly preserve ancient cultural life; they are proud of preserving Egyptian or oriental culture, which has become diluted to such an extent that it is now no more than a symbol. Those symbols are no longer understood, but in the upper echelons they carry a certain weight. But this is the old spiritual, cultural life which has not grown up on home soil [Plate 20, right]. And then on the other hand there is a spiritual, cultural life which has grown up on the soil of the economic life, but which as yet has only the tiniest flowering; it blooms with the tiniest flowers on the soil of the economic life.

[Plate 20]

Those who study and understand these things know full well that Locke,[107] Hume, Mill, Spencer, Darwin and others are these small flowers emerging from the economic life. The ideas of someone like Mill or Spencer can easily be derived from economic life. Social democracy then raised them up to be a theory while regarding the spiritual, cultural life as a manifestation of economic life. All this is initially present, all of it is derived from so-called practical life, or rather from life's routines, not from true practical life. They all travel along side by side: Darwinism, Spencerism, Millism, Humeism together with the watered-down mystery teachings carried on by sectarian developments, the Theosophical Society, the Quakers and so on. The economic life which is seeking to develop has thus far grown only small blooms; it has not yet travelled far. Spiritual, cultural life as such, the life of rights as such: these are unfamiliar plants! And, please note, they are all the more unfamiliar the further one travels westwards in European civilization.

In Central Europe, on the other hand, there has always been some kind of what I would call a reaction, a struggle against whatever was Greek spiritual, cultural life on the one hand and the Roman Catholic life of rights on the other. There has always been a degree of rebellion here. One example of this rebellion has been the philosophy of central Europe. In England nothing is really known about central European philosophy. Hegel[108] cannot really be translated into English; it's not possible. Nothing is known of what he has to say. In England people talk of German philosophy as Germanism, meaning something with which sensible people do not concern themselves.

Especially in German philosophy, however, with the exception of one episode—when Kant was thoroughly ruined by Hume, so that this horrible Kant-Hume element was brought into German philosophy where it really wreaked havoc in Central European heads—with the exception of this one episode there is always a follow-on flowering after the rebellion, especially in Fichte, Schelling, Hegel. And Goethe, too, who wanted to allow nothing of that final echo of Roman Catholic jurisprudence to enter into the laws of what we call natural science, was searching for a free spiritual life.

In that shabby gown and the peculiar headdresses from olden times which judges still wear—they are now petitioning to do away with them—you can also sense, as in natural science and in natural law 'the law', which still exists in jurisprudence! The very expression 'natural law' is meaningless for Goethe's natural science which is concerned solely with the archetypal phenomenon, the archetypal fact. Here we have the beginning of the battle—but of course everything is as yet only at the very beginning—the first foray towards a free spiritual science: Goethean natural science.

And here in Central Europe we also have the initial foray towards an independent life of rights and the state. Read Wilhelm von

Humboldt's essay. That man is even a Prussian minister for education. Read his essay. It used to cost only 20 pfennigs in the Reclam edition. Read that essay on endeavours to determine the limits of state competency. If you do, you will be encountering the first attempt to bring about an independent life of rights and the state, an independent political life. Unfortunately the endeavour never progressed beyond that initial point which lies back in the first half of the nineteenth century or even the end of the eighteenth century. Nevertheless, one must bear in mind that important impulses did exist in Central Europe which pointed in that direction, impulses which could be taken as a starting point and should not remain untested, for they may be able to lead on towards the impulse for a threefold social organism.

In one of his first books, Nietzsche wrote the words I quoted on the first page of my book about him,[109] words which hint at the tragedy of German spiritual and cultural life. He was endeavouring in his essay about David Strauss to characterize the events of 1870/71, the founding of the German Reich, with the words: 'Extirpation of the German spirit in favour of the German Reich.' Since then the throat of the German spirit has been well and truly severed. And since over the last five to six years three quarters of the world have been attacking the Germany of that time—I don't want to go into detail here about the causes or the perpetrators. The configuration, the global situation is what is relevant—it was, even then, already the corpse of the German spiritual and cultural life.

Yesterday I described some facts impartially, so I hope you did not understand me to mean that there is not still a great deal which is present in this German spiritual and cultural life which must be taken into account and needs to be taken into account despite the country's future Gypsy-like characteristics. For what was it, basically, which led to the downfall of the Germans? This question, too, calls for an impartial answer. The downfall of the Germans was brought about by the way in which they wanted to share in materialism without having any talent for materialism. Herman Grimm[110] once gave an excellent description of a German characteristic when he said: On the whole the Germans hold back when it would be better for them to stride ahead, and they rush terribly ahead when it would be better for them to hold back. This is a very good description of one inner characteristic of the German people. Throughout the centuries the Germans have had great energy while lacking the ability to keep going with this energy.

Goethe was able to present the original phenomenon without being able to reach back to the beginnings of spiritual and cultural science. He was able to develop great cultural force for example in his *Faust* or in his *Wilhelm Meister* which would have been capable of revolutionizing the world if he had gone about it in the right way. But instead of this, the external personality of this genius managed merely to grow fat and develop a double chin in Weimar, to become a corpulent privy councillor who was also an extremely industrious minister while at the same time being no great shakes in political life.

It really would be important in the world to realize that such phenomena as Goethe and Humboldt[111] everywhere represent starting points and that it really would be to the detriment of the world if it were unable to take hold of what lives within German evolution, which has by no means yet been developed in the way it should be. German people lack something which others have built up to excess the further westwards one goes, and that is the inclination to ascend to the very limits of abstraction. The fact that others talk of the Germans having 'abstractions' in their spiritual and cultural life stems from an inability to experience the truth and also from the way those others have squeezed out the living element themselves and are thus unable to experience it.

But the Germans are not given to pressing forward to the final limits of abstraction. This was demonstrated specifically in their political life, in that most unfortunate of all political lives. If they had from the beginning had the talent for monarchism, which the French have retained so brilliantly right up to the present time, they would never have become so fatally attracted to 'Wilhelmism'. They would not have needed to set up or maintain that peculiar caricature of a monarch. Although the French refer to themselves as republicans they have in their midst a secret monarch who holds the state together and keeps a tight rein on people's feelings: strictly speaking, the spirit of Louis XIV[112] is present everywhere. It is now decadent, surely, but it exists nonetheless. There is indeed still a secret monarch among the people of France, and it shows in all their cultural manifestations.

And the talent for abstraction which showed itself in Woodrow Wilson is that talent at its most extreme in external political life. Those Fourteen Points[113] promulgated by the world's schoolmaster, which bear the imprint of everything impractical and unenforceable in every word, can only have sprung from a mind utterly given over to the abstract and entirely lacking in any sense for reality.

There will surely one day be two things which the future history of culture will have difficulty in comprehending. I have often characterized the one for you in the words of Herman Grimm,[114] and that is the Kant-Laplace theory which some people still believe in today. Herman Grimm put it beautifully in his *Goethe*: The day will come when that sickness which people nowadays call science will cease to be believable, namely its description of everything we have around us today having arisen out of an archetypal fog. And this is supposed to continue until everything once more reverts back into the sun! Really, a rotting bone circled by a hungry dog is a more appetizing idea than this fantasy of how the world came into being. So said Herman Grimm. Of course the time will come when the scientific madness of the nineteenth and twentieth centuries will have great difficulty in explaining this Kant-Laplace theory.[115]

The second difficult fact to be explained will be the unbelievable point of there once having been a great many individuals who took seriously the humbug of Woodrow Wilson's Fourteen Points at a time which was socially in such difficulties.

When we look more closely at what goes on side by side in the world we find the economic life, the political life of rights and the spiritual, cultural life all entangled with one another. If we want to avoid perishing beneath the utterly degenerate spiritual life and life of rights we shall have to turn towards the threefold social organism which builds up the economic life out of independent roots, the economic life which wants to come about but which cannot come up if there is no life of rights and no spiritual, cultural life which can come towards it in freedom. These things have deep roots in the whole of human evolution and in human social life. We shall have to search for these roots. People must today be made aware of the fact that down there, down on the ground, the economic life is creeping along, interwoven with Anglo-American habits of thought, and that it will only be able to send tendrils upwards if it works in harmony with the whole world, with whatever capabilities others have. Otherwise the attainment of world domination will be its doom.

If the world continues along its current path together with the degenerating spiritual life coming over from the Orient, then this spiritual life, having been at one end the loftiest truth, will hurtle at the other end into the most frightful mendacity. Nietzsche was obliged to describe how already the Greeks had to safeguard themselves against the mendacity of life by means of their art.[116] Art is indeed ultimately the child of the gods which saves humanity from descending into mendacity. But if this first strand of culture is pursued one-sidedly it leads into mendacity. During the past five to six years there has been more lying within civilized society than in the whole of human history. Almost no truth at all has been spoken in public life; hardly a single sentence heard worldwide has been true. Whereas this stream leads into mendacity [see drawing on p. 199 (Plate 20)], this middle stream leads into self-interest. And as for an economic life such as that now present in England and America which ought to become worldwide, if it does not bother to allow itself to be filled with the independent spiritual-cultural life and with the independent life of rights it will lead into the third abyss of human life, into the third of those three. The first abyss is mendacity, the degeneration of humanity through Ahriman. The second is self-interest, the degeneration of humanity through Lucifer. And the third is sickness and death in the physical realm and the sickness of culture and the death of culture in the cultural realm.

The Anglo-American world may well attain global dominance;

but without threefolding this global dominance will flood the world with cultural death and cultural sickness. These are the gift of the Asuras[117] just as mendacity is a gift of Ahriman and self-interest is a gift of Lucifer. Thus that third gift fittingly taking its place at the side of the other two is the gift of the Asuras!

From all this we should gain enthusiasm which will fire us up to search diligently now for ways of explaining to as many people as possible what is going on. It is the duty of those who understand these matters to explain them to others. We must do whatever we can to counteract that folly which regards itself as wisdom and as having achieved so much; we must present that folly with the practical aspect of anthroposophical spiritual science.

If I have succeeded in awakening in you the feeling of how profoundly seriously these things must be regarded, then perhaps I have achieved something of my intention in speaking to you here. When we meet again in a few weeks' time we shall continue to speak about these things. Today it was my intention to evoke in you a feeling of how the most important social task we now have is to enlighten others in the widest circles.

APPENDICES

Introduction to the Lecture of 28 November 1919

I shall begin with a brief introduction to today's lecture in order to inform you about certain things which are happening just now. Let me read you a notice included by our friend Dr Stein in the recent issue of *Dreigliederung des sozialen Organismus*,[118] a short article entitled 'New Elective Affinities':

> On 11 November Canon Laun[119] gave an utterly insignificant talk at the Stuttgart Sieglehaus on the subject of 'Theosophy and Christianity'. There would be no call for us to take any notice of this were it not for the fact that it revealed a certain tendency, namely that the speaker was following the sequence of thoughts—or rather the order of sentences—contained in Professor Traub's pamphlet[120] entitled 'Steiner—Philosopher and Theosophist'. Traub was of course not mentioned, but symptomatically it was interesting to observe a Canon of the Catholic Church making common cause behind the scenes with a Protestant professor. The Catholic and the Protestant parties (for these are surely no longer religions) join forces against Steiner. When in full view they do battle against each other, but behind the scenes they get on well. The weapons employed by the speaker will be seen to be obvious when I mention that there was no opportunity for discussion after the talk and that the speaker advised those who wanted to know more about Steiner to consult his opponents, whom he listed, but not Steiner's writings since these had been placed on the Index by the Pope. Dr W.J. Stein.

You can see how necessary it is to form independent judgements about individuals just now and how inappropriate it is to assess matters superficially, which does, unfortunately, frequently occur in our circles. We cannot repeat often enough: These times *are indeed* extremely serious and it is insufficient to continue in a new form with old ways of believing in authority merely out of a comfortable complacency.

Conclusion of the Lecture of 30 November 1919

In this respect (recognizing the importance even of small impulses), my dear friends, one must also exemplify everyday matters. One cannot get to the bottom of things if one does not look at the example of everyday matters. We would be taking things too lightly if we did not look thoroughly into the everyday. In recent weeks I have so often emphasized that it *is absolutely* necessary for someone seriously seeking to discover what is needed anthroposophically, for a new view of the world, that he should *take seriously* the matter of representing the truth even in everyday life. Anyone can remain silent about things and keep as much to himself as he wishes. But *if he does* say something he must strive to ensure that what he puts into words is in keeping with what is going on. I can still hear myself, scarcely more than a fortnight ago,[121] emphasizing the importance of being truthful also outwardly. And yet so much of this kind has again come towards me within our own movement over the last fortnight. I am only mentioning this now because it is truly grotesque.

Last Thursday, at short notice, I had to give a lecture to the teachers in Basel.[122] This was quite simply an ordinary fact: I was to give a lecture to the Basel teachers. Someone else, who is present here at this moment, heard on that day that the plan was for me to repeat that lecture again on the following Saturday, which would have been yesterday. I was to repeat the same lecture. I heard about this, but there was absolutely no truth in it. And yet somebody drew the conclusion that I would after all not be doing it because it would clash with a synod and therefore the attendance would not be adequate. There was no reason why such a rumour should arise since no one had any intention of arranging anything. I am mentioning this as an example of what is said here and there day after day in our circles, namely that something is going to take place when it is not. When you look into it there is absolutely nothing there, and yet such rumours are put about. My dear friends, my advice to be entirely serious with respect to the truth is not expressed merely as something with which to fill the empty air. The advice is given because it is a fact that for the sake of the right attitude of soul in anthroposophical work it is essential to be absolutely accurate in external matters; what one says must be in keeping with even the most external matters of everyday life. Such things really must be taken seriously even if they appear to be of minor importance.

Introduction to the Lecture of 7 December 1919

My dear friends, once again I am obliged to begin by bothering you with a brief explanation. Since this is my last talk before we depart[123]—our absence will no doubt be shorter this time—I really must give you this for me rather unpalatable information. It is about another in the series of numerous attacks we have been experiencing and differs somewhat from the others already mentioned in that it is considerably more vicious than others have been. A journal is published not far from here: *Suisse-Belgique Outremer*. In the current issue there is an article[124] on *Towards Social Renewal* beginning with the following words:

> Quel abîme, si nous passons d'un Emil Waxweiler à un Rudolf Steiner! L'un est, au premier abord, obscure dans sa terminologie, mais sa pensée est d'une clarté aigue. L'autre développe ses pensées en une langue que ses intimes pourron trouver claire: mais sa pensée nous paraît éminemment obscure! L'écrivain allemand est théosophe. On affirme qu'il fut le conseiller intime, le confident et l'inspirateur de Guillaume II, par déférence nous ne répéterons point l'expression de 'Ras-

poutine' de Guillaume II, par laquelle nous l'avons endendu désigner.

{What an abyss it is that opens up when we move on from an Emil Waxweiler[125] to a Rudolf Steiner! The one is at first glance obscure in his terminology, but his thoughts are brilliantly clear. The other develops his ideas in a language which his followers may find comprehensible: but to us they appear to be exceptionally obscure! The German writer is a theosophist. One is assured that he was the intimate adviser, confidant and inspirer of Wilhelm II;[126] out of tact we refrain from using the designation 'the Rasputin'[127] of Wilhelm II, which we have also heard.}

Well, my dear friends, let's begin with the logic which in this case also has to do with morality so that since we have recently been discussing various moral questions it also fits in quite well with our other considerations. So, the logic, which also has to do with morality: A vicious rumour is put about accompanied by an assurance that one has no intention of spreading it; one does not want to make an assertion and then one does just that. For many people today this is logical.

So let me counter this with the facts. Our friends will remember that over the decades I have given many lectures, right back into the eighties of the last century. You therefore know that I have only ever held *one* stance towards that 'Guillaume II', which was to ignore him entirely; the only possibility was to ignore him absolutely. This attitude to 'Guillaume II' was not even unique to Germany, for it was also prevalent in other countries, so it is not surprising that I, too, ignored him absolutely.

Since I received this article yesterday evening I have been thinking about my relationship with 'Guillaume II', and I can describe it quite simply. I saw him once in the royal box in the dress circle of a Berlin theatre; I was as far away from him as those of you here in the back row are distant from me now. Then, as I was walking along the Friedrichstrasse one day he rode by surrounded by his generals and with his marshal's baton under his arm. And the last time I saw him he was walking in the procession following the coffin of Grand Duchess Sophie of Sachsen-Weimar. I have never exchanged a single word with him nor been anywhere near him. *That*, my dear friends, is *the truth*.

Nowadays, of course, it is possible for the truth to be distorted to such an extent not only by chaps enjoying a pint and a game of cards or by ladies nattering over a cup of coffee, but by people who write in 'journals'. And, my dear friends, these journals are read without any attention being paid to the attitude regarding the truth manifested in the whole journalistic business. In view of such a degree of corruption, one can thus not avoid wondering what chances there are for a spiritual movement which says, not as a fibbing joke but out of the inmost needs of its existence: 'Wisdom lies solely in the truth'?[128]

My dear friends, it has frequently been necessary for us to point out, especially in view of what has been going on in the last few weeks, that if what we call spiritual science really wants to enter into the world it will be essential for there to be a solid ground of the most honest and upright truthfulness upon which it can base what it wants to tell the world. I have often said that even in the most trivial matters it is necessary, for those who want to participate in a spiritual movement like ours, to ensure that even in the most insignificant announcements about everyday matters absolute truthfulness must be present in the wording. When absolute meticulousness is not present even in the most unimportant everyday matters, this has an inner power to grow, it has its own vitality which grows until it can outdo any measure of ordinary behaviour so that finally such things can be printed and duplicated on paper with black ink which in the end render our culture corrupt. So long as battle is not joined in a serious and honest way against everything emanating from that direction, humanity will continue to slip into things which are already becoming apparent.

My dear friends, we must look squarely at these symptoms of what is going on in the world. That is why it will be necessary ever and again to rebuke every infringement of the truth, whether small or large. Those who know what is connected with the personality of

Rasputin also know how vicious the neck of the woods is out of which such slanders are coined. So you see that it is not only from the angle of the Church, whence attacks are becoming ever more virulent, but also from non-Church quarters that everything we are endeavouring to bring into cultural life in the way of spiritual science is being threatened. As I have often said, if only we could find a more potent way of expressing ourselves than my own words have hitherto been, if only we could find a more potent way of expressing ourselves in order to counteract what is so very much in opposition to the dissemination of truth in the world. We need more strength because regrettably the souls of most people are asleep with regard to the truth we are hoping to bring to them here; the souls of most of the people very soon again forget the immense gravity which lies behind these things once they have been told about them.

So this is what I want to mention here as a matter of principle: Please, my dear friends, try to use the few weeks in which I shall probably not be lecturing here to meditate earnestly about the sense of truth and a truthful attitude of mind, about the power of a sense for the truth and about the immense corruption emanating from the sense for untruth which is so intensively pervading the world. Please believe me when I say that human thoughts are genuine forces and that untruths, however small, are *fatal* for what one must call the spirit which fosters the evolution of the Earth. In the long run one cannot contribute to this fostering of Earth evolution if one again and again has to come up against sheer untruthfulness.

It was necessary to say this today as a preamble in order to explain to you, my dear friends, what might become the cause of the esoteric gradually seeping away out of our spiritual-scientific movement. Please do not believe that this is unimportant. It is necessary for each one of you to deliberate seriously and to ask meditatively the question concerning the power of the truth. For untruth comes on the one hand in small things, in everyday announcements, and on the other in morally corrupt lack of logic as demonstrated by that article. Quantitatively these things might vary, but qualitatively they are identical.

NOTES

1. See Rudolf Steiner, *Soziales Verständnis aus geisteswissenschaftlicher Erkenntnis* (GA 191).
2. See *Anthroposophy in the Light of Goethe's Faust*, Steinerbooks, Great Barrington 2014 (CW 272/273, Vol. I).
3. *Paradise Lost*, a religious poem in 12 'books' by John Milton (1608–74). *Der Messias*, a musical-lyrical epic in 20 songs by Friedrich Gottlieb Klopstock (1724–1803).
4. Rudolf Steiner, lectures of 1 and 2 November 1919 in *The Influences of Lucifer and Ahriman*, Anthroposophic Press, New York 1993 (in GA 191).
5. The 'Canones contra Photium' stated that the human being possesses 'not two souls' but 'unum animam rationabilem et intellectualem'. The Catholic philosopher Otto Willmann, who was greatly esteemed by Rudolf Steiner, wrote in his three-volume work *Geschichte des Idealismus*, 1st edition, Brunswick 1894, in #54 'Der christliche Idealismus als Vollendung des Antiken' (Vol.II, page 111): 'The perversion committed by the Gnostics in connection with the Pauline distinction between the pneumatic and the psychic human being, by declaring the former to be an expression of perfection and the latter as representing Christians caught up in canonical law, brought about the express *rejection of the trichotomy* by the Church.'
6. *Stimmen der Zeit*, formerly *Stimmen aus Maria-Laach*, a monthly Catholic journal dealing with the cultural life of the present time published by Herdersche Verlagshandlung, Freiburg im Breisgau. Otto Zimmermann SJ polemicized for years in this journal against Rudolf Steiner and anthroposophy. In the 1919 November issue he wrote an article 'The Church's Condemnation of Theosophy' in which he broadened the resolution of the Council of Rome to include anthroposophy.
7. Friedrich Nietzsche (1844–1900), for example in *The Antichrist—the Curse of Christendom*: 'and one counts this time after the *dies nefastus* as from the first day of Christianity—but why not from its last day?—from today?—a reassessment of all values.'
8. See Note 2.
9. See Rudolf Steiner, *Rudolf Steiner, An Autobiography*, SteinerBooks, New York 1991 (CW 28).
10. This refers to the end in 1899 of what is known as Kali Yuga, the age of darkness, the completion of which has led spiritually into a new age of light.
11. See *The Fall of the Spirits of Darkness*, Rudolf Steiner Press, Bristol 1993 (CW 177).
12. This refers to the commencement of the Michael Age in the year 1879. See Note 11.

13. John, 21:25.
14. Matthew, 28:20.
15. See *Die Polarität von Dauer und Entwickelung im Menschenleben*, lecture of 8 September 1918 in Dornach (CW 184).
16. Rudolf Steiner is here referring to the well-known Austrian geologist Eduard Suess (1831–1914): *Das Antlitz der Erde*, 3 vols, Vienna 1883–1901.
17. See Note 1, lecture of 15 November 1919.
18. See Rudolf Steiner *Architecture as a Synthesis of the Arts*, Rudolf Steiner Press, London 1999 (CW 286/287).
19. Ernst Haeckel (1834–1919), natural scientist. See his work *Anthropogenie, Exoteric Scientific Lectures*, Leipzig 1874.
20. See Rudolf Steiner, *Art in the Light of Mystery Wisdom*, Rudolf Steiner Press, London 1970 (CW 271).
21. Archimedes (*c.* 287–212 BC), eminent mathematician, physicist and technologist in the age of Greek antiquity.
22. During the building of the first Goetheanum, these lectures were given in the carpenters' workshop, a large wooden barrack on the building site.
23. Mark 1:15.
24. Renatus Cartesius, actually René Descartes (1596–1650), French philosopher and mathematician. *The Principles of Philosophy*, Amsterdam 1644.
25. Adolf von Harnack (Dorpat 1851–1930 Berlin). German Protestant Church historian. Rudolf Steiner is here referring to Harnack's *What is Christianity?*, 16 lectures (1899–1900) at Berlin University, published in English in 1901.
26. The League of Nations was founded at the instigation of American President Woodrow Wilson in 1919; an international organization for the preservation of peace and the status quo resulting from World War I. Seat in Geneva. Formally dissolved in 1946.
27. Rudolf Steiner made some comments before beginning this lecture. See p. 207.
28. Socrates (469–399 BC); Plato (427–347 BC); Aristotle (384–322 BC): Concerning these three great Greek philosophers, see Rudolf Steiner 'The World Conception of the Greek Philosophers' in *The Riddles of Philosophy*, Anthroposophic Press, New York 1973 (CW 18).
29. Augustine (354–430). From 395 Bishop of Roman Africa. One of the great Roman Church Fathers.
30. Aeschylus (525–456 BC), Greek tragedian.
31. Galileo Galilei (1564–1642), Italian scientist.
32. Giordano Bruno (1548–1600). The Italian Renaissance philosopher, who brought about the division between philosophy and theology, was burnt at the stake as a heretic in Rome.
33. Chimborazo, an extinct volcano in the Ecuadorean Andes, height: 6,310 m.
34. Georg Wilhelm Friedrich Hegel (1770–1831). His 'Philosophy of Nature' forms the second part of his *Encyclopaedia of the Philosophical Sciences*, first published 1817.
35. See Immanuel Kant (1724–1804) *Metaphysical Foundations of Natural Science*, 1786, Preface.
36. See Note 25.

37. *De Monarchia* was first published in Basel in 1559.
38. Op cit., Book Two, Chapter III.
39. Herman Grimm (1828–1901), German art historian. On Dante's *Monarchia*: in 'Dante und die letzten Kämpfe in Italien' (Essays, 1st Series).
40. Not known.
41. Wilhelm Wundt (1832–1920), founder of the German Institute for Experimental Psychology, author of *Völkerpsychologie,* 'Ethnic Psychology' in 10 volumes.
42. See Note 5.
43. See Note 29.
44. John Calvin (1509–64), Genevan theologian and reformer.
45. See Note 16.
46. See Rudolf Steiner's essay 'Zu dem "Fragment" über die Natur' in *Methodische Grundlagen der Anthroposophie 1884–1901. Gesammelte Aufsätze zur Philosophie, Naturwissenschaft, Ästhetik und Seelenkunde* (GA 30).
47. Theobald von Bethmann-Hollweg (1856–1921); 1909–17 Chancellor of the German Reich. *Betrachtungen zum Weltkriege, Part I: Vor dem Kriege; Part II: Während des Krieges*, Berlin 1919–21.
48. Gottlieb von Jagow (1863–1935), Prussian minister of state from 1914, *Ursachen und Ausbruch des Weltkrieges*, 1919.
49. Georges Clemenceau (1841–1929), French prime minister 1917–20.
50. Thomas Woodrow Wilson (1856–1924), 1913–21 President of the United States of America. On 8 January 1918, as head of the Entente, he enumerated his 'Fourteen Points' for the reconstruction of the world after World War I. *The Speeches of Woodrow Wilson* (English and German), Berne 1919.
51. Alfred von Tirpitz (1849–1930), German admiral, Chief of Staff of the Navy High Command, chief builder of the German navy, *My Memoirs*, Leipzig 1919.
52. Erich Ludendorff (1865–1937), Hindenburg's General Chief of Staff in World War I; 1916 First Quartermaster General; 1918 dismissed for wishing to continue with the war. *My War Memoirs 1914–18, 1919*. See Rudolf Steiner's lecture of 14 November 1919 in *Soziales Verständnis aus geisteswissenschaftlicher Erkenntnis* (GA 191).
53. See Ludendorff's description in *My War Memoirs 1914–1918*. 'Lüttich' (Liège), pp.19–31, 3rd edition 1919.
54. Rudolf Steiner, *Towards Social Renewal*, Rudolf Steiner Press, London 1999 (CW 23).
55. Rudolf Steiner, 'Culture, Law and Economics' in *The Renewal of the Social Organism*, Anthroposophic Press, New York, and Rudolf Steiner Press, London (in CW 24).
56. *Goethes Naturwissenschaftliche Schriften*, edited and with comments by Rudolf Steiner, published by Kürschner in *Deutsche National-Literatur*, 5 vols, GA 1a–e, Vol. III on the theory of colour, p. 105: 'If one looks at a bright picture it will make a powerful, enduring impression, and as it fades this is accompanied by a colour phenomenon.' On the same page there is a footnote by Rudolf Steiner: 'All types of after-image show a coloured fading which, although this cannot as yet be explained anatomically, proves that the full spectrum of colours is prefigured in the eye ...'

57. Genesis, 2:7.
58. See Rudolf Steiner's lecture in Berlin, 12 December 1911 in *The Wisdom of Man, of the Soul, and of the Spirit*, Anthroposophic Press, New York 1993 (in GA 115). See also *A Psychology of Body, Soul and Spirit*, Anthroposophic Press 1993.
59. 'The ultimate would be to grasp that everything factual is in itself theoretical. The blue of the sky reveals to us the basic law of chromatics. One need not seek anything beyond the phenomena; they themselves are the theory.' In *Goethes Naturwissenschaftliche Schriften*, fifth volume 'Sprüche in Prosa', p. 376.
60. Gustav Theodor Fechner (1801–87), see Rudolf Steiner, *The Riddles of Philosophy*, Anthroposophic Press, New York 1973 (CW 18).
61. Spoken by Mephistopheles in Goethe's *Faust Part 1*, 'In the Study'. See also Rudolf Steiner's lecture with the same title given on 25 October 1906, in *Supersensible Knowledge*, Anthroposophic Press, New York, and Rudolf Steiner Press, London, 1987 (GA 55).
62. Mentioned in R. Hagen *Die erste deutsche Eisenbahn* (1885, p. 45). See also Friedrich Harkorf 'Eisenbahnen' in the journal *Hermann*, No. 26, 1835.
63. This reference is to W.J. Stein. See Appendix p. 207.
64. The remarks with which Rudolf Steiner closed this lecture are here included in the Appendix on p. 208.
65. The poem is by Johann Gottfried von Herder (1744–1803), English in *The Explorers and Other Poems*, The University of Sydney. Translation by Catherine Martin.
66. Rudolf Steiner, *An Introduction to Waldorf Education*, Anthroposophic Press, New York, and Rudolf Steiner Press, London 1985 (in GA 24).
67. Lex Duodecim Tabularum, records of Roman law written on bronze tablets displayed on the Forum Romanum as the basis of all laws. Only fragments remain.
68. Leopold von Ranke (1795–1886), German historian.
69. See Note 25 and the lecture of 28 November 1919 in this volume.
70. The reference is to comments made by the geologist Eduard Suess mentioned in the lecture of 23 November 1919 in this volume. See Note 16.
71. Theodor Svedberg (1884–1971), a Swedish chemist and Nobel Prize winner. His book *Matter* was published in 1912.
72. Rudolf Steiner made some comments before beginning this lecture. See Appendix p. 209.
73. See Note 56.
74. See also Rudolf Steiner, *Riddles of the Soul*, Mercury Press, Spring Valley 1996, chapter 'The Physical and Spiritual Dependencies of Man's Being' (CW 21).
75. Alexander Helphand (1867–1924), who called himself Parvus-Helphand, a Russian socialist, for many years a refugee in Germany and chief editor of *Die Sächsische Arbeiterzeitung*, Dresden. After World War I he played an important part in the Bolshevik revolution and in bringing about the Treaty of Brest-Litovsk (1918). See Georg Wolf, *Warten aufs letzte Gefecht*, Cologne 1961.

76. See Note 52.
77. Paul von Hindenburg (1847–1934), in World War I field marshal and from 1916 General Chief of Staff. German President 1925–34.
78. Richard Avenarius (1843–96), German philosopher.
79. Ernst Mach (1836–1916), German physicist and philosopher.
80. The lecture on 'The economic nature of research in physics' took place on 25 May 1882. See Ernst Mach *Populärwissenschaftliche Vorlesungen*, Leipzig 1896, pp. 208–30. Among other books, Mach also wrote *Die Analyse der Empfindungen und das Verhältnis des Physischen zum Psychischen*, Jena 1900.
81. Karl Polanyi (1886–1964), Hungarian-American political economist. His article in the weekly journal *Neue Erde*, Year I, Issue 31/32 of 12 October 1919 was headed 'Crisis of Ideology: On F.W. Förster's *Machinery of Commonality*.' This is mentioned in Karl Polanyi, *For a New West*, Polity Press, Cambridge 2014. Two of the passages quoted there ('The amalgamation ... swamp', p. 458, and 'The result: ... is over', p. 461) are translated by Ciaran Cronin. The rest of the translation here is by J.C.
82. Eugen Kolisko (Vienna 1893–1939 London), physician and teacher at the Free Waldorf School in Stuttgart. See the journal *Dreigliederung des sozialen Organismus*, No. 20, November 1919, article 'Kritik des Marxismus'.
83. Rudolf Steiner was planning to go to Stuttgart, but at that time permission to leave and re-enter Switzerland was required for every journey.
84. See Note 18.
85. 1 Corinthians, 1:20 and 3:19.
86. Depictions are shown in *Der Baugedanke des Goetheanum*, Verlag Freies Geistesleben, Stuttgart 1958. Looseleaf in the volume is a translation of Rudolf Steiner's lecture of 19 June 1921: *The Architectural Conception of the Goetheanum with Explanations of Pictures of the Building*.
87. Regarding tabes dorsalis see Rudolf Steiner, *Course for Young Doctors*, Mercury Press, New York 1994, and *Understanding Healing*, Rudolf Steiner Press 2013, lecture of 2 January 1924 (CW 314).
88. See for example Carl von Linné, *Philosophia botanica*, Stockholm 1751, No. 77.
89. Karl Lamprecht (1856–1915), German historian, *Moderne Geschichtswissenschaft*, Berlin 1909.
90. Pericles (*c*. 500–429 BC), Athenian statesman.
91. Rudolf Steiner, *Four Mystery Dramas*, Scene 4 in the first drama 'The Portal of Initiation', Rudolf Steiner Press, London 1997 (CW 14).
92. Friedrich Traub, *Rudolf Steiner als Philosoph und Theosoph*, Tübingen 1919. Rudolf Steiner also spoke about this pamphlet in his lecture of 16 November 1919, in *Die Anthroposophie und ihre Gegner* (GA 255b). See also Note 27.
93. Dr Walter Johannes Stein (Vienna 1891–1957 London), teacher at the Stuttgart Waldorf School, writer, lecturer. See Rudolf Steiner, *The Cosmic New Year*, Rudolf Steiner Publishing Co., London 1938 (CW 195).
94. Rudolf Steiner, *The Fourth Dimension, Sacred Geometry, Alchemy and Mathematics*, Anthroposophic Press, Great Barrington 2001 (GA 324a).
95. Public lecture on 10 November 1919 in Rudolf Steiner, *Die Befreiung des Menschenwesens als Grundlage für eine soziale Neugestaltung* (GA 329).

96. See Note 5.
97. See Diogenes Laertius, Book VI, Chapter II on Diogenes.
98. See Note 24.
99. See Note 25.
100. *Fercher von Steinwands sämtliche Werke in 3 Bänden*, Vol.3 'Zigeuner'. Rudolf Steiner read from this chapter at Dornach on 15 November 1918, see Lecture Three in *Entwicklungsgeschichtliche Unterlagen zur Bildung eines sozialen Urteils* (GA 185a).
101. Rudolf Steiner, *Die soziale Grundforderung unserer Zeit—in geänderter Zeitlage* (GA 186). The lecture of 12 December 1918 in English is: *Social and Antisocial Forces*, Mercury Press, New York 1982. Also in *The Challenge of the Times*, Anthroposophic Press, New York 1961.
102. See Note 83.
103. See Rudolf Steiner, *The Riddle of Humanity*, Rudolf Steiner Press, London 1990; *The Karma of Vocation*, Anthroposophic Press, New York 1984 (GA 172); *The Karma of Untruthfulness, Vols.I and II*, Rudolf Steiner Press, London (GA 173 and 174); *Life Beyond Death*, Rudolf Steiner Press 1995. Also *Kosmische und Menschliche Geschichte* (GA 170–174b); *Die geistigen Hintergründe der sozialen Frage*) (GA 189–191); and other volumes of lectures between 1917 and 1919.
104. See Note 103. Also Rudolf Steiner, *Towards Social Renewal*, Rudolf Steiner Press, London 2009 (GA 23); *The Renewal of the Social Organism*, Anthroposophic Press, New York and Rudolf Steiner Press, London 1985 (in GA 24).
105. Plato *Phaedrus* 242.
106. Founded in New York in 1875, the Theosophical Society moved its headquarters to Adyar near Madras in India a few years later. In her first book, *Isis Unveiled*, its founder, H.P. Blavatsky, was as yet more connected with western occultism, but she soon turned increasingly to Indian wisdom. See Rudolf Steiner's descriptions in *The Occult Movement of the Nineteenth Century and its Relation to Modern Culture*, Rudolf Steiner Press, London 1973 (in GA 254) and also *The Anthroposophic Movement*, Rudolf Steiner Press, Bristol 1993 (GA 258).
107. John Locke (1632–1704, English philosopher; David Hume (1711–76), Scottish philosopher and historian; John Stuart Mill (1806–73), English philosopher and politician; Herbert Spencer (1820–1903), English philosopher; Charles Robert Darwin (1809–82), English naturalist, founder of the evolutionary theory named after him.
108. Georg Friedrich Wilhelm Hegel (1770–1831); Immanuel Kant (1724–1804); Johann Gottlieb Fichte (1767–1814); Friedrich Joseph von Schelling (1775–1854); all the great German philosophers of the eighteenth to nineteenth century. See Rudolf Steiner, *The Riddles of Philosophy*, Anthroposophic Press, New York 1973 (GA 18), and *The Riddle of Man*, Mercury Press, New York 1990 (GA 20).
109. Rudolf Steiner, *Friedrich Nietzsche, Fighter for Freedom*, Spiritual Science Library, New York 1985 (GA 5).
110. Herman Grimm in his essay 'Heinrich von Treitschkes Deutsche Geschichte' in *Beiträge zur Deutschen Kulturgeschichte*, Berlin 1897.

111. Wilhelm von Humboldt (1767–1835), German philologist, diplomat and man of letters.
112. Louis XIV (1638–1715), the Sun King, the culmination of absolutist monarchy in Europe ('L'État c'est Moi').
113. See Note 50.
114. Herman Grimm, *Goethe*, lectures given at the Royal University in Berlin, 2 vols, 1877, 8th edition, Stuttgart and Berlin 1903, Vol. II, Lecture 23, pp. 171ff.
115. According to the Nebular Hypothesis of the philosopher and mathematician Immanuel Kant (1724–1804) and the theories developed independently of Kant by the French mathematician and astronomer Pierre Simon Laplace (1749–1827), the earth was formed out of a kind of archetypal fog.
116. Nietzsche, *The Birth of Tragedy from the Spirit of Music* (1871).
117. See Rudolf Steiner's lecture in Berlin on 22 March 1909 in *The Deed of Christ*, Rudolf Steiner Publishing Co., London 1954 (in GA 107).

Notes to the Appendix

118. Monthly journal: *Dreigliederung des sozialen Organismus*, No. 21, Stuttgart, November 1919.
119. The talk is available in print: *Moderne Theosophie und katholisches Christentum*, Rottenburg, Wilhelm Bader 1920.
120. See Note 92.
121. This refers to the lecture given on 16 November 1919 in which Rudolf Steiner dealt in detail with Professor Traub's pamphlet, drawing attention specifically to the untruths expressed in it. See Notes 27 and 92 and the lecture of 16 November 1919 in *Die Anthroposophie und ihre Gegner* (GA 255b).
122. Rudolf Steiner, *The Spirit of the Waldorf School*, Anthroposophic Press, New York 1995, lecture of 27 November 1919 (GA 297).
123. The departure for Stuttgart was delayed by a further ten days. See Note 83.
124. By Adolphe Ferrière (1879–1960), dr. en sociologie *La loi du progrès économique et la justice sociale*. 'II. L'organisme sociale'. In the journal *Suisse-Belgique Outremer*, 1st year, No. 3/4, July/August 1919, pp. 19ff.
125. Emil Waxweiler, Director of the 'Institut de sociologie' in Brussels; author of *Esquisse d'une sociologie*, Brussels and Paris 1906, and *La Belgique neutre et loyal*.
126. Wilhelm II (1859–1941), German Kaiser 1888–1918.
127. Rasputin (1871–1916), a Russian monk who was very influential at the court of the Czar.
128. This quotation from Goethe, 'Wisdom is solely in the truth', was the motto of the statutes of the Anthroposophical Society from 1913 to 1923.

RUDOLF STEINER'S COLLECTED WORKS

The German Edition of Rudolf Steiner's Collected Works (the *Gesamtausgabe* [GA] published by Rudolf Steiner Verlag, Dornach, Switzerland) presently runs to 354 titles, organized either by type of work (written or spoken), chronology, audience (public or other), or subject (education, art, etc.). For ease of comparison, the Collected Works in English [CW] follows the German organization exactly. A complete listing of the CWs follows with literal translations of the German titles. Other than in the case of the books published in his lifetime, titles were rarely given by Rudolf Steiner himself, and were often provided by the editors of the German editions. The titles in English are not necessarily the same as the German; and, indeed, over the past seventy-five years have frequently been different, with the same book sometimes appearing under different titles.

For ease of identification and to avoid confusion, we suggest that readers looking for a title should do so by CW number. Because the work of creating the Collected Works of Rudolf Steiner is an ongoing process, with new titles being published every year, we have not indicated in this listing which books are presently available. To find out what titles in the Collected Works are currently in print, please check our website at www.rudolfsteinerpress.com (or www.steinerbooks.org for US readers).

Written Work

CW 1	Goethe: Natural-Scientific Writings, Introduction, with Footnotes and Explanations in the text by Rudolf Steiner
CW 2	Outlines of an Epistemology of the Goethean World View, with Special Consideration of Schiller
CW 3	Truth and Science
CW 4	The Philosophy of Freedom
CW 4a	Documents to 'The Philosophy of Freedom'
CW 5	Friedrich Nietzsche, A Fighter against His Time
CW 6	Goethe's Worldview
CW 6a	Now in CW 30
CW 7	Mysticism at the Dawn of Modern Spiritual Life and Its Relationship with Modern Worldviews
CW 8	Christianity as Mystical Fact and the Mysteries of Antiquity
CW 9	Theosophy: An Introduction into Supersensible World Knowledge and Human Purpose
CW 10	How Does One Attain Knowledge of Higher Worlds?
CW 11	From the Akasha-Chronicle

CW 12	Levels of Higher Knowledge
CW 13	Occult Science in Outline
CW 14	Four Mystery Dramas
CW 15	The Spiritual Guidance of the Individual and Humanity
CW 16	A Way to Human Self-Knowledge: Eight Meditations
CW 17	The Threshold of the Spiritual World. Aphoristic Comments
CW 18	The Riddles of Philosophy in Their History, Presented as an Outline
CW 19	Contained in CW 24
CW 20	The Riddles of the Human Being: Articulated and Unarticulated in the Thinking, Views and Opinions of a Series of German and Austrian Personalities
CW 21	The Riddles of the Soul
CW 22	Goethe's Spiritual Nature And Its Revelation In 'Faust' and through the 'Fairy Tale of the Snake and the Lily'
CW 23	The Central Points of the Social Question in the Necessities of Life in the Present and the Future
CW 24	Essays Concerning the Threefold Division of the Social Organism and the Period 1915–1921
CW 25	Cosmology, Religion and Philosophy
CW 26	Anthroposophical Leading Thoughts
CW 27	Fundamentals for Expansion of the Art of Healing according to Spiritual-Scientific Insights
CW 28	The Course of My Life
CW 29	Collected Essays on Dramaturgy, 1889–1900
CW 30	Methodical Foundations of Anthroposophy: Collected Essays on Philosophy, Natural Science, Aesthetics and Psychology, 1884–1901
CW 31	Collected Essays on Culture and Current Events, 1887–1901
CW 32	Collected Essays on Literature, 1884–1902
CW 33	Biographies and Biographical Sketches, 1894–1905
CW 34	Lucifer-Gnosis: Foundational Essays on Anthroposophy and Reports from the Periodicals 'Lucifer' and 'Lucifer-Gnosis,' 1903–1908
CW 35	Philosophy and Anthroposophy: Collected Essays, 1904–1923
CW 36	The Goetheanum-Idea in the Middle of the Cultural Crisis of the Present: Collected Essays from the Periodical 'Das Goetheanum,' 1921–1925
CW 37	Now in CWs 260a and 251
CW 38	Letters, Vol. 1: 1881–1890
CW 39	Letters, Vol. 2: 1890–1925
CW 40	Truth-Wrought Words
CW 40a	Sayings, Poems and Mantras; Supplementary Volume
CW 42	Now in CWs 264–266
CW 43	Stage Adaptations
CW 44	On the Four Mystery Dramas. Sketches, Fragments and Paralipomena on the Four Mystery Dramas
CW 45	Anthroposophy: A Fragment from the Year 1910

Public Lectures

CW 51	On Philosophy, History and Literature
CW 52	Spiritual Teachings Concerning the Soul and Observation of the World
CW 53	The Origin and Goal of the Human Being
CW 54	The Riddles of the World and Anthroposophy
CW 55	Knowledge of the Supersensible in Our Times and Its Meaning for Life Today
CW 56	Knowledge of the Soul and of the Spirit
CW 57	Where and How Does One Find the Spirit?
CW 58	The Metamorphoses of the Soul Life. Paths of Soul Experiences: Part One
CW 59	The Metamorphoses of the Soul Life. Paths of Soul Experiences: Part Two
CW 60	The Answers of Spiritual Science to the Biggest Questions of Existence
CW 61	Human History in the Light of Spiritual Research
CW 62	Results of Spiritual Research
CW 63	Spiritual Science as a Treasure for Life
CW 64	Out of Destiny-Burdened Times
CW 65	Out of Central European Spiritual Life
CW 66	Spirit and Matter, Life and Death
CW 67	The Eternal in the Human Soul. Immortality and Freedom
CW 68	Public lectures in various cities, 1906–1918
CW 69	Public lectures in various cities, 1906–1918
CW 70	Public lectures in various cities, 1906–1918
CW 71	Public lectures in various cities, 1906–1918
CW 72	Freedom—Immortality—Social Life
CW 73	The Supplementing of the Modern Sciences through Anthroposophy
CW 73a	Specialized Fields of Knowledge and Anthroposophy
CW 74	The Philosophy of Thomas Aquinas
CW 75	Public lectures in various cities, 1906–1918
CW 76	The Fructifying Effect of Anthroposophy on Specialized Fields
CW 77a	The Task of Anthroposophy in Relation to Science and Life: The Darmstadt College Course
CW 77b	Art and Anthroposophy. The Goetheanum-Impulse
CW 78	Anthroposophy, Its Roots of Knowledge and Fruits for Life
CW 79	The Reality of the Higher Worlds
CW 80	Public lectures in various cities, 1922
CW 81	Renewal-Impulses for Culture and Science—Berlin College Course
CW 82	So that the Human Being Can Become a Complete Human Being
CW 83	Western and Eastern World-Contrast. Paths to Understanding It through Anthroposophy
CW 84	What Did the Goetheanum Intend and What Should Anthroposophy Do?

Lectures to the Members of the Anthroposophical Society

CW 88	Concerning the Astral World and Devachan
CW 89	Consciousness—Life—Form. Fundamental Principles of a Spiritual-Scientific Cosmology
CW 90	Participant Notes from the Lectures during the Years 1903–1905
CW 91	Participant Notes from the Lectures during the Years 1903–1905
CW 92	The Occult Truths of Ancient Myths and Sagas
CW 93	The Temple Legend and the Golden Legend
CW 93a	Fundamentals of Esotericism
CW 94	Cosmogony. Popular Occultism. The Gospel of John. The Theosophy in the Gospel of John
CW 95	At the Gates of Theosophy
CW 96	Origin-Impulses of Spiritual Science. Christian Esotericism in the Light of New Spirit-Knowledge
CW 97	The Christian Mystery
CW 98	Nature Beings and Spirit Beings—Their Effects in Our Visible World
CW 99	The Theosophy of the Rosicrucians
CW 100	Human Development and Christ-Knowledge
CW 101	Myths and Legends. Occult Signs and Symbols
CW 102	The Working into Human Beings by Spiritual Beings
CW 103	The Gospel of John
CW 104	The Apocalypse of John
CW 104a	From the Picture-Script of the Apocalypse of John
CW 105	Universe, Earth, the Human Being: Their Being and Development, as well as Their Reflection in the Connection between Egyptian Mythology and Modern Culture
CW 106	Egyptian Myths and Mysteries in Relation to the Active Spiritual Forces of the Present
CW 107	Spiritual-Scientific Knowledge of the Human Being
CW 108	Answering the Questions of Life and the World through Anthroposophy
CW 109	The Principle of Spiritual Economy in Connection with the Question of Reincarnation. An Aspect of the Spiritual Guidance of Humanity
CW 110	The Spiritual Hierarchies and Their Reflection in the Physical World. Zodiac, Planets and Cosmos
CW 111	Contained in CW 109
CW 112	The Gospel of John in Relation to the Three Other Gospels, Especially the Gospel of Luke
CW 113	The Orient in the Light of the Occident. The Children of Lucifer and the Brothers of Christ
CW 114	The Gospel of Luke
CW 115	Anthroposophy—Psychosophy—Pneumatosophy
CW 116	The Christ-Impulse and the Development of 'I'-Consciousness
CW 117	The Deeper Secrets of the Development of Humanity in Light of the Gospels

CW 118 The Event of the Christ-Appearance in the Etheric World
CW 119 Macrocosm and Microcosm. The Large World and the Small World. Soul-Questions, Life-Questions, Spirit-Questions
CW 120 The Revelation of Karma
CW 121 The Mission of Individual Folk-Souls in Connection with Germanic-Nordic Mythology
CW 122 The Secrets of the Biblical Creation-Story. The Six-Day Work in the First Book of Moses
CW 123 The Gospel of Matthew
CW 124 Excursus in the Area of the Gospel of Mark
CW 125 Paths and Goals of the Spiritual Human Being. Life Questions in the Light of Spiritual Science
CW 126 Occult History. Esoteric Observations of the Karmic Relationships of Personalities and Events of World History
CW 127 The Mission of the New Spiritual Revelation. The Christ-Event as the Middle-Point of Earth Evolution
CW 128 An Occult Physiology
CW 129 Wonders of the World, Trials of the Soul, and Revelations of the Spirit
CW 130 Esoteric Christianity and the Spiritual Guidance of Humanity
CW 131 From Jesus to Christ
CW 132 Evolution from the View Point of the Truth
CW 133 The Earthly and the Cosmic Human Being
CW 134 The World of the Senses and the World of the Spirit
CW 135 Reincarnation and Karma and their Meaning for the Culture of the Present
CW 136 The Spiritual Beings in Celestial Bodies and the Realms of Nature
CW 137 The Human Being in the Light of Occultism, Theosophy and Philosophy
CW 138 On Initiation. On Eternity and the Passing Moment. On the Light of the Spirit and the Darkness of Life
CW 139 The Gospel of Mark
CW 140 Occult Investigation into the Life between Death and New Birth. The Living Interaction between Life and Death
CW 141 Life between Death and New Birth in Relationship to Cosmic Facts
CW 142 The Bhagavad Gita and the Letters of Paul
CW 143 Experiences of the Supersensible. Three Paths of the Soul to Christ
CW 144 The Mysteries of the East and of Christianity
CW 145 What Significance Does Occult Development of the Human Being Have for the Sheaths—Physical Body, Etheric Body, Astral Body, and Self?
CW 146 The Occult Foundations of the Bhagavad Gita
CW 147 The Secrets of the Threshold
CW 148 Out of Research in the Akasha: The Fifth Gospel
CW 149 Christ and the Spiritual World. Concerning the Search for the Holy Grail

CW 150	The World of the Spirit and Its Extension into Physical Existence; The Influence of the Dead in the World of the Living
CW 151	Human Thought and Cosmic Thought
CW 152	Preliminary Stages to the Mystery of Golgotha
CW 153	The Inner Being of the Human Being and Life Between Death and New Birth
CW 154	How does One Gain an Understanding of the Spiritual World? The Flowing in of Spiritual Impulses from out of the World of the Deceased
CW 155	Christ and the Human Soul. Concerning the Meaning of Life. Theosophical Morality. Anthroposophy and Christianity
CW 156	Occult Reading and Occult Hearing
CW 157	Human Destinies and the Destiny of Peoples
CW 157a	The Formation of Destiny and the Life after Death
CW 158	The Connection Between the Human Being and the Elemental World. Kalevala—Olaf Åsteson—The Russian People—The World as the Result of the Influences of Equilibrium
CW 159	The Mystery of Death. The Nature and Significance of Middle Europe and the European Folk Spirits
CW 160	In CW 159
CW 161	Paths of Spiritual Knowledge and the Renewal of the Artistic Worldview
CW 162	Questions of Art and Life in Light of Spiritual Science
CW 163	Coincidence, Necessity and Providence. Imaginative Knowledge and the Processes after Death
CW 164	The Value of Thinking for a Knowledge That Satisfies the Human Being. The Relationship of Spiritual Science to Natural Science
CW 165	The Spiritual Unification of Humanity through the Christ-Impulse
CW 166	Necessity and Freedom in the Events of the World and in Human Action
CW 167	The Present and the Past in the Human Spirit
CW 168	The Connection between the Living and the Dead
CW 169	World-being and Selfhood
CW 170	The Riddle of the Human Being. The Spiritual Background of Human History. Cosmic and Human History, Vol. 1
CW 171	Inner Development-Impulses of Humanity. Goethe and the Crisis of the 19th Century. Cosmic and Human History, Vol. 2
CW 172	The Karma of the Vocation of the Human Being in Connection with Goethe's Life. Cosmic and Human History, Vol. 3
CW 173	Contemporary-Historical Considerations: The Karma of Untruthfulness, Part One. Cosmic and Human History, Vol. 4
CW 174	Contemporary-Historical Considerations: The Karma of Untruthfulness, Part Two. Cosmic and Human History, Vol. 5
CW 174a	Middle Europe between East and West. Cosmic and Human History, Vol. 6
CW 174b	The Spiritual Background of the First World War. Cosmic and Human History, Vol. 7

CW 175	Building Stones for an Understanding of the Mystery of Golgotha. Cosmic and Human Metamorphoses
CW 176	Truths of Evolution of the Individual and Humanity. The Karma of Materialism
CW 177	The Spiritual Background of the Outer World. The Fall of the Spirits of Darkness. Spiritual Beings and Their Effects, Vol. 1
CW 178	Individual Spiritual Beings and their Influence in the Soul of the Human Being. Spiritual Beings and their Effects, Vol. 2
CW 179	Spiritual Beings and Their Effects. Historical Necessity and Freedom. The Influences on Destiny from out of the World of the Dead. Spiritual Beings and Their Effects, Vol. 3
CW 180	Mystery Truths and Christmas Impulses. Ancient Myths and their Meaning. Spiritual Beings and Their Effects, Vol. 4
CW 181	Earthly Death and Cosmic Life. Anthroposophical Gifts for Life. Necessities of Consciousness for the Present and the Future.
CW 182	Death as Transformation of Life
CW 183	The Science of the Development of the Human Being
CW 184	The Polarity of Duration and Development in Human Life. The Cosmic Pre-History of Humanity
CW 185	Historical Symptomology
CW 185a	Historical-Developmental Foundations for Forming a Social Judgement
CW 186	The Fundamental Social Demands of Our Time—In Changed Situations
CW 187	How Can Humanity Find the Christ Again? The Threefold Shadow-Existence of our Time and the New Christ-Light
CW 188	Goetheanism, a Transformation-Impulse and Resurrection-Thought. Science of the Human Being and Science of Sociology
CW 189	The Social Question as a Question of Consciousness. The Spiritual Background of the Social Question, Vol. 1
CW 190	Impulses of the Past and the Future in Social Occurrences. The Spiritual Background of the Social Question, Vol. 2
CW 191	Social Understanding from Spiritual-Scientific Cognition. The Spiritual Background of the Social Question, Vol. 3
CW 192	Spiritual-Scientific Treatment of Social and Pedagogical Questions
CW 193	The Inner Aspect of the Social Riddle. Luciferic Past and Ahrimanic Future
CW 194	The Mission of Michael. The Revelation of the Actual Mysteries of the Human Being
CW 195	Cosmic New Year and the New Year Idea
CW 196	Spiritual and Social Transformations in the Development of Humanity
CW 197	Polarities in the Development of Humanity: West and East Materialism and Mysticism Knowledge and Belief
CW 198	Healing Factors for the Social Organism
CW 199	Spiritual Science as Knowledge of the Foundational Impulses of Social Formation

CW 200 The New Spirituality and the Christ-Experience of the 20th Century

CW 201 The Correspondences Between Microcosm and Macrocosm. The Human Being—A Hieroglyph of the Universe. The Human Being in Relationship with the Cosmos: 1

CW 202 The Bridge between the World-Spirituality and the Physical Aspect of the Human Being. The Search for the New Isis, the Divine Sophia. The Human Being in Relationship with the Cosmos: 2

CW 203 The Responsibility of Human Beings for the Development of the World through their Spiritual Connection with the Planet Earth and the World of the Stars. The Human Being in Relationship with the Cosmos: 3

CW 204 Perspectives of the Development of Humanity. The Materialistic Knowledge-Impulse and the Task of Anthroposophy. The Human Being in Relationship with the Cosmos: 4

CW 205 Human Development, World-Soul, and World-Spirit. Part One: The Human Being as a Being of Body and Soul in Relationship to the World. The Human Being in Relationship with the Cosmos: 5

CW 206 Human Development, World-Soul, and World-Spirit. Part Two: The Human Being as a Spiritual Being in the Process of Historical Development. The Human Being in Relationship with the Cosmos: 6

CW 207 Anthroposophy as Cosmosophy. Part One: Characteristic Features of the Human Being in the Earthly and the Cosmic Realms. The Human Being in Relationship with the Cosmos: 7

CW 208 Anthroposophy as Cosmosophy. Part Two: The Forming of the Human Being as the Result of Cosmic Influence. The Human Being in Relationship with the Cosmos: 8

CW 209 Nordic and Central European Spiritual Impulses. The Festival of the Appearance of Christ. The Human Being in Relationship with the Cosmos: 9

CW 210 Old and New Methods of Initiation. Drama and Poetry in the Change of Consciousness in the Modern Age

CW 211 The Sun Mystery and the Mystery of Death and Resurrection. Exoteric and Esoteric Christianity

CW 212 Human Soul Life and Spiritual Striving in Connection with World and Earth Development

CW 213 Human Questions and World Answers

CW 214 The Mystery of the Trinity: The Human Being in Relationship with the Spiritual World in the Course of Time

CW 215 Philosophy, Cosmology, and Religion in Anthroposophy

CW 216 The Fundamental Impulses of the World-Historical Development of Humanity

CW 217 Spiritually Active Forces in the Coexistence of the Older and Younger Generations. Pedagogical Course for Youth

CW 217a	Youth's Cognitive Task
CW 218	Spiritual Connections in the Forming of the Human Organism
CW 219	The Relationship of the World of the Stars to the Human Being, and of the Human Being to the World of the Stars. The Spiritual Communion of Humanity
CW 220	Living Knowledge of Nature. Intellectual Fall and Spiritual Redemption
CW 221	Earth-Knowing and Heaven-Insight
CW 222	The Imparting of Impulses to World-Historical Events through Spiritual Powers
CW 223	The Cycle of the Year as Breathing Process of the Earth and the Four Great Festival-Seasons. Anthroposophy and the Human Heart (Gemüt)
CW 224	The Human Soul and its Connection with Divine-Spiritual Individualities. The Internalization of the Festivals of the Year
CW 225	Three Perspectives of Anthroposophy. Cultural Phenomena observed from a Spiritual-Scientific Perspective
CW 226	Human Being, Human Destiny, and World Development
CW 227	Initiation-Knowledge
CW 228	Science of Initiation and Knowledge of the Stars. The Human Being in the Past, the Present, and the Future from the Viewpoint of the Development of Consciousness
CW 229	The Experiencing of the Course of the Year in Four Cosmic Imaginations
CW 230	The Human Being as Harmony of the Creative, Building, and Formative World-Word
CW 231	The Supersensible Human Being, Understood Anthroposophically
CW 232	The Forming of the Mysteries
CW 233	World History Illuminated by Anthroposophy and as the Foundation for Knowledge of the Human Spirit
CW 233a	Mystery Sites of the Middle Ages: Rosicrucianism and the Modern Initiation-Principle. The Festival of Easter as Part of the History of the Mysteries of Humanity
CW 234	Anthroposophy. A Summary after 21 Years
CW 235	Esoteric Observations of Karmic Relationships in 6 Volumes, Vol. 1
CW 236	Esoteric Observations of Karmic Relationships in 6 Volumes, Vol. 2
CW 237	Esoteric Observations of Karmic Relationships in 6 Volumes, Vol. 3: The Karmic Relationships of the Anthroposophical Movement
CW 238	Esoteric Observations of Karmic Relationships in 6 Volumes, Vol. 4: The Spiritual Life of the Present in Relationship to the Anthroposophical Movement
CW 239	Esoteric Observations of Karmic Relationships in 6 Volumes, Vol. 5

CW 240	Esoteric Observations of Karmic Relationships in 6 Volumes, Vol. 6
CW 243	The Consciousness of the Initiate
CW 245	Instructions for an Esoteric Schooling
CW 250	The Building-Up of the Anthroposophical Society. From the Beginning to the Outbreak of the First World War
CW 251	The History of the Goetheanum Building-Association
CW 252	Life in the Anthroposophical Society from the First World War to the Burning of the First Goetheanum
CW 253	The Problems of Living Together in the Anthroposophical Society. On the Dornach Crisis of 1915. With Highlights on Swedenborg's Clairvoyance, the Views of Freudian Psychoanalysts, and the Concept of Love in Relation to Mysticism
CW 254	The Occult Movement in the 19th Century and Its Relationship to World Culture. Significant Points from the Exoteric Cultural Life around the Middle of the 19th Century
CW 255	Rudolf Steiner during the First World War
CW 255a	Anthroposophy and the Reformation of Society. On the History of the Threefold Movement
CW 255b	Anthroposophy and Its Opponents, 1919–1921
CW 256	How Can the Anthroposophical Movement Be Financed?
CW 256a	Futurum, Inc. / International Laboratories, Inc.
CW 256b	The Coming Day, Inc.
CW 257	Anthroposophical Community-Building
CW 258	The History of and Conditions for the Anthroposophical Movement in Relationship to the Anthroposophical Society. A Stimulus to Self-Contemplation
CW 259	The Year of Destiny 1923 in the History of the Anthroposophical Society. From the Burning of the Goetheanum to the Christmas Conference
CW 260	The Christmas Conference for the Founding of the General Anthroposophical Society
CW 260a	The Constitution of the General Anthroposophical Society and the School for Spiritual Science. The Rebuilding of the Goetheanum
CW 261	Our Dead. Addresses, Words of Remembrance, and Meditative Verses, 1906–1924
CW 262	Rudolf Steiner and Marie Steiner-von Sivers: Correspondence and Documents, 1901–1925
CW 263/1	Rudolf Steiner and Edith Maryon: Correspondence: Letters, Verses, Sketches, 1912–1924
CW 264	On the History and the Contents of the First Section of the Esoteric School from 1904 to 1914. Letters, Newsletters, Documents, Lectures
CW 265	On the History and from the Contents of the Ritual-Knowledge Section of the Esoteric School from 1904 to 1914. Documents, and Lectures from the Years 1906 to 1914, as well as on New Approaches to Ritual-Knowledge Work in the Years 1921–1924

CW 266/1	From the Contents of the Esoteric Lessons. Volume 1: 1904–1909. Notes from Memory of Participants. Meditation texts from the notes of Rudolf Steiner
CW 266/2	From the Contents of the Esoteric Lessons. Volume 2: 1910–1912. Notes from Memory of Participants
CW 266/3	From the Contents of the Esoteric Lessons. Volume 3: 1913, 1914 and 1920–1923. Notes from Memory of Participants. Meditation texts from the notes of Rudolf Steiner
CW 267	Soul-Exercises: Vol. 1: Exercises with Word and Image Meditations for the Methodological Development of Higher Powers of Knowledge, 1904–1924
CW 268	Soul-Exercises: Vol. 2: Mantric Verses, 1903–1925
CW 269	Ritual Texts for the Celebration of the Free Christian Religious Instruction. The Collected Verses for Teachers and Students of the Waldorf School
CW 270	Esoteric Instructions for the First Class of the School for Spiritual Science at the Goetheanum 1924, 4 Volumes
CW 271	Art and Knowledge of Art. Foundations of a New Aesthetic
CW 272	Spiritual-Scientific Commentary on Goethe's 'Faust' in Two Volumes. Vol. 1: Faust, the Striving Human Being
CW 273	Spiritual-Scientific Commentary on Goethe's 'Faust' in Two Volumes. Vol. 2: The Faust-Problem
CW 274	Addresses for the Christmas Plays from the Old Folk Traditions
CW 275	Art in the Light of Mystery-Wisdom
CW 276	The Artistic in Its Mission in the World. The Genius of Language. The World of Self-Revealing Radiant Appearances—Anthroposophy and Art. Anthroposophy and Poetry
CW 277	Eurythmy. The Revelation of the Speaking Soul
CW 277a	The Origin and Development of Eurythmy
CW 278	Eurythmy as Visible Song
CW 279	Eurythmy as Visible Speech
CW 280	The Method and Nature of Speech Formation
CW 281	The Art of Recitation and Declamation
CW 282	Speech Formation and Dramatic Art
CW 283	The Nature of Things Musical and the Experience of Tone in the Human Being
CW 284/285	Images of Occult Seals and Pillars. The Munich Congress of Whitsun 1907 and Its Consequences
CW 286	Paths to a New Style of Architecture. 'And the Building Becomes Human'
CW 287	The Building at Dornach as a Symbol of Historical Becoming and an Artistic Transformation Impulse
CW 288	Style-Forms in the Living Organic
CW 289	The Building-Idea of the Goetheanum: Lectures with Slides from the Years 1920–1921
CW 290	The Building-Idea of the Goetheanum: Lectures with Slides from the Years 1920–1921

CW 291	The Nature of Colours
CW 291a	Knowledge of Colours. Supplementary Volume to 'The Nature of Colours'
CW 292	Art History as Image of Inner Spiritual Impulses
CW 293	General Knowledge of the Human Being as the Foundation of Pedagogy
CW 294	The Art of Education, Methodology and Didactics
CW 295	The Art of Education: Seminar Discussions and Lectures on Lesson Planning
CW 296	The Question of Education as a Social Question
CW 297	The Idea and Practice of the Waldorf School
CW 297a	Education for Life: Self-Education and the Practice of Pedagogy
CW 298	Rudolf Steiner in the Waldorf School
CW 299	Spiritual-Scientific Observations on Speech
CW 300a	Conferences with the Teachers of the Free Waldorf School in Stuttgart, 1919 to 1924, in 3 Volumes, Vol. 1
CW 300b	Conferences with the Teachers of the Free Waldorf School in Stuttgart, 1919 to 1924, in 3 Volumes, Vol. 2
CW 300c	Conferences with the Teachers of the Free Waldorf School in Stuttgart, 1919 to 1924, in 3 Volumes, Vol. 3
CW 301	The Renewal of Pedagogical-Didactical Art through Spiritual Science
CW 302	Knowledge of the Human Being and the Forming of Class Lessons
CW 302a	Education and Teaching from a Knowledge of the Human Being
CW 303	The Healthy Development of the Human Being
CW 304	Methods of Education and Teaching Based on Anthroposophy
CW 304a	Anthroposophical Knowledge of the Human Being and Pedagogy
CW 305	The Soul-Spiritual Foundational Forces of the Art of Education. Spiritual Values in Education and Social Life
CW 306	Pedagogical Praxis from the Viewpoint of a Spiritual-Scientific Knowledge of the Human Being. The Education of the Child and Young Human Beings
CW 307	The Spiritual Life of the Present and Education
CW 308	The Method of Teaching and the Life-Requirements for Teaching
CW 309	Anthroposophical Pedagogy and Its Prerequisites
CW 310	The Pedagogical Value of a Knowledge of the Human Being and the Cultural Value of Pedagogy
CW 311	The Art of Education from an Understanding of the Being of Humanity
CW 312	Spiritual Science and Medicine
CW 313	Spiritual-Scientific Viewpoints on Therapy
CW 314	Physiology and Therapy Based on Spiritual Science
CW 315	Curative Eurythmy
CW 316	Meditative Observations and Instructions for a Deepening of the Art of Healing
CW 317	The Curative Education Course

CW 318 The Working Together of Doctors and Pastors
CW 319 Anthroposophical Knowledge of the Human Being and Medicine
CW 320 Spiritual-Scientific Impulses for the Development of Physics 1: The First Natural-Scientific Course: Light, Colour, Tone, Mass, Electricity, Magnetism
CW 321 Spiritual-Scientific Impulses for the Development of Physics 2: The Second Natural-Scientific Course: Warmth at the Border of Positive and Negative Materiality
CW 322 The Borders of the Knowledge of Nature
CW 323 The Relationship of the various Natural-Scientific Fields to Astronomy
CW 324 Nature Observation, Mathematics, and Scientific Experimentation and Results from the Viewpoint of Anthroposophy
CW 324a The Fourth Dimension in Mathematics and Reality
CW 325 Natural Science and the World-Historical Development of Humanity since Ancient Times
CW 326 The Moment of the Coming Into Being of Natural Science in World History and Its Development Since Then
CW 327 Spiritual-Scientific Foundations for Success in Farming. The Agricultural Course
CW 328 The Social Question
CW 329 The Liberation of the Human Being as the Foundation for a New Social Form
CW 330 The Renewal of the Social Organism
CW 331 Work-Council and Socialization
CW 332 The Alliance for Threefolding and the Total Reform of Society. The Council on Culture and the Liberation of the Spiritual Life
CW 332a The Social Future
CW 333 Freedom of Thought and Social Forces
CW 334 From the Unified State to the Threefold Social Organism
CW 335 The Crisis of the Present and the Path to Healthy Thinking
CW 336 The Great Questions of the Times and Anthroposophical Spiritual Knowledge
CW 337a Social Ideas, Social Reality, Social Practice, Vol. 1: Question-and-Answer Evenings and Study Evenings of the Alliance for the Threefold Social Organism in Stuttgart, 1919–1920
CW 337b Social Ideas, Social Realities, Social Practice, Vol. 2: Discussion Evenings of the Swiss Alliance for the Threefold Social Organism
CW 338 How Does One Work on Behalf of the Impulse for the Threefold Social Organism?
CW 339 Anthroposophy, Threefold Social Organism, and the Art of Public Speaking
CW 340 The National-Economics Course. The Tasks of a New Science of Economics, Volume 1
CW 341 The National-Economics Seminar. The Tasks of a New Science of Economics, Volume 2

CW 342 Lectures and Courses on Christian Religious Work, Vol. 1: Anthroposophical Foundations for a Renewed Christian Religious Working

CW 343 Lectures and Courses on Christian Religious Work, Vol. 2: Spiritual Knowledge—Religious Feeling—Cultic Doing

CW 344 Lectures and Courses on Christian Religious Work, Vol. 3: Lectures at the Founding of the Christian Community

CW 345 Lectures and Courses on Christian Religious Work, Vol. 4: Concerning the Nature of the Working Word

CW 346 Lectures and Courses on Christian Religious Work, Vol. 5: The Apocalypse and the Work of the Priest

CW 347 The Knowledge of the Nature of the Human Being According to Body, Soul and Spirit. On Earlier Conditions of the Earth

CW 348 On Health and Illness. Foundations of a Spiritual-Scientific Doctrine of the Senses

CW 349 On the Life of the Human Being and of the Earth. On the Nature of Christianity

CW 350 Rhythms in the Cosmos and in the Human Being. How Does One Come To See the Spiritual World?

CW 351 The Human Being and the World. The Influence of the Spirit in Nature. On the Nature of Bees

CW 352 Nature and the Human Being Observed Spiritual-Scientifically

CW 353 The History of Humanity and the World-Views of the Folk Cultures

CW 354 The Creation of the World and the Human Being. Life on Earth and the Influence of the Stars

SIGNIFICANT EVENTS IN THE LIFE OF RUDOLF STEINER

1829: June 23: birth of Johann Steiner (1829–1910)—Rudolf Steiner's father—in Geras, Lower Austria.

1834: May 8: birth of Franciska Blie (1834–1918)—Rudolf Steiner's mother—in Horn, Lower Austria. 'My father and mother were both children of the glorious Lower Austrian forest district north of the Danube.'

1860: May 16: marriage of Johann Steiner and Franciska Blie.

1861: February 25: birth of *Rudolf Joseph Lorenz Steiner* in Kraljevec, Croatia, near the border with Hungary, where Johann Steiner works as a telegrapher for the South Austria Railroad. Rudolf Steiner is baptized two days later, February 27, the date usually given as his birthday.

1862: Summer: the family moves to Mödling, Lower Austria.

1863: The family moves to Pottschach, Lower Austria, near the Styrian border, where Johann Steiner becomes stationmaster. 'The view stretched to the mountains ... majestic peaks in the distance and the sweet charm of nature in the immediate surroundings.'

1864: November 15: birth of Rudolf Steiner's sister, Leopoldine (d. November 1, 1927). She will become a seamstress and live with her parents for the rest of her life.

1866: July 28: birth of Rudolf Steiner's deaf-mute brother, Gustav (d. May 1, 1941).

1867: Rudolf Steiner enters the village school. Following a disagreement between his father and the schoolmaster, whose wife falsely accused the boy of causing a commotion, Rudolf Steiner is taken out of school and taught at home.

1868: A critical experience. Unknown to the family, an aunt dies in a distant town. Sitting in the station waiting room, Rudolf Steiner sees her 'form,' which speaks to him, asking for help. 'Beginning with this experience, a new soul life began in the boy, one in which not only the outer trees and mountains spoke to him, but also the worlds that lay behind them. From this moment on, the boy began to live with the spirits of nature...'

1869: The family moves to the peaceful, rural village of Neudörfl, near Wiener-Neustadt in present-day Austria. Rudolf Steiner attends the village school. Because of the 'unorthodoxy' of his writing and spelling, he has to do 'extra lessons.'

1870: Through a book lent to him by his tutor, he discovers geometry: 'To grasp something purely in the spirit brought me inner happiness. I know that I first learned happiness through geometry.' The same tutor allows him to draw, while other students still struggle with their reading and writing. 'An artistic element' thus enters his education.

1871: Though his parents are not religious, Rudolf Steiner becomes a 'church child,' a favourite of the priest, who was 'an exceptional character.' 'Up to the age of ten or eleven, among those I came to know, he was far and away the most significant.' Among other things, he introduces Steiner to Copernican, heliocentric cosmology. As an altar boy, Rudolf Steiner serves at Masses, funerals, and Corpus Christi processions. At year's end, after an incident in which he escapes a thrashing, his father forbids him to go to church.

1872: Rudolf Steiner transfers to grammar school in Wiener-Neustadt, a five-mile walk from home, which must be done in all weathers.

1873–75: Through his teachers and on his own, Rudolf Steiner has many wonderful experiences with science and mathematics. Outside school, he teaches himself analytic geometry, trigonometry, differential equations, and calculus.

1876: Rudolf Steiner begins tutoring other students. He learns bookbinding from his father. He also teaches himself stenography.

1877: Rudolf Steiner discovers Kant's *Critique of Pure Reason*, which he reads and rereads. He also discovers and reads von Rotteck's *World History*.

1878: He studies extensively in contemporary psychology and philosophy.

1879: Rudolf Steiner graduates from high school with honours. His father is transferred to Inzersdorf, near Vienna. He uses his first visit to Vienna 'to purchase a great number of philosophy books'—Kant, Fichte, Schelling, and Hegel, as well as numerous histories of philosophy. His aim: to find a path from the 'I' to nature.

October 1879–1883: Rudolf Steiner attends the Technical College in Vienna—to study mathematics, chemistry, physics, mineralogy, botany, zoology, biology, geology, and mechanics—with a scholarship. He also attends lectures in history and literature, while avidly reading philosophy on his own. His two favourite professors are Karl Julius Schröer (German language and literature) and Edmund Reitlinger (physics). He also audits lectures by Robert Zimmermann on aesthetics and Franz Brentano on philosophy. During this year he begins his friendship with Moritz Zitter (1861–1921), who will help support him financially when he is in Berlin.

1880: Rudolf Steiner attends lectures on Schiller and Goethe by Karl Julius Schröer, who becomes his mentor. Also 'through a remarkable combination of circumstances,' he meets Felix Koguzki, a 'herb gatherer' and healer, who could 'see deeply into the secrets of nature.' Rudolf Steiner will meet and study with this 'emissary of the Master' throughout his time in Vienna.

1881: January: '... I didn't sleep a wink. I was busy with philosophical problems until about 12:30 a.m. Then, finally, I threw myself down on my couch. All my striving during the previous year had been to research whether the following statement by Schelling was true or not: *Within everyone dwells a secret, marvelous capacity to draw back from the stream of time—out of the self clothed in all that comes to us from outside—into our innermost being and there, in the immutable form of the Eternal, to look into ourselves*. I believe, and I am still quite certain of it, that I discovered this capacity in myself; I had long had an inkling of it. Now the whole of idealist philosophy stood before me in modified form. What's a sleepless night compared to that!'

Rudolf Steiner begins communicating with leading thinkers of the day, who send him books in return, which he reads eagerly.

July: 'I am not one of those who dives into the day like an animal in human form. I pursue a quite specific goal, an idealistic aim—knowledge of the truth! This cannot be done offhandedly. It requires the greatest striving in the world, free of all egotism, and equally of all resignation.'

August: Steiner puts down on paper for the first time thoughts for a 'Philosophy of Freedom.' 'The striving for the absolute: this human yearning is freedom.' He also seeks to outline a 'peasant philosophy,' describing what the worldview of a 'peasant'—one who lives close to the earth and the old ways—really is.

1881–1882: Felix Koguzki, the herb gatherer, reveals himself to be the envoy of another, higher initiatory personality, who instructs Rudolf Steiner to penetrate Fichte's philosophy and to master modern scientific thinking as a preparation for right entry into the spirit. This 'Master' also teaches him the double (evolutionary and involutionary) nature of time.

1882: Through the offices of Karl Julius Schröer, Rudolf Steiner is asked by Joseph Kürschner to edit Goethe's scientific works for the *Deutschen National-Literatur* edition. He writes 'A Possible Critique of Atomistic Concepts' and sends it to Friedrich Theodor Vischer.

1883: Rudolf Steiner completes his college studies and begins work on the Goethe project.

1884: First volume of Goethe's *Scientific Writings* (CW 1) appears (March). He lectures on Goethe and Lessing, and Goethe's approach to science. In July, he enters the household of Ladislaus and Pauline Specht as tutor to the four Specht boys. He will live there until 1890. At this time, he meets Josef Breuer (1842–1925), the co-author with Sigmund Freud of *Studies in Hysteria*, who is the Specht family doctor.

1885: While continuing to edit Goethe's writings, Rudolf Steiner reads deeply in contemporary philosophy (Eduard von Hartmann, Johannes Volkelt, and Richard Wahle, among others).

1886: May: Rudolf Steiner sends Kürschner the manuscript of *Outlines of Goethe's Theory of Knowledge* (CW 2), which appears in October, and which he sends out widely. He also meets the poet Marie Eugenie Delle Grazie and writes 'Nature and Our Ideals' for her. He attends her salon, where he meets many priests, theologians, and philosophers, who will become his friends. Meanwhile, the director of the Goethe Archive in Weimar requests his collaboration with the *Sophien* edition of Goethe's works, particularly the writings on colour.

1887: At the beginning of the year, Rudolf Steiner is very sick. As the year progresses and his health improves, he becomes increasingly 'a man of letters,' lecturing, writing essays, and taking part in Austrian cultural life. In August–September, the second volume of Goethe's *Scientific Writings* appears.

1888: January–July: Rudolf Steiner assumes editorship of the 'German Weekly' (*Deutsche Wochenschrift*). He begins lecturing more intensively, giving, for example, a lecture titled 'Goethe as Father of a New Aesthetics.' He meets and becomes soul friends with Friedrich Eckstein (1861–1939), a vegetarian, philosopher of symbolism, alchemist, and musician, who will introduce him to various spiritual currents (including Theosophy) and with whom he will meditate and interpret esoteric and alchemical texts.

1889: Rudolf Steiner first reads Nietzsche (*Beyond Good and Evil*). He encounters Theosophy again and learns of Madame Blavatsky in the Theosophical circle around Marie Lang (1858–1934). Here he also meets well-known figures of Austrian life, as well as esoteric figures like the occultist Franz Hartmann and Karl Leinigen-Billigen (translator of C.G. Harrison's *The Transcendental Universe*). During this period, Steiner first reads A.P. Sinnett's *Esoteric Buddhism* and Mabel Collins's *Light on the Path*. He also begins travelling, visiting Budapest, Weimar, and Berlin (where he meets philosopher Eduard von Hartmann).

1890: Rudolf Steiner finishes volume 3 of Goethe's scientific writings. He begins his doctoral dissertation, which will become *Truth and Science* (CW 3). He also meets the poet and feminist Rosa Mayreder (1858–1938), with whom he can exchange his most intimate thoughts. In September, Rudolf Steiner moves to Weimar to work in the Goethe-Schiller Archive.

1891: Volume 3 of the Kürschner edition of Goethe appears. Meanwhile, Rudolf Steiner edits Goethe's studies in mineralogy and scientific writings for the *Sophien* edition. He meets Ludwig Laistner of the Cotta Publishing Company, who asks for a book on the basic question of metaphysics. From this will result, ultimately, *The Philosophy of Freedom* (CW 4), which will be published not by Cotta but by Emil Felber. In October, Rudolf Steiner takes the oral exam for a doctorate in philosophy, mathematics, and mechanics at Rostock University, receiving his doctorate on the twenty-sixth. In November, he gives his first lecture on Goethe's 'Fairy Tale' in Vienna.

1892: Rudolf Steiner continues work at the Goethe-Schiller Archive and on his *Philosophy of Freedom*. *Truth and Science*, his doctoral dissertation, is published. Steiner undertakes to write introductions to books on Schopenhauer and Jean Paul for Cotta. At year's end, he finds lodging with Anna Eunike, née Schulz (1853–1911), a widow with four daughters and a son. He also develops a friendship with Otto Erich Hartleben (1864–1905) with whom he shares literary interests.

1893: Rudolf Steiner begins his habit of producing many reviews and articles. In March, he gives a lecture titled 'Hypnotism, with Reference to Spiritism.' In September, volume 4 of the Kürschner edition is completed. In November, *The Philosophy of Freedom* appears. This year, too, he meets John Henry Mackay (1864–1933), the anarchist, and Max Stirner, a scholar and biographer.

1894: Rudolf Steiner meets Elisabeth Förster Nietzsche, the philosopher's sister, and begins to read Nietzsche in earnest, beginning with the as yet unpublished *Antichrist*. He also meets Ernst Haeckel (1834–1919). In the fall, he begins to write *Nietzsche, A Fighter against His Time* (CW 5).

1895: May, *Nietzsche, A Fighter against His Time* appears.

1896: January 22: Rudolf Steiner sees Friedrich Nietzsche for the first and only time. Moves between the Nietzsche and the Goethe-Schiller Archives, where he completes his work before year's end. He falls out with Elisabeth Förster Nietzsche, thus ending his association with the Nietzsche Archive.

1897: Rudolf Steiner finishes the manuscript of *Goethe's Worldview* (CW 6). He moves to Berlin with Anna Eunike and begins editorship of the *Magazin für Literatur*. From now on, Steiner will write countless reviews, literary and philosophical articles, and so on. He begins lecturing at the 'Free Literary Society.' In September, he attends the Zionist Congress in Basel. He sides with Dreyfus in the Dreyfus affair.

1898: Rudolf Steiner is very active as an editor in the political, artistic, and theatrical life of Berlin. He becomes friendly with John Henry Mackay and poet Ludwig Jacobowski (1868–1900). He joins Jacobowski's circle of writers, artists, and scientists—'The Coming Ones' (*Die Kommenden*)—and contributes lectures to the group until 1903. He also lectures at the 'League for College Pedagogy.' He writes an article for Goethe's sesquicentennial, 'Goethe's Secret Revelation,' on the 'Fairy Tale of the Green Snake and the Beautiful Lily.'

1898–99: 'This was a trying time for my soul as I looked at Christianity. . . . I was able to progress only by contemplating, by means of spiritual perception, the evolution of Christianity. . . . Conscious knowledge of real Christianity began to dawn in me around the turn of the century. This seed continued to develop. My soul trial occurred shortly before the beginning of the twentieth century. It was decisive for my soul's development that I stood spiritually before the Mystery of Golgotha in a deep and solemn celebration of knowledge.'

1899: Rudolf Steiner begins teaching and giving lectures and lecture cycles at the Workers' College, founded by Wilhelm Liebknecht (1826–1900). He will continue to do so until 1904. Writes: *Literature and Spiritual Life in the Nineteenth Century; Individualism in Philosophy*; *Haeckel and His Opponents; Poetry in the Present;* and begins what will become (fifteen years later) *The Riddles of Philosophy* (CW 18). He also meets many artists and writers, including Käthe Kollwitz, Stefan Zweig, and Rainer Maria Rilke. On October 31, he marries Anna Eunike.

1900: 'I thought that the turn of the century must bring humanity a new light. It seemed to me that the separation of human thinking and willing from the spirit had peaked. A turn or reversal of direction in human evolution seemed to me a necessity.' Rudolf Steiner finishes *World and Life Views in the Nineteenth Century* (the second part of what will become *The Riddles of Philosophy*) and dedicates it to Ernst Haeckel. It is published in March. He continues lecturing at *Die Kommenden*, whose leadership he assumes after the death of Jacobowski. Also, he gives the Gutenberg Jubilee lecture before 7,000 typesetters and printers. In September, Rudolf Steiner is invited by Count and Countess Brockdorff to lecture in the Theosophical Library. His first lecture is on Nietzsche. His second lecture is titled 'Goethe's Secret Revelation.' October 6, he begins a lecture cycle on the mystics that will become *Mystics after Modernism* (CW 7). November-December: 'Marie von Sivers appears in the audience....' Also in November, Steiner gives his first lecture at the Giordano Bruno Bund (where he will continue to lecture until May, 1905). He speaks on Bruno and modern Rome, focusing on the importance of the philosophy of Thomas Aquinas as monism.

1901: In continual financial straits, Rudolf Steiner's early friends Moritz Zitter and Rosa Mayreder help support him. In October, he begins the lecture cycle *Christianity as Mystical Fact* (CW 8) at the Theosophical Library. In November, he gives his first 'Theosophical lecture' on Goethe's 'Fairy Tale' in Hamburg at the invitation of Wilhelm Hubbe-Schleiden. He also attends a gathering to celebrate the founding of the Theosophical Society at Count and Countess Brockdorff's. He gives a lecture cycle, 'From Buddha to Christ,' for the circle of the *Kommenden*. November 17, Marie von Sivers asks Rudolf Steiner if Theosophy needs a Western-Christian spiritual movement (to complement Theosophy's Eastern emphasis). 'The question was posed. Now, following spiritual laws, I could begin to give an answer....' In December, Rudolf Steiner writes his first article for a Theosophical publication. At year's end, the Brockdorffs and possibly Wilhelm Hubbe-Schleiden ask Rudolf Steiner to join the Theosophical Society and undertake the leadership of the German section. Rudolf Steiner agrees, on the condition that Marie von Sivers (then in Italy) work with him.

1902: Beginning in January, Rudolf Steiner attends the opening of the Workers' School in Spandau with Rosa Luxemberg (1870–1919). January 17, Rudolf Steiner joins the Theosophical Society. In April, he is asked to become general secretary of the German Section of the Theosophical Society, and works on preparations for its founding. In July, he visits London for a Theosophical congress. He meets Bertram Keightly, G.R.S. Mead, A.P. Sinnett, and Annie Besant, among others. In September, *Christianity as Mystical Fact* appears. In October, Rudolf Steiner gives his first public lecture on Theosophy ('Monism and Theosophy') to about three hundred people at the Giordano Bruno Bund. On October 19–21, the German Section of the Theosophical Society has its first meeting; Rudolf Steiner is the general secretary, and Annie Besant attends. Steiner lectures on practical karma studies. On October 23, Annie Besant inducts Rudolf Steiner into the Esoteric School of the Theosophical Society. On October 25, Steiner begins a weekly series of lectures: 'The Field of Theosophy.' During this year, Rudolf Steiner also first meets Ita Wegman (1876–1943), who will become his close collaborator in his final years.

1903: Rudolf Steiner holds about 300 lectures and seminars. In May, the first issue of the periodical *Luzifer* appears. In June, Rudolf Steiner visits

London for the first meeting of the Federation of the European Sections of the Theosophical Society, where he meets Colonel Olcott. He begins to write *Theosophy* (CW 9).

1904: Rudolf Steiner continues lecturing at the Workers' College and elsewhere (about 90 lectures), while lecturing intensively all over Germany among Theosophists (about 140 lectures). In February, he meets Carl Unger (1878–1929), who will become a member of the board of the Anthroposophical Society (1913). In March, he meets Michael Bauer (1871–1929), a Christian mystic, who will also be on the board. In May, *Theosophy* appears, with the dedication: 'To the spirit of Giordano Bruno.' Rudolf Steiner and Marie von Sivers visit London for meetings with Annie Besant. June: Rudolf Steiner and Marie von Sivers attend the meeting of the Federation of European Sections of the Theosophical Society in Amsterdam. In July, Steiner begins the articles in *Luzifer-Gnosis* that will become *How to Know Higher Worlds* (CW 10) and *Cosmic Memory* (CW 11). In September, Annie Besant visits Germany. In December, Steiner lectures on Freemasonry. He mentions the High Grade Masonry derived from John Yarker and represented by Theodore Reuss and Karl Kellner as a blank slate 'into which a good image could be placed.'

1905: This year, Steiner ends his non-Theosophical lecturing activity. Supported by Marie von Sivers, his Theosophical lecturing—both in public and in the Theosophical Society—increases significantly: 'The German Theosophical Movement is of exceptional importance.' Steiner recommends reading, among others, Fichte, Jacob Boehme, and Angelus Silesius. He begins to introduce Christian themes into Theosophy. He also begins to work with doctors (Felix Peipers and Ludwig Noll). In July, he is in London for the Federation of European Sections, where he attends a lecture by Annie Besant: 'I have seldom seen Mrs. Besant speak in so inward and heartfelt a manner. . . .' 'Through Mrs. Besant I have found the way to H.P. Blavatsky.' September to October, he gives a course of thirty-one lectures for a small group of esoteric students. In October, the annual meeting of the German Section of the Theosophical Society, which still remains very small, takes place. Rudolf Steiner reports membership has risen from 121 to 377 members. In November, seeking to establish esoteric 'continuity,' Rudolf Steiner and Marie von Sivers participate in a 'Memphis-Misraim' Masonic ceremony. They pay forty-five marks for membership. 'Yesterday, you saw how little remains of former esoteric institutions.' 'We are dealing only with a "framework". . . for the present, nothing lies behind it. The occult powers have completely withdrawn.'

1906: Expansion of Theosophical work. Rudolf Steiner gives about 245 lectures, only 44 of which take place in Berlin. Cycles are given in Paris, Leipzig, Stuttgart, and Munich. Esoteric work also intensifies. Rudolf Steiner begins writing *An Outline of Esoteric Science* (CW 13). In January, Rudolf Steiner receives permission (a patent) from the Great Orient of the Scottish A & A Thirty-Three Degree Rite of the Order of the Ancient

Freemasons of the Memphis-Misraim Rite to direct a chapter under the name 'Mystica Aeterna.' This will become the 'Cognitive-Ritual Section' (also called 'Misraim Service') of the Esoteric School. (See: *Freemasonry and Ritual Work: The Misraim Service*, CW 265). During this time, Steiner also meets Albert Schweitzer. In May, he is in Paris, where he visits Edouard Schuré. Many Russians attend his lectures (including Konstantin Balmont, Dimitri Mereszkovski, Zinaida Hippius, and Maximilian Woloshin). He attends the General Meeting of the European Federation of the Theosophical Society, at which Col. Olcott is present for the last time. He spends the year's end in Venice and Rome, where he writes and works on his translation of H.P. Blavatsky's *Key to Theosophy*.

1907: Further expansion of the German Theosophical Movement according to the Rosicrucian directive to 'introduce spirit into the world'—in education, in social questions, in art, and in science. In February, Col. Olcott dies in Adyar. Before he dies, Olcott indicates that 'the Masters' wish Annie Besant to succeed him: much politicking ensues. Rudolf Steiner supports Besant's candidacy. April-May: preparations for the Congress of the Federation of European Sections of the Theosophical Society—the great, watershed Whitsun 'Munich Congress,' attended by Annie Besant and others. Steiner decides to separate Eastern and Western (Christian-Rosicrucian) esoteric schools. He takes his esoteric school out of the Theosophical Society (Besant and Rudolf Steiner are 'in harmony' on this). Steiner makes his first lecture tours to Austria and Hungary. That summer, he is in Italy. In September, he visits Edouard Schuré, who will write the introduction to the French edition of *Christianity as Mystical Fact* in Barr, Alsace. Rudolf Steiner writes the autobiographical statement known as the 'Barr Document.' In *Luzifer-Gnosis*, 'The Education of the Child' appears.

1908: The movement grows (membership: 1,150). Lecturing expands. Steiner makes his first extended lecture tour to Holland and Scandinavia, as well as visits to Naples and Sicily. Themes: St. John's Gospel, the Apocalypse, Egypt, science, philosophy, and logic. *Luzifer-Gnosis* ceases publication. In Berlin, Marie von Sivers (with Johanna Mücke (1864–1949) forms the *Philosophisch-Theosophisch* (after 1915 *Philosophisch-Anthroposophisch*) *Verlag* to publish Steiner's work. Steiner gives lecture cycles titled *The Gospel of St. John* (CW 103) and *The Apocalypse* (104).

1909: *An Outline of Esoteric Science* appears. Lecturing and travel continues. Rudolf Steiner's spiritual research expands to include the polarity of Lucifer and Ahriman; the work of great individualities in history; the Maitreya Buddha and the Bodhisattvas; spiritual economy (CW 109); the work of the spiritual hierarchies in heaven and on earth (CW 110). He also deepens and intensifies his research into the Gospels, giving lectures on the Gospel of St. Luke (CW 114) with the first mention of two Jesus children. Meets and becomes friends with Christian Morgenstern (1871–1914). In April, he lays the foundation stone for the Malsch model—the building that will lead to the first Goetheanum. In May, the International Congress of the Federation of European Sections of the

Theosophical Society takes place in Budapest. Rudolf Steiner receives the Subba Row medal for *How to Know Higher Worlds*. During this time, Charles W. Leadbeater discovers Jiddu Krishnamurti (1895–1986) and proclaims him the future 'world teacher,' the bearer of the Maitreya Buddha and the 'reappearing Christ.' In October, Steiner delivers seminal lectures on 'anthroposophy,' which he will try, unsuccessfully, to rework over the next years into the unfinished work, *Anthroposophy (A Fragment)* (CW 45).

1910: New themes: *The Reappearance of Christ in the Etheric* (CW 118); *The Fifth Gospel; The Mission of Folk Souls* (CW 121); *Occult History* (CW 126); the evolving development of etheric cognitive capacities. Rudolf Steiner continues his Gospel research with *The Gospel of St. Matthew* (CW 123). In January, his father dies. In April, he takes a month-long trip to Italy, including Rome, Monte Cassino, and Sicily. He also visits Scandinavia again. July–August, he writes the first mystery drama, *The Portal of Initiation* (CW 14). In November, he gives 'psychosophy' lectures. In December, he submits 'On the Psychological Foundations and Epistemological Framework of Theosophy' to the International Philosophical Congress in Bologna.

1911: The crisis in the Theosophical Society deepens. In January, 'The Order of the Rising Sun,' which will soon become 'The Order of the Star in the East,' is founded for the coming world teacher, Krishnamurti. At the same time, Marie von Sivers, Rudolf Steiner's co-worker, falls ill. Fewer lectures are given, but important new ground is broken. In Prague, in March, Steiner meets Franz Kafka (1883–1924) and Hugo Bergmann (1883-1975). In April, he delivers his paper to the Philosophical Congress. He writes the second mystery drama, *The Soul's Probation* (CW 14). Also, while Marie von Sivers is convalescing, Rudolf Steiner begins work on *Calendar 1912/1913*, which will contain the 'Calendar of the Soul' meditations. On March 19, Anna (Eunike) Steiner dies. In September, Rudolf Steiner visits Einsiedeln, birthplace of Paracelsus. In December, Friedrich Rittelmeyer, future founder of the Christian Community, meets Rudolf Steiner. The *Johannes-Bauverein*, the 'building committee,' which would lead to the first Goetheanum (first planned for Munich), is also founded, and a preliminary committee for the founding of an independent association is created that, in the following year, will become the Anthroposophical Society. Important lecture cycles include *Occult Physiology* (CW 128); *Wonders of the World* (CW 129); *From Jesus to Christ* (CW 131). Other themes: esoteric Christianity; Christian Rosenkreutz; the spiritual guidance of humanity; the sense world and the world of the spirit.

1912: Despite the ongoing, now increasing crisis in the Theosophical Society, much is accomplished: *Calendar 1912/1913* is published; eurythmy is created; both the third mystery drama, *The Guardian of the Threshold* (CW 14) and *A Way of Self-Knowledge* (CW 16) are written. New (or renewed) themes included life between death and rebirth and karma and reincarnation. Other lecture cycles: *Spiritual Beings in the Heavenly Bodies and in the Kingdoms of Nature* (CW 136); *The Human Being in the Light of Occultism, Theosophy, and Philosophy* (CW 137); *The Gospel of St. Mark* (CW 139); and *The Bhagavad Gita and the Epistles of Paul* (CW 142). On May 8, Rudolf Steiner celebrates White Lotus Day, H.P. Blavatsky's death day, which he had faithfully observed for the past decade, for the last time. In August, Rudolf Steiner suggests the 'independent association' be called the 'Anthroposophical Society.' In September, the first eurythmy course takes place. In October, Rudolf Steiner declines recognition of a Theosophical Society lodge dedicated to the Star of the East and decides to expel all Theosophical Society members belonging to the order. Also, with Marie von Sivers, he first visits Dornach, near Basel, Switzerland, and they stand on the hill where the Goetheanum will be built. In November, a Theosophical Society lodge is opened by direct mandate from Adyar (Annie Besant). In December, a meeting of the German section occurs at which it is decided that belonging to the Order of the Star of the East is incompatible with membership in the Theosophical Society. December 28: informal founding of the Anthroposophical Society in Berlin.

1913: Expulsion of the German section from the Theosophical Society. February 2–3: Foundation meeting of the Anthroposophical Society. Board members include: Marie von Sivers, Michael Bauer, and Carl Unger. September 20: Laying of the foundation stone for the *Johannes Bau* (Goetheanum) in Dornach. Building begins immediately. The third mystery drama, *The Soul's Awakening* (CW 14), is completed. Also: *The Threshold of the Spiritual World* (CW 147). Lecture cycles include: *The Bhagavad Gita and the Epistles of Paul* and *The Esoteric Meaning of the Bhagavad Gita* (CW 146), which the Russian philosopher Nikolai Berdyaev attends; *The Mysteries of the East and of Christianity* (CW 144); *The Effects of Esoteric Development* (CW 145); and *The Fifth Gospel* (CW 148). In May, Rudolf Steiner is in London and Paris, where anthroposophical work continues.

1914: Building continues on the *Johannes Bau* (Goetheanum) in Dornach, with artists and co-workers from seventeen nations. The general assembly of the Anthroposophical Society takes place. In May, Rudolf Steiner visits Paris, as well as Chartres Cathedral. June 28: assassination in Sarajevo ('Now the catastrophe has happened!'). August 1: War is declared. Rudolf Steiner returns to Germany from Dornach—he will travel back and forth. He writes the last chapter of *The Riddles of Philosophy*. Lecture cycles include: *Human and Cosmic Thought* (CW 151); *Inner Being of Humanity between Death and a New Birth* (CW 153); *Occult Reading and Occult Hearing* (CW 156). December 24: marriage of Rudolf Steiner and Marie von Sivers.

1915: Building continues. Life after death becomes a major theme, also art. Writes: *Thoughts during a Time of War* (CW 24). Lectures include: *The Secret of Death* (CW 159); *The Uniting of Humanity through the Christ Impulse* (CW 165).

1916: Rudolf Steiner begins work with Edith Maryon (1872–1924) on the sculpture 'The Representative of Humanity' ('The Group'—Christ, Lucifer, and Ahriman). He also works with the alchemist Alexander von Bernus on the quarterly *Das Reich*. He writes *The Riddle of Humanity* (CW 20). Lectures include: *Necessity and Freedom in World History and Human Action* (CW 166); *Past and Present in the Human Spirit* (CW 167); *The Karma of Vocation* (CW 172); *The Karma of Untruthfulness* (CW 173).

1917: Russian Revolution. The U.S. enters the war. Building continues. Rudolf Steiner delineates the idea of the 'threefold nature of the human being' (in a public lecture March 15) and the 'threefold nature of the social organism' (hammered out in May-June with the help of Otto von Lerchenfeld and Ludwig Polzer-Hoditz in the form of two documents titled *Memoranda*, which were distributed in high places). August–September: Rudolf Steiner writes *The Riddles of the Soul* (CW 20). Also: commentary on 'The Chymical Wedding of Christian Rosenkreutz' for Alexander Bernus (*Das Reich*). Lectures include: *The Karma of Materialism* (CW 176); *The Spiritual Background of the Outer World: The Fall of the Spirits of Darkness* (CW 177).

1918: March 18: peace treaty of Brest-Litovsk—'Now everything will truly enter chaos! What is needed is cultural renewal.' June: Rudolf Steiner visits Karlstein (Grail) Castle outside Prague. Lecture cycle: *From Symptom to Reality in Modern History* (CW 185). In mid-November, Emil Molt, of the Waldorf-Astoria Cigarette Company, has the idea of founding a school for his workers' children.

1919: Focus on the threefold social organism: tireless travel, countless lectures, meetings, and publications. At the same time, a new public stage of Anthroposophy emerges as cultural renewal begins. The coming years will see initiatives in pedagogy, medicine, pharmacology, and agriculture. January 27: threefold meeting: ' We must first of all, with the money we have, found free schools that can bring people what they need.' February: first public eurythmy performance in Zurich. Also: 'Appeal to the German People' (CW 24), circulated March 6 as a newspaper insert. In April, *Towards Social Renewal* (CW 23) appears—'perhaps the most widely read of all books on politics appearing since the war.' Rudolf Steiner is asked to undertake the 'direction and leadership' of the school founded by the Waldorf-Astoria Company. Rudolf Steiner begins to talk about the 'renewal' of education. May 30: a building is selected and purchased for the future Waldorf School. August–September, Rudolf Steiner gives a lecture course for Waldorf teachers, *The Foundations of Human Experience (Study of Man)* (CW 293). September 7: Opening of the first Waldorf School. December (into January): first science course, the *Light Course* (CW 320).

1920: The Waldorf School flourishes. New threefold initiatives. Founding of limited companies *Der Kommende Tag* and *Futurum A.G.* to infuse spiritual values into the economic realm. Rudolf Steiner also focuses on the sciences. Lectures: *Introducing Anthroposophical Medicine* (CW 312); *The Warmth Course* (CW 321); *The Boundaries of Natural Science* (CW 322); *The Redemption of Thinking* (CW 74). February: Johannes Werner

Klein—later a co-founder of the Christian Community—asks Rudolf Steiner about the possibility of a 'religious renewal,' a 'Johannine church.' In March, Rudolf Steiner gives the first course for doctors and medical students. In April, a divinity student asks Rudolf Steiner a second time about the possibility of religious renewal. September 27–October 16: anthroposophical 'university course.' December: lectures titled *The Search for the New Isis* (CW 202).

1921: Rudolf Steiner continues his intensive work on cultural renewal, including the uphill battle for the threefold social order. 'University' arts, scientific, theological, and medical courses include: *The Astronomy Course* (CW 323); *Observation, Mathematics, and Scientific Experiment* (CW 324); the *Second Medical Course* (CW 313); *Colour*. In June and September-October, Rudolf Steiner also gives the first two 'priests' courses' (CW 342 and 343). The 'youth movement' gains momentum. Magazines are founded: *Die Drei* (January), and—under the editorship of Albert Steffen (1884–1963)—the weekly, *Das Goetheanum* (August). In February–March, Rudolf Steiner takes his first trip outside Germany since the war (Holland). On April 7, Steiner receives a letter regarding 'religious renewal,' and May 22–23, he agrees to address the question in a practical way. In June, the Klinical-Therapeutic Institute opens in Arlesheim under the direction of Dr. Ita Wegman. In August, the Chemical-Pharmaceutical Laboratory opens in Arlesheim (Oskar Schmiedel and Ita Wegman are directors). The Clinical Therapeutic Institute is inaugurated in Stuttgart (Dr. Ludwig Noll is director); also the Research Laboratory in Dornach (Ehrenfried Pfeiffer and Günther Wachsmuth are directors). In November–December, Rudolf Steiner visits Norway.

1922: The first half of the year involves very active public lecturing (thousands attend); in the second half, Rudolf Steiner begins to withdraw and turn toward the Society—'The Society is asleep.' It is 'too weak' to do what is asked of it. The businesses—*Der Kommende Tag* and *Futurum A.G.*—fail. In January, with the help of an agent, Steiner undertakes a twelve-city German lecture tour, accompanied by eurythmy performances. In two weeks he speaks to more than 2,000 people. In April, he gives a 'university course' in The Hague. He also visits England. In June, he is in Vienna for the East–West Congress. In August–September, he is back in England for the Oxford Conference on Education. Returning to Dornach, he gives the lectures *Philosophy, Cosmology, and Religion* (CW 215), and gives the third priests' course (CW 344). On September 16, The Christian Community is founded. In October–November, Steiner is in Holland and England. He also speaks to the youth: *The Youth Course* (CW 217). In December, Steiner gives lectures titled *The Origins of Natural Science* (CW 326), and *Humanity and the World of Stars: The Spiritual Communion of Humanity* (CW 219). December 31: Fire at the Goetheanum, which is destroyed.

1923: Despite the fire, Rudolf Steiner continues his work unabated. A very hard year. Internal dispersion, dissension, and apathy abound. There is conflict—between old and new visions—within the Society. A wake-up call is needed, and Rudolf Steiner responds with renewed lecturing vitality. His focus: the spiritual context of human life; initiation science; the course of the year; and community building. As a foundation for an artistic school, he creates a series of pastel sketches. Lecture cycles: *The Anthroposophical Movement; Initiation Science* (CW 227) (in England at the Penmaenmawr Summer School); *The Four Seasons and the Archangels* (CW 229); *Harmony of the Creative Word* (CW 230); *The Supersensible Human* (CW 231), given in Holland for the founding of the Dutch society. On November 10, in response to the failed Hitler-Ludendorff putsch in Munich, Steiner closes his Berlin residence and moves the *Philosophisch-Anthroposophisch Verlag* (Press) to Dornach. On December 9, Steiner begins the serialization of his *Autobiography: The Course of My Life* (CW 28) in *Das Goetheanum*. It will continue to appear weekly, without a break, until his death. Late December–early January: Rudolf Steiner re-founds the Anthroposophical Society (about 12,000 members internationally) and takes over its leadership. The new board members are: Marie Steiner, Ita Wegman, Albert Steffen, Elisabeth Vreede, and Günther Wachsmuth. (See *The Christmas Meeting for the Founding of the General Anthroposophical Society*, CW 260). Accompanying lectures: *Mystery Knowledge and Mystery Centres* (CW 232); *World History in the Light of Anthroposophy* (CW 233). December 25: the Foundation Stone is laid (in the hearts of members) in the form of the 'Foundation Stone Meditation.'

1924: January 1: having founded the Anthroposophical Society and taken over its leadership, Rudolf Steiner has the task of 'reforming' it. The process begins with a weekly newssheet ('What's Happening in the Anthroposophical Society') in which Rudolf Steiner's 'Letters to Members' and 'Anthroposophical Leading Thoughts' appear (CW 26). The next step is the creation of a new esoteric class, the 'first class' of the 'University of Spiritual Science' (which was to have been followed, had Rudolf Steiner lived longer, by two more advanced classes). Then comes a new language for Anthroposophy—practical, phenomenological, and direct; and Rudolf Steiner creates the model for the second Goetheanum. He begins the series of extensive 'karma' lectures (CW 235–40); and finally, responding to needs, he creates two new initiatives: biodynamic agriculture and curative education. After the middle of the year, rumours begin to circulate regarding Steiner's health. Lectures: January–February, *Anthroposophy* (CW 234); February: *Tone Eurythmy* (CW 278); June: *The Agriculture Course* (CW 327); June–July: *Speech Eurythmy* (CW 279); *Curative Education* (CW 317); August: (England, 'Second International Summer School'), *Initiation Consciousness: True and False Paths in Spiritual Investigation* (CW 243); September: *Pastoral Medicine* (CW 318). On September 26, for the first time, Rudolf Steiner cancels a lecture. On September 28, he gives his last lecture. On September 29, he withdraws to his studio in the carpenter's shop; now he is definitively ill. Cared for by Ita Wegman, he continues working, however, and writing the weekly installments of his *Autobiography* and *Letters to the Members/Leading Thoughts* (CW 26).

1925: Rudolf Steiner, while continuing to work, continues to weaken. He finishes *Extending Practical Medicine* (CW 27) with Ita Wegman.
On March 30, around ten in the morning, Rudolf Steiner dies

INDEX

COLOUR PLATES

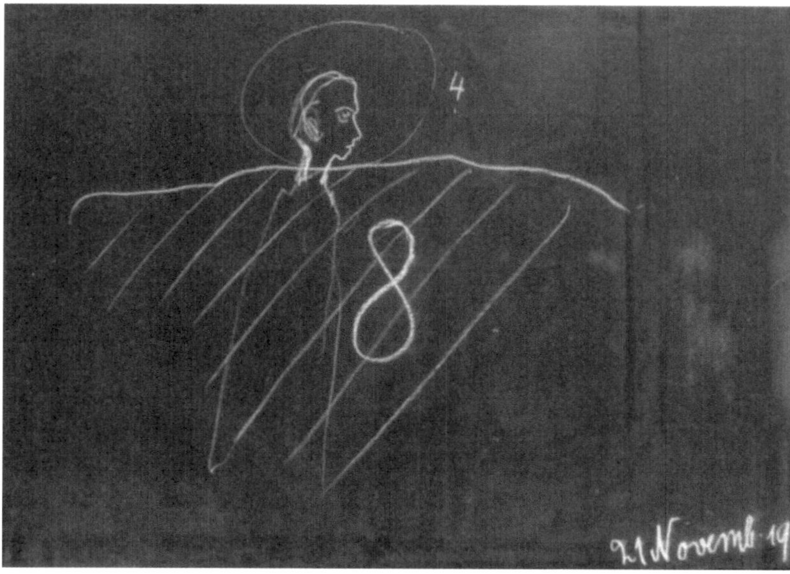

Plate 1

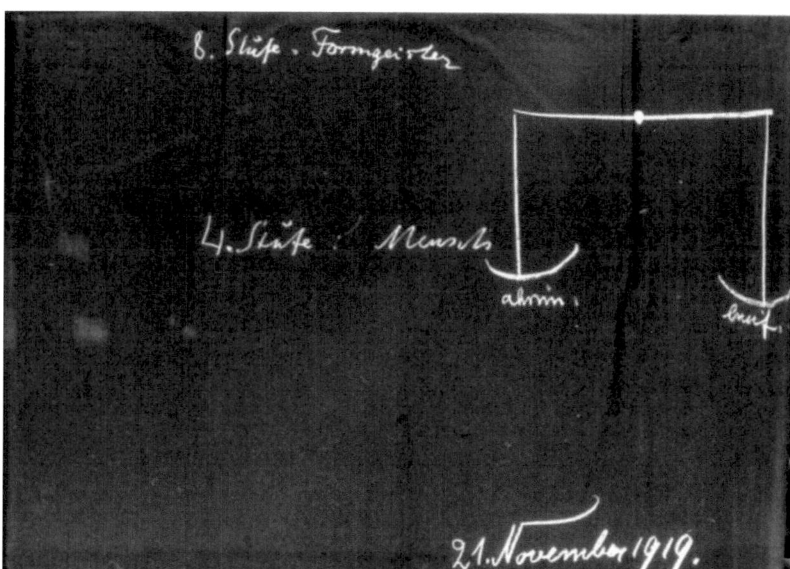

Plate 2

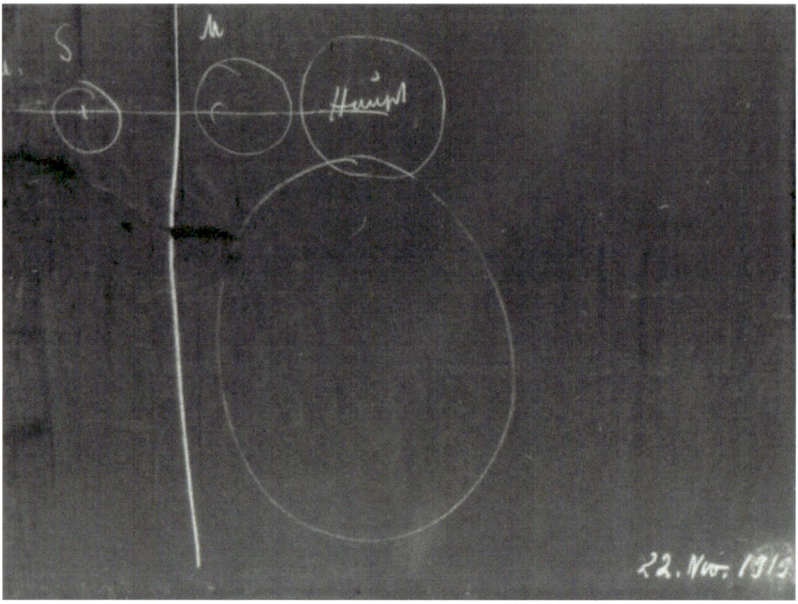

Plate 3

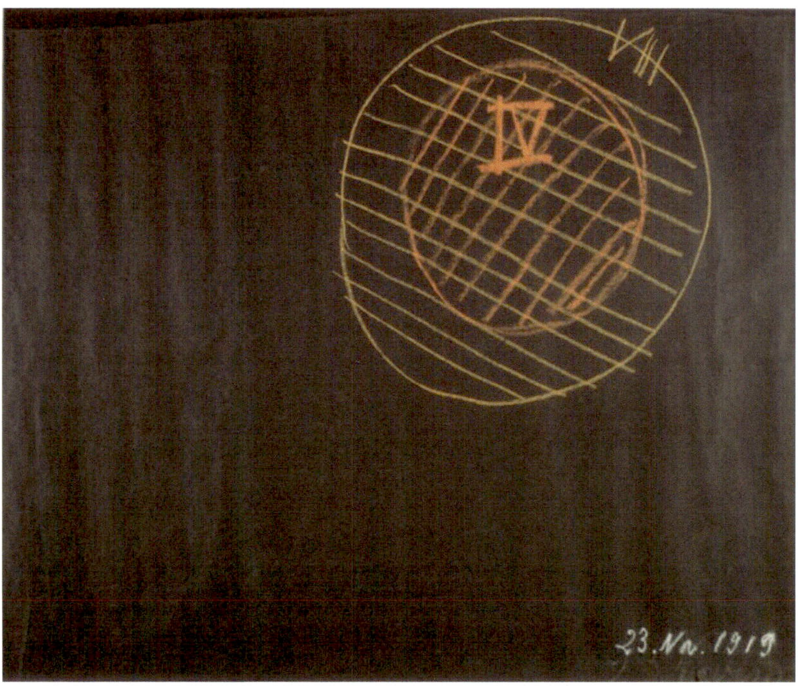

Plate 4

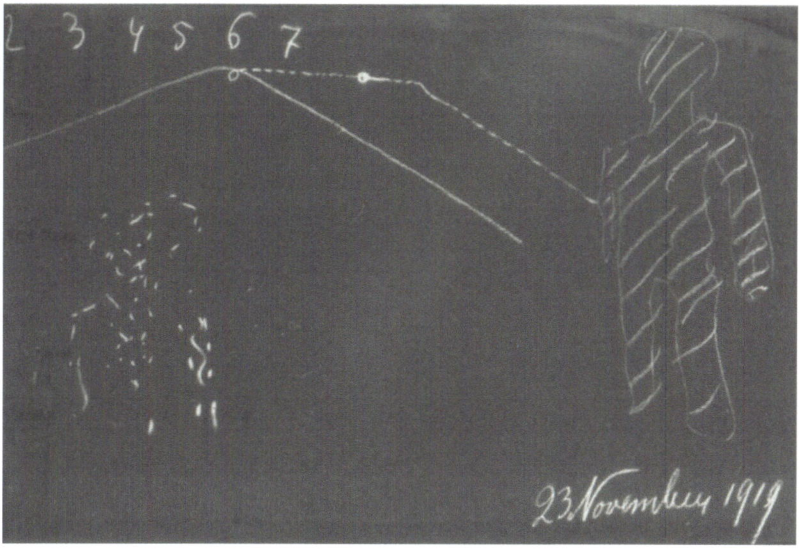

Plate 5

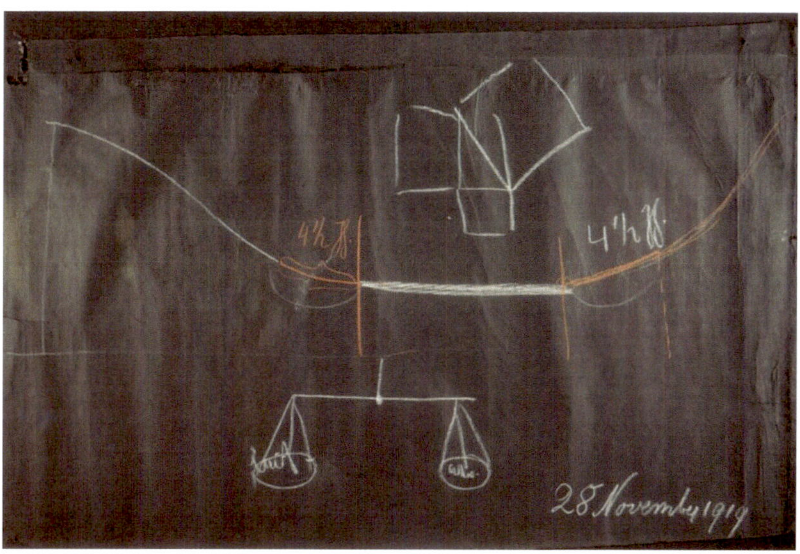

Plate 6

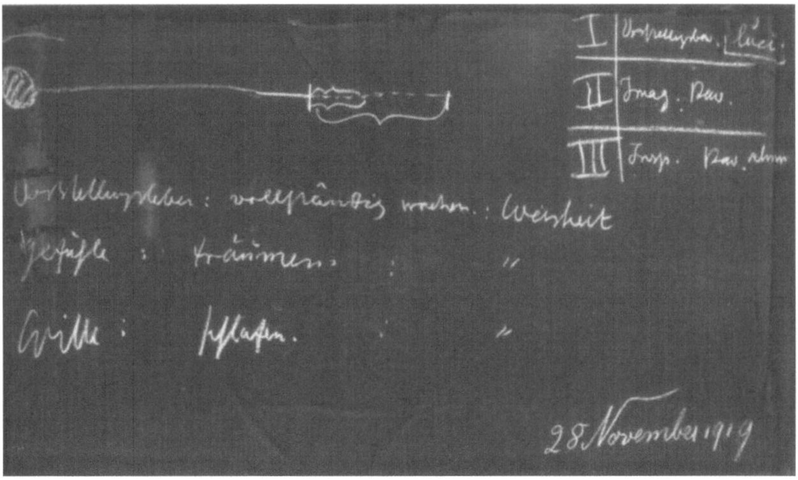

Plate 7

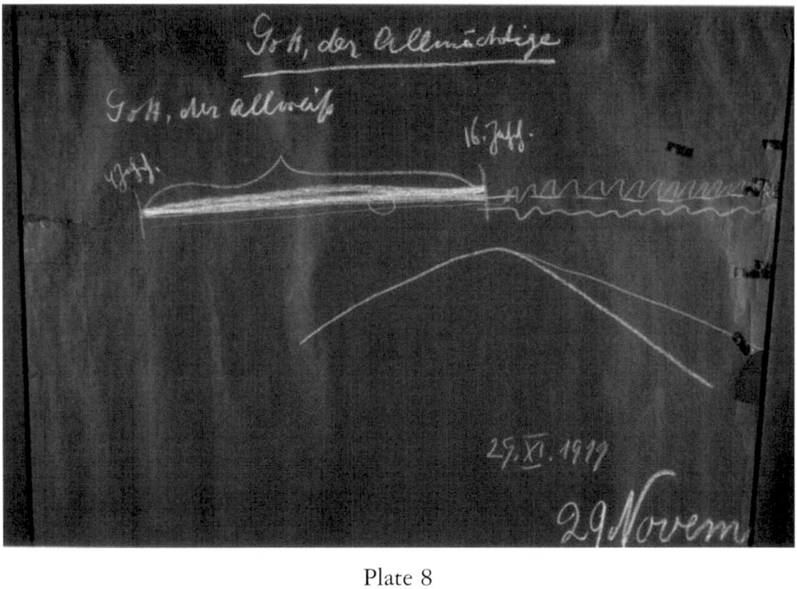

Plate 8

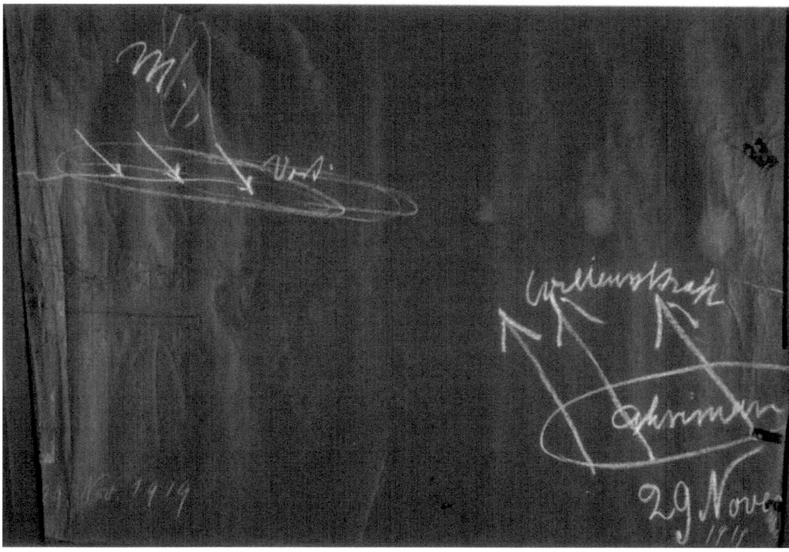

Plate 9

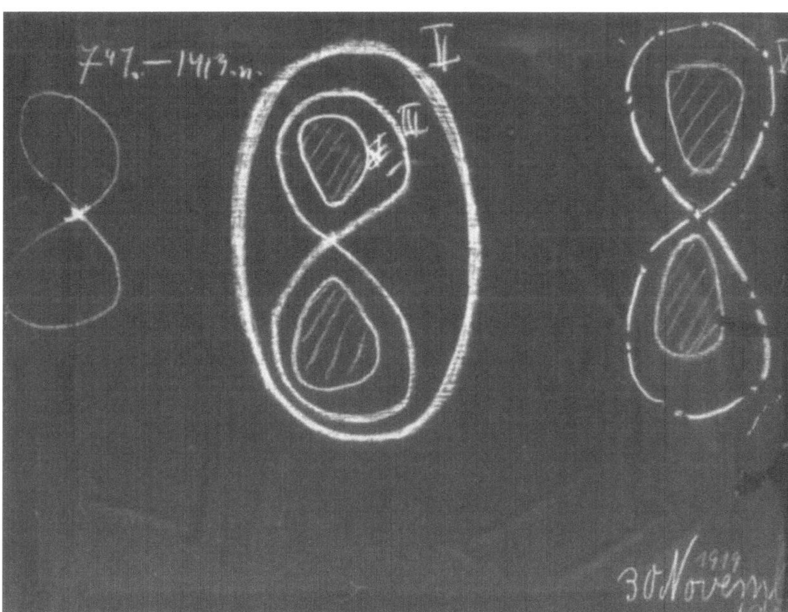

Plate 10

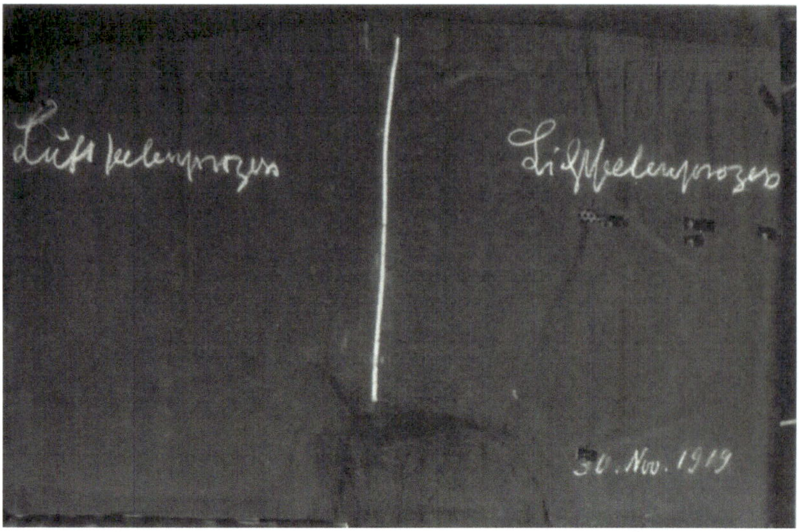

Plate 11

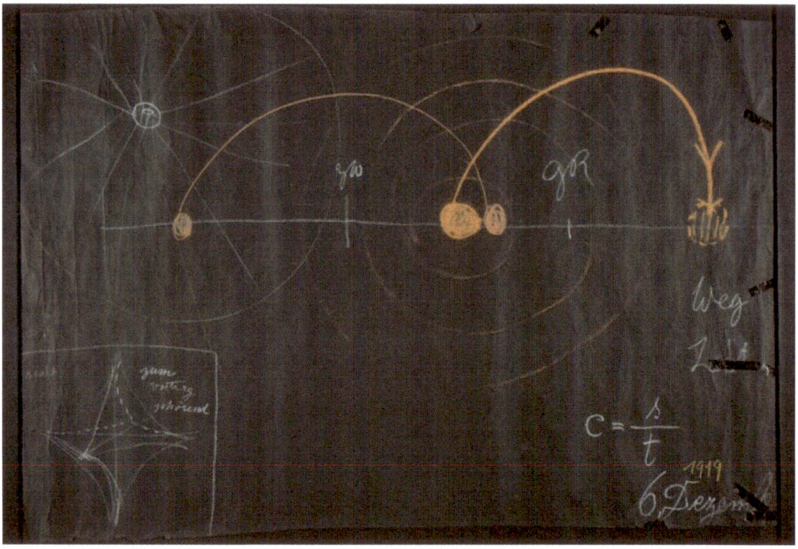

Plate 12

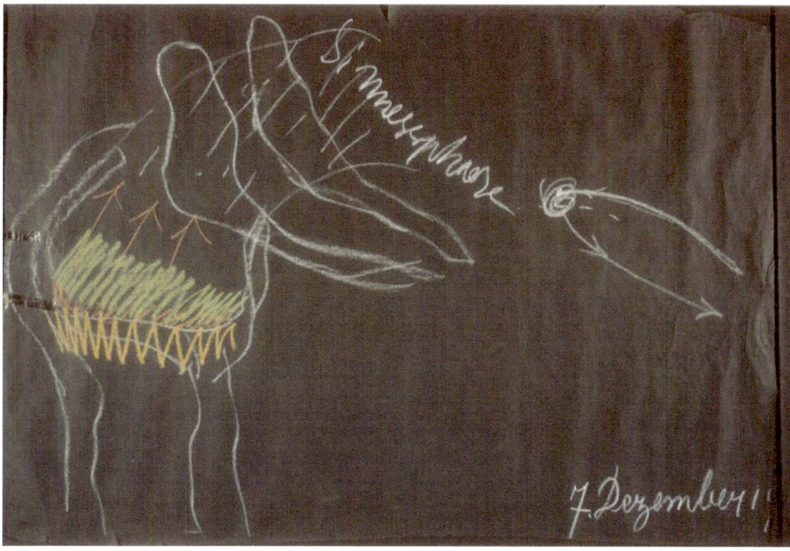

Plate 13

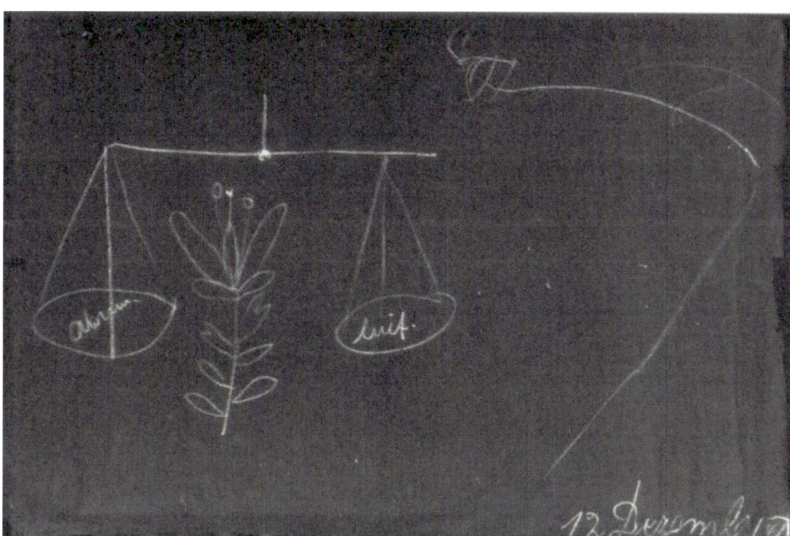

Plate 14

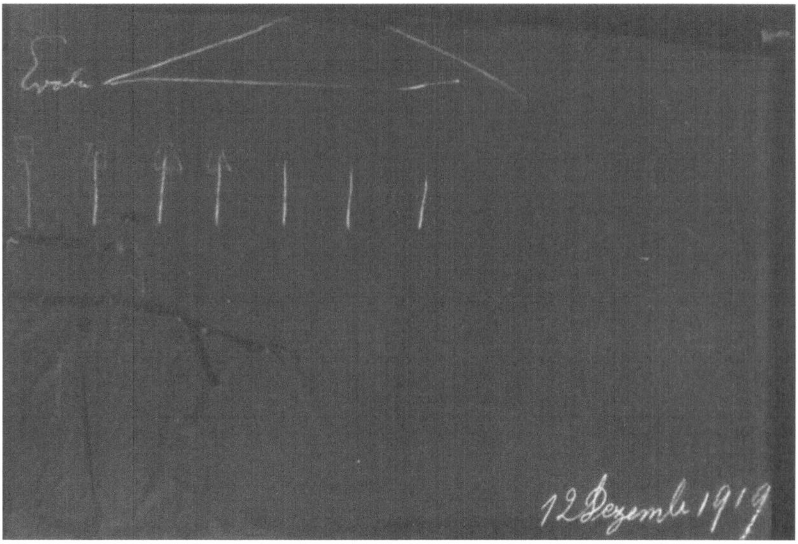

Plate 15

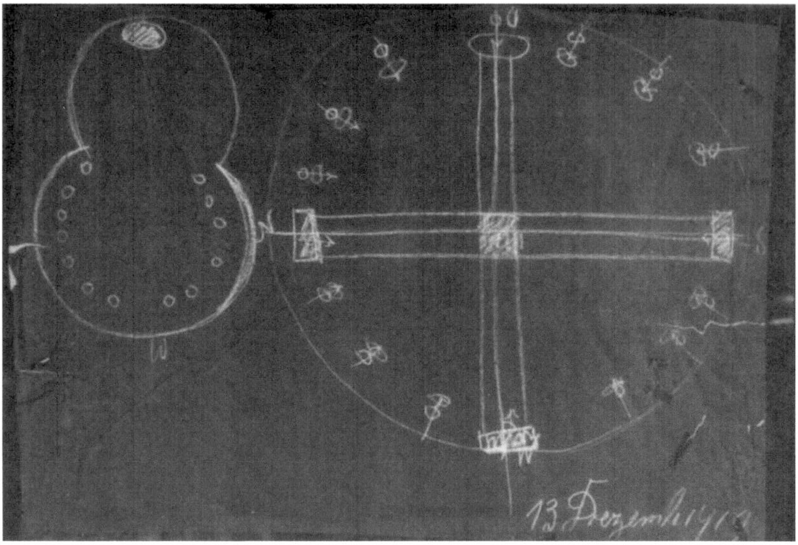

Plate 16

Plate 17

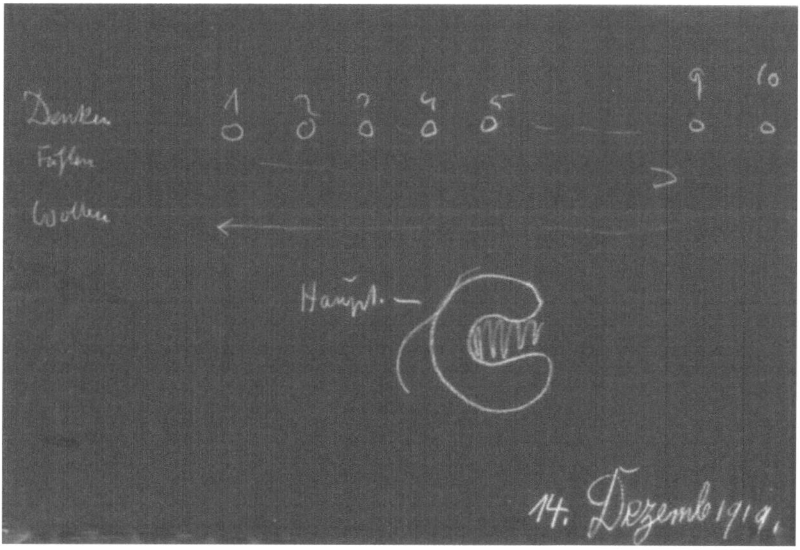

Plate 18

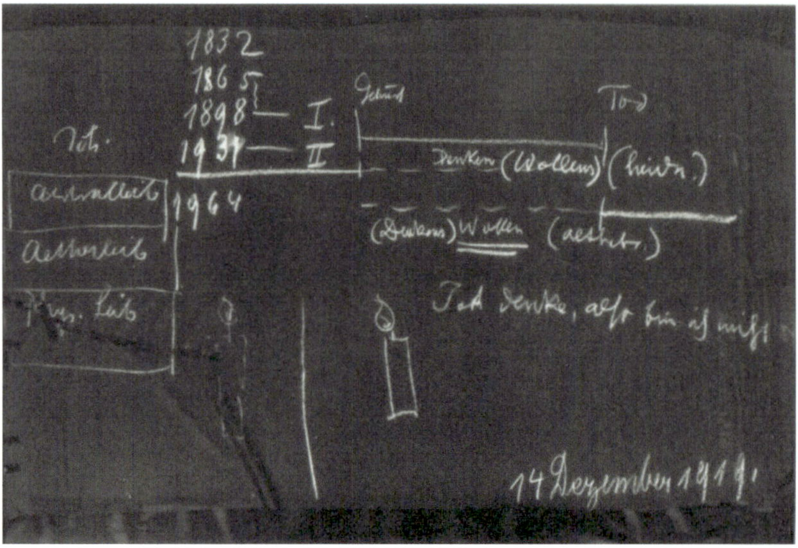

Plate 19

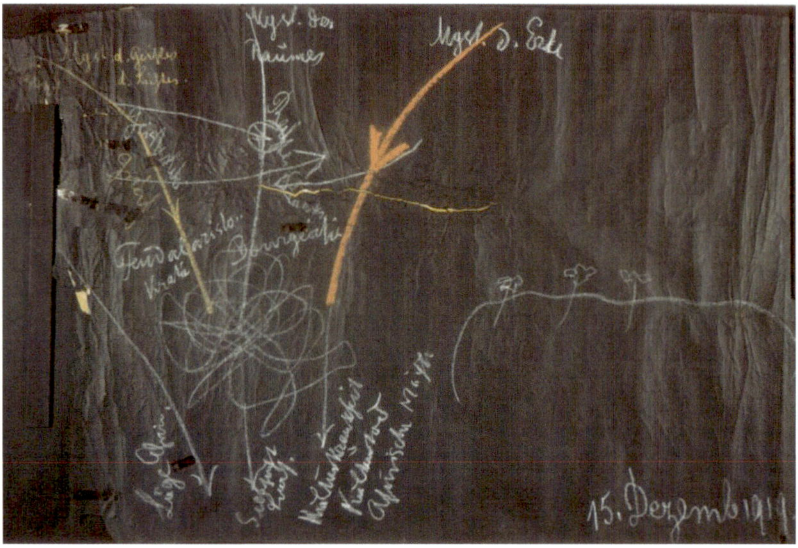

Plate 20

A NOTE FROM RUDOLF STEINER PRESS

We are an independent publisher and registered charity (non-profit organisation) dedicated to making available the work of Rudolf Steiner in English translation. We care a great deal about the content of our books and have hundreds of titles available – as printed books, ebooks and in audio formats.

As a publisher devoted to anthroposophy…

- We continually commission translations of previously unpublished works by Rudolf Steiner and invest in re-translating, editing and improving our editions.
- We are committed to making anthroposophy available to all by publishing introductory books as well as contemporary research.
- Our new print editions and ebooks are carefully checked and proofread for accuracy, and converted into all formats for all platforms.
- Our translations are officially authorised by Rudolf Steiner's estate in Dornach, Switzerland, to whom we pay royalties on sales, thus assisting their critical work.

So, look out for Rudolf Steiner Press as a mark of quality and support us today by buying our books, or contact us should you wish to sponsor specific titles or to support the charity with a gift or legacy.